Reynolds Cahoon and his Stalwart Sons

REYNOLDS CAHOON

AND HIS

STALWART SONS

. . . . .

Utah Pioneers

GENEALOGICAL SOCIETY
OF THE CHURCH OF JESUS CHRIST
OF LATTER-DAY SAINTS

Compiled and Edited By
STELLA CAHOON SHURTLEFF
and
BRENT FARRINGTON CAHOON

iii

To Our Beloved Father,
Daniel Farrington Cahoon,
Grandson of Reynolds Cahoon,
This Book Is Lovingly Dedicated.

PREFACE

This book is meant to be more than a tribute to Reynolds Cahoon and his family. It is an effort to paint a word portrait of a typical Mormon Pioneer, or better still, to portray a life-like picture of a religious people dedicated to a profound way of life.

It is a story of men and women whose stout hearts and spiritual force carved commonwealths out of the raw materials of a rugged and ruthless West. It is their own story, for the most part, taken from the journals they kept of their sorrows and success; the suffering they endured in defense of their religion.

We, the descendants of the Utah Pioneers, are justly proud of our heritage. No other people have made any greater contribution to the spiritual betterment of life, no others have better exemplified the Christian belief that we are our "brother's keeper."

The date of publication of this book is significant. As it goes to press, ground is being broken for the construction of a Memorial Theatre commemorating the original Salt Lake "Playhouse" built in 1862 — a tribute to the cultural life of our Utah Pioneers.

Since Reynolds Cahoon and his sons played important roles, not as actors, but as participants in the activities of the original Salt Lake Theatre, we thought it timely to publish, as a separate book, part of the manuscript of a forth-coming book, "The Cahoon Story," a comprehensive Family History dating from the Colquhoun (Cahoon) Clan in the Highlands of Scotland, during the 12th Century, down to the present day.

ACKNOWLEDGEMENT

In compiling the information and historical data of this book, Reynolds Cahoon and His Stalwart Sons, we are indebted to many good people and many worthy organizations

To our relatives who have furnished biographies, journals, photographs and valuable family records for our use, to Harold B. Carruth, Alan T. Calhoun and William H. Cahoon for their aid in genealogical research, and to Mary L. S. Putnam for the arrangement of our Index, we express sincere thanks.

To the Church Historian's Office for permission to seek out facts and verify events contained in its treasured records, and to the Genealogical Society in Salt Lake City for its help and counsel, we are particularly grateful.

To the authors and writers of books and articles about Utah and the Mormon Pioneers, to which we have so often referred, we give special thanks and acknowledgment

To all these and many others who have given so generously of their time and information in the preparation of this book, the descendants of Reynolds Cahoon are deeply indebted.

.

ILLUSTRATIONS

Printed By
PARAGON PRESS, INC.
Salt Lake City, Utah

REYNOLDS CAHOON

THIRZA STILES CAHOON
First wife of Reynolds Cahoon

LUCINA ROBERTS and REYNOLDS CAHOON
*This is understood to be a photo of Reynolds and
his second wife. It has not been authenticated.*

REYNOLDS CAHOON

✦

Alike are life and death when life in death survives
And the interrupted breath inspires a thousand lives
Were a star quenched on high, for ages would its light
Still traveling downward from the sky, shine on our mortal sight
So when a great man dies, for ages beyond our ken,
The light he leaves behind him lies upon the paths of men
—LONGFELLOW

✦

We pay tribute to Reynolds Cahoon, our Utah Pioneer Ancestor, and relate, in part, the story of his life. He was among those known stalwarts of his time — tried and found true. His name ranks high in the history of a new Westen Civilization and the ushering in of the fullness of the Gospel of Jesus Christ. He was a builder of the magnificent temples of his time. Through revelation and by the Will of the Lord, he was given an inheritance in the Land of Zion while he was yet alive, and because he kept the commandments of God, death to him is but a sweet repose, a rest from toil and labor, a refreshing sleep from which he shall awake to receive a greater inheritance. "The architect may rest, but his House stands there, a monument to his genius and diligence."

Reynolds Cahoon was a descendant of a line of patriotic christian people who had dedicated themselves to the service of their God and their country at the risk of their own lives. Many made the supreme sacrifice. Of Reynolds, we state in all truth that he was, as were they, among the world's noblemen who continued steadfast to that pure Christian faith and loyalty for which his projenitors had suffered the severest hardships.

Reynolds was a soldier in the War of 1812. His first known American ancestor, William Cahoon(e) of Block Island, Rhode Island, gave his life in 1675 defending the Masachusetts Colonies in the cruel King Philip's War. William Cahoon Jr., father of Reynolds, served in the American Revolution under Capt. Slocum in the regiment of Col. Asa Barnes. He enlisted October 11, 1781 at Williamstown, Berkshire County, Massachusetts and marched to Saratoga "by order of General Stark, on Alarm."*

Massachusetts Soldiers and Sailors, Vol 3, page 11

1

We accept William Cahoon(e) of Block Island as our first known American ancestor and have designated him as William[1]. "The Cahoon Story" tells us there were Cahoon immigrants as early as 1635, but our exact relationship to them has not been established. We do have authentic proof, however, tracing back to William[1] of Block Island 1661.

Reynolds Cahoon was the sixth generation in America. The known generations from Reynolds are as follows: Reynolds [6], son of William Jr.[5], son of William[4], son of Ebenezer[3], son of Joseph[2], son of William[1] Cahoon. This information is taken from the records kept by Daniel Farrington[8] Cahoon, son of Andrew[7], son of Reynolds[6]. Daniel Farrington Cahoon compiled a history of Reynolds and it is from his writings and family record that this Life Sketch of Reynolds is taken.

Daniel Farrington was born January 5th, 1863 in Murray, Salt Lake County, Utah He died at the home of his daughter, Stella Cahoon Shurtleff, Los Angeles, California, July 14th, 1945. He married Naamah Tripp, the lovely daughter of Enoch Bartlett Tripp and Jessie Eddins. Daniel F. and Naamah Tripp Cahoon devoted their lives to the service of their God and the Gospel of the Church of Jesus Christ of Latter-day Saints.

It was the sincere wish of "D. F.," as he was affectionately known, that his work, when finished, might be a benefit to his children and serve as a bond of union between them and their ancestors. He was most particular as to the truth of all that he recorded therein, for "he had the firm conviction that many would read his writings with pleasure, that God would bless his work that it might be a humble means of confirming them in the love of the Lord. And that, through the blessings of his Heavenly Father, this memoir might be an instrument for the advancement of the Glory of God and our eternal welfare."

Daniel Farrington tells us that Reynolds requested William Farrington Cahoon, his eldest son, to write a few facts regarding his (Reynolds) life. The following is what he wrote:

"My father, Reynolds Cahoon, was the son of William Cahoon Jr. and Mehitable Hodge. William Jr. was son of William Sen. whose forefathers came to America from Scotland and settled in Rhode Island and from thence scattered abroad in different parts of the land and I have no record of them. My father was born April 30, 1790 at Cambridge, Washington County, New York. He married December 11, 1810 in

New Port, New York, to Thirza Stiles, daughter of Daniel
Olds Stiles, son of John Stiles. They were married by Hon.
John Stiles. Reynolds moved to Harpersfield, Ohio, then a
new country and began farming in the year 1811."

REYNOLDS, A SOLDIER IN WAR OF 1812

After forty peaceful years, war with England broke out
again. English cruisers boarded American merchantmen on
pretense of searching for sailors. In 1796-97, the American
Minister at London had made application for release of 271
seamen, American citizens. England did not stop at this, she
boarded and impressed American seamen in American waters.
In 1807 an American frigate, the Chesapeake, was attacked
by the English An American citizen was carried to England
and thrown into Dorsmoor prison. All Western Massachusetts
passed resolutions condemning such action and war was declared by the President of the United States, June 19, 1812.
The Treaty of Ghent put a stop to all such procedure and
the second war with England was at an end.

Regarding this, William F. writes:

"In the winter of 1812, my father Reynolds was called by
the Government of the United States to go to Buffalo, New
York to assist in driving the British from Buffalo, who had
crossed Lake Erie from Canada and burned the city. Upon
arriving at Erie, they found that the British had crossed
back over the Lake and he was released and returned home."
Then William F. continues, "Reynolds lived in Harpersfield
about twelve years. Five children were born at this place.
In the year 1825 he moved about thirty miles farther west
near the town of Kirtland and went into the business of tan-
ning leather and making shoes. In this business, he was quite
prosperous and accumulated considerable amounts of property.

REYNOLDS HEARS ABOUT MORMONISM

"During this time, a great stir was created over what was
known as the 'Golden Bible,' or Book of Mormon. He soon
became satisfied that the book was of Divine Origin, and
that God had commenced this great and marvelous work as
was spoken of by the inspired men of former days. He soon
went and was baptized, 12 Oct. 1830 and confirmed a member
of the Church of Jesus Christ of Latter-day Saints. He was
baptized by Parley P. Pratt, one of the four elders who had
been appointed by revelation to go to the Western Boundaries

of the United States, preaching by the way. He was ordained an 'Elder' by Sidney Rigdon and went on a mission calling the people to repent and be baptized. He was ordained a 'High Priest' by Lyman Wight. His missionary companion was Samuel Smith, Joseph's brother.

"In a short time he had used most of his property in preaching and assisting others to build up and establish the work of God in this dispensation of the fullness of time. He was soon ordained to go and preach the Gospel of Faith to all the world. In 1831 in company with Samuel H. Smith and twenty-four elders, he traveled to Missouri, preaching by the way. He returned in Sept. and in Dec. was ordained a counsellor to Bishop Whitney. He was called by revelation, one of the three committeemen to build a 'House to the Lord' in Kirtland in 1832. He and Hyrum Smith commenced their labors in May by counsel of the prophet Joseph.

"They had not a dollar to help them labor on the building but according to promise they soon had means to forward the building. They proceeded then until the Temple was finished. In the Autumn of 1837 he was ordained by president Marks as the President's Counselor in the Stake of Kirtland and in month of March 1838 moved into Missouri and was with the Saints in their troubles there. In Nauvoo, he was appointed, in company of brother A. Cutler and E. Higbee, a committee to build a "House to the Lord" in Nauvoo.

"My father's calling, ordinations and a brief sketch of his labors in the Church up to 1845 are thus recorded. He was faithful and true He labored with and for the Church and was driven with them from Nauvoo and came out to Utah with the people of God, having fought the good fight and won the prize, Eternal Life."

To attempt to write the story of Reynolds Cahoon by simply reciting the incidents immediately connected with his life would be entirely inadequate and leave the tale without a suitable background. One must go back to the early days of the Church of Jesus Christ of Latter-day Saints, for it was just six months after the organization of the "Mormon" Church, that Reynolds and his wife, Thirza, became members and from that day on his life and the history of that church are inseparable. What a dramatic story!

His life being a religious history, it becomes necessary to acquaint ourselves, more or less, with the principles of the religious organization with which he had affiliated himself. This church is the Church of Jesus Christ of Latter-day Saints, commonly known as the Mormon Church and was organized on the sixth day of April 1830 at Fayette, New York. The first President of the church was Joseph Smith, the Prophet, with whom Reynolds and his family were closely associated.

*"Joseph Smith was born in year 1805 in State of Vermont. His father moved to New York. There was in the place where they lived an unusual excitement on the subject of religion. The many different sects, the Methodists, Baptists, Presbyterians and others were holding religious revivals, all claiming to be right and all teaching different religious beliefs. Great multitudes united themselves to the different religious parties which created no small stir and division amongst the people. Priest was contending against priest, convert against convert.

"This great excitement caused Joseph Smith to reflect very seriously and in his own words, he says, 'In the midst of this war of words and tumult of opinions I often said to myself, 'What is to be done? Who of all these parties is right, or are they all wrong together? If any one of them be right, which is it and how shall I know it?' While I was laboring under extreme difficulties caused by the contests of these parties of religionists, I was one day reading the Epistle of James, first chapter, fifth verse which reads: 'If any of you lack wisdom, let him ask of God, that giveth to all men liberally, and upbraideth not: and it shall be given him.'

"Never did any passage of scripture come with more power to the heart of man than this did at this time to mine. I reflected on it again and again, knowing that if any person needed wisdom of God, I did. At length I came to the conclusion that I must either remain in darkness or else I must do as James directs, ask of God. So in accordance with this, my determination to ask God, I retired to the woods to make the attempt."

What he saw and experienced is recorded in detail in L.D.S. Church Publications, including the appearance of "two personages, whose brightness and glory defy all description . . . One of them spake unto me . . . and said, pointing to the other — 'This is My Beloved Son. Hear Him' "

*See "Joseph Smith's Own Story."

Joseph said, "I asked the Personages who stood above me in the light, which of all the sects was right — and which I should join. I was answered that I must join none of them . . . and many other things did God say unto me." The declarations that followed indicated the need for "restoration" of the Gospel of Jesus Christ, which some among the religious "reformers" had long recognized.

Joseph Smith's story continues: "Some weeks after I had this vision, I took occasion to give an account of the vision to one of the preachers who was very active in the aforementioned religious excitement and was greatly surprised at his behavior. He treated my communication with great contempt . . . the story excited great prejudice against me and was the cause of great persecution . . . But this did not destroy the reality of my vision. I have actually seen a light, in the midst of that light I saw two personages and they did in reality speak to me.

"Who am I that I can withstand God? Why does the world think to make me deny what I have actually seen, for I had seen a vision, I knew it and I knew God knew it and I could not deny it, neither dare I do it, at least by so doing I would offend God and come under condemnation . . . I had found the testimony of James to be true."

Moroni's Visit*

The visit of the angel is related by Joseph. He tells that while in prayer, a Personage appeared in his room, calling him by name and said he was a messenger sent from God. He explained that he was Moroni and that God had a great work for Joseph to do. He told of a book, written on gold plates, giving an account of the former inhabitants of this continent, and the source from whence they sprang. He also said that the fullness of the everlasting Gospel was contained in it, as delivered by the Savior to the ancient inhabitants.

He explained that there were two stones in silver bows, deposited with the plates. And that these stones, fastened to a breastplate, constituted what is called the Urim and Thummin. The possession and use of these stones was what constituted "Seers" in ancient or former times; and that God had prepared them for the purpose of translating the book. Moroni also related the prophecies of the Old Testament.

*Sept. 21, 1823 — 3 years later than the first vision.

After many visits of instruction and previous planning, the angel Moroni delivered the plates into the hands of Joseph Smith on September 22nd, 1827, at the Hill Cumorah situated in western New York.

THE BOOK OF MORMON

The Book of Mormon was first published in 1830 and takes its title from a man whose name was Mormon, one of the prophets whose writing are contained in the book. It is a translation of the sacred literature of sevaral nations on this American continent from approximately 2200 B.C. to 400 A.D. "Mor," the anglo-saxon word means more; "Mon," the Egyptian word means good — "More Good".

The book was translated into the English language through Divine assistance by Joseph Smith, the man who is accepted by over one-million Latter-day Saints as a Prophet, Seer and Revelator of God and one who was commissioned of God to effect a "restoration" of the Gospel of Jesus Christ.

MORONI'S PROMISE

This quotation from the writings of Moroni is directed to any who shall read the book:

"And when ye shall receive these things, I would exhort you that ye would ask God, the Eternal Father, in the name of Christ, if these things are not true; and if ye shall ask with a sincere heart, with real intent, having faith in Christ, He will manifest the truth of it unto you, by the Power of the Holy Ghost."*

Both the Bible and the Book of Mormon embellish Mormon pulpits and both books are accepted as holy scripture The Bible is basic to "Mormon" belief. The King James version is officially used and is believed to be the word of God as far as it is translated correctly.

The following paragraphs introduce us to the principles of the church to which Reynolds Cahoon and his family belonged. In explaining these principles, one may refer to "The Articles of Faith of the Church of Jesus Christ of Latter-day Saints" as written in the year 1842, by Joseph Smith. At the request of Mr. John Wentworth, editor and proprietor of the newspaper, the Chicago Democrat, Joseph made a statement

---

*Book of Mormon, Moroni 10:4

outlining the beliefs of the church members and these are known as the Articles of Faith.

First, they believe in the Trinity: three literal, distinct personalities — God the Eternal Father, His son Jesus the Christ and the Holy Ghost — the latter being a Personage of spirit. They believe in Divine Revelation; all that God has revealed; all that He does now reveal and that He will yet reveal many great and important things.

They claim no authority by succession from any other church, but that they have received Authority by direct Divine Bestowal. They are Christians in both the name of the church and in unqualified acceptance and worship of Jesus Christ and believe in the miraculous Conception.

They believe in Universal Salvation and that Exaltation must be earned by obedience to laws, ordinances and commandments of the Kingdom of God They believe in Faith in God, Repentance and Baptism by immersion; also in a simple Confirmation by the laying on of hands for the gift of the Holy Ghost; and in Communion as a simple manner of partaking of the Sacrament.*

They believe in the same organization that existed in the Primitive Church, viz: apostles, prophets, pastors, teachers, evangelists, etc. They believe in Salvation for the dead, in Celestial Marriage and in many other principles for eternal progression embracing all truth.

In fact, Reynolds and the other men who were associated with Joseph Smith were not naturally enthusiasts in the matter of religion; nor were they men who could be deceived. They were of Puritan ancestry and demanded the conviction of their reason before yielding their faith.

Mammoth volumes might be filled with the narratives, travels, vicissitudes and difficulties to which the Church of Jesus Christ of Latter-day Saints has been subjected, however, the foregoing brief introduction is ample to give us an insight into the foundation of this church. The following pages comprise a story of the life of Reynolds Cahoon with separate biographies of his wives and children.

Elder Reynolds Cahoon Ordained High Priest

On June 13, 1831, the fourth General Conference of this church was held at Kirtland, Ohio. These conferences are

---

*Notes taken from "What is a Mormon?" by Richard L Evans.

part of the divinely instituted organization of the church. Two-thousand members were in attendance and several Elders were ordained High Priests. Reynolds Cahoon writes in his private journal:

"Several were selected by revelation through President Smith and ordained to the High Priesthood after the Order of God, which is after the Order of Melchizedek. This was the first occasion in which the priesthood had been revealed and conferred upon Elders in this dispensation, except as being held by Joseph Smith and Oliver Cowdery, although the office is the same in a certain degree, but not in the fulness. On this occasion I was ordained to His Holy Ordinance and called by President Smith."

More than thirty missionaries were called on missions to preach the gospel and baptize by the way. They were to travel two by two. The revelation pertaining to the calling of Reynolds Cahoon was given June 7, 1831 and is recorded in the Doctrine and Covenants, Section 52, Verse 30:

"Let My Servants Reynolds Cahoon and Samuel H. Smith also take their journey."

Samuel H. Smith, brother of the Prophet, was one of the eight witnesses to the divine origin of the Book of Mormon and one of the charter members of the Church. At the time of this mission he was about twenty-three years of age. Reynolds was forty-one. Regarding their mission which was into Missouri, Lucy Smith, mother of Samuel and Joseph, gives us a few details that help us to envision the trip.

"Joseph was requested by Parley P. Pratt and his company who were then in Missouri to send Elders to assist them. Joseph inquired of the Lord and received the Revelation contained in Times and Seasons, Vol. 4, p. 416, in which Samuel H. Smith and Reynolds Cahoon were appointed to go together to Missouri. They immediately departed on their Mission. Before they had proceeded far, they called at a town, the name of which I do not remember, where they found William E. McClellin who was employed as a clerk in a store. After making a little inquiry, they found that Mr. McClellin was anxious to hear them preach and that he was willing to make exertion to obtain a house and congregation for them, for the name of the Latter-day Saints was new to him, and he felt curious to hear what the principles of our faith were.

"Shortly after they left, McClellin became very uneasy respecting his new acquaintances; he felt that it was his duty to have gone with them and assisted them on their journey. This feeling worked so strongly in his breast as to deprive him of rest all the ensuing night, and before morning, he concluded to set out for Missouri at the hazard of business, character and everything else. Accordingly after settling with his employer, he started in pursuit of Samuel and Brother Cahoon He passed them on the way, and got to Missouri and was baptized before they arrived. On their route Samuel and brother Cahoon suffered great hardships, such as want of rest and food. At the time they started for Missouri nearly fifty others started for the same place, all taking different routes. When they arrived they dedicated the spot for the Temple."

A journey of a thousand miles from Kirtland to Independence during these days was quite an undertaking. Of this trip Samuel writes:

"In 1831 I was called by revelation to go to Missouri in company with Reynolds Cahoon. Called on Wm. McClellin . . preached the gospel without purse or script, enduring much for want of food and rest . . . Elders met on the spot for the temple and dedicated the ground in Jackson County Brother Cahoon and I spent several days in Jackson County. attended several conferences and were with Joseph when he received several revelations, returned home in September.

Soon after, they took their mission into the Southern county of Ohio. Reynolds labored there six weeks. Samuel preached through the winter. From Reynolds Cahoon's Private Journal,* we read:

"Thursday, June 9, 1831. Elder Samuel H. Smith and Reynolds Cahoon left Kirtland, Ohio for Missouri, in obedience to a commandment. Journeyed to Northfield Preached Sabbath, June 12". July 14", spent our last penny for lodging. August, reached Lexington August 4", continued to Independence. I found some of the brethren and there my mortal eyes beheld great and marvelous things such as I had not ever expected to see in this world We had a glorious meeting on the Sabbath."

The return journey is of special significance and a source of great satisfaction to Elders Reynolds and Samuel. They

*This Journal is at the Church Historians Office, No 610 — Reynolds Cahoon Journal 1831-1832

sincerely believed that through Joseph Smith, the Lord had truly spoken these special words of praise regarding them:

"And let them journey together, or two by two, as seemeth them good, only let my servant Reynolds Cahoon and my servant Samuel H. Smith, with whom I am well pleased, be not separated until they return to their homes, and this for a wise purpose in me.*

EXCERPTS FROM REYNOLDS PRIVATE JOURNAL

Reynolds writes in his own Private Journal, and the same is recorded in the Church Journal History of Aug. 15th, 1831. We quote Reynolds' own words:

"After tarrying in Independence a number of days, engaged in exploring that region of country, the Lord commanded us to return . . . we crossed the Missouri River Aug 13", where we found Brother Hyrum Smith and others . . . In Fayette, we met Brother Joseph Smith, Oliver Cowdery and Sidney Rigdon who took the stage, while Samuel H. Smith and myself journed by land . . . We found Brother Thomas B. Marsh who was very sick. We prayed with him and laid hands on him (meaning administered to) . . . we found a number of men working on the road and in one of their camps we held a meeting . . . we traveled on, not knowing what the day would bring forth . . . the people requested us to stop and preach . . . we found people very anxious to know the truth . . . we held many meetings on our Westward journey. We found the region of the country in a state of excitement over the Book of Mormon. People were searching the scripture and came to hear what further testimony we had to give. September 4", we baptized three members . . . I went with my brother-in-law, J. Patten. We visited many cities and arrived home Wednesday Sept. 28 1831."

Upon his arrival home, Reynolds was appointed as one of the Elders to instruct the Saints the ancient manner of conducting meetings, and he and David Whitmore were appointed to obtain means in order that Joseph Smith and Sidney Rigdon might continue the translation of the Scriptures (or revision of the Bible).

---

*History of the Church — Vol. I, page 205 and Doctrine and Covenants — Sec. 61, Verse 35.

SECOND MISSIONARIES TO ENTER ILLINOIS

Church historians tell us that Samuel H. Smith and Reynolds Cahoon were the second missionaries to enter Illinois and the first to enter Kentucky. Having left Kirtland, Ohio, June 9, 1831, they arrived in the latter part of the month at Cincinnati where they crossed the Ohio River into Kentucky and traveled in that state about twenty miles in a westerly direction by way of Burlington and then recrossed the Ohio River to Rising Sun, Indiana.

The time was drawing near for the Church to establish itself in the center Stake of Zion (Independence, Missouri), the land which Joseph Smith had dedicated for both the Lamanites (Indians) and the gentiles and where a temple was to be erected.

The members were to receive recommends before they departed and they were guided by revelation in each instance. The members were anxiously awaiting their appointed time.

At a special Conference in Hiram, after Reynolds had opened the meeting by prayer, he said, "The question which I wish settled is, whether it is the will of the Lord that I should go to Zion in the spring." The conference voted that it was the mind of the conference that "Our brother Reynolds be not sent up to Zion the coming spring . . . that he is not commanded by anything yet written."

Joseph Smith had been told that he would be given power to discern by the Spirit, those who should go to the Land of Zion (Missouri) and those of the Lord's disciples who should tarry. Believing this sincerely, Reynolds asks the above question of November 11th, wishing only to be obedient in all things. If Reynolds were with us today he would in all probability, instruct us, his grandchildren, as follows:

"Truly the Bible tells us, 'The Lord revealeth His secrets unto His servants the prophets.' The Lord does not stand personally in the midst of His children to direct their affairs, but He speaks through His inspired servants. There must be one directing will. This is necessary in earthly concerns — a factory, a ship, a railroad system. It is equally necessary in the Kingdom of God. Be obedient! Even the Son learned obedience before He became the author of eternal salvation."

"I Shall Show Unto Three of You"

We now understand why Reynolds was retained in Kirtland — the first Temple was to be built there. The Lord had spoken: "Verily I say, it is My will that you build a House. If you keep My commandments you shall have power to build it . . . Let the House be built, not after the manner of the world, for I give not unto you that you shall live after the manner of the world. Therefore, let it be built after the manner which I shall show unto three of you, whom ye shall appoint and ordain unto this power."

"It was a very important undertaking. A Temple of the Lord had not been built anywhere upon the earth since Herod's reconstruction of Solomon's Temple on Mount Moriah It was imperative that a man of proved integrity and reliability should be placed in charge of the labor. The Church now numbered perhaps, fifteen hundred souls. From among that number, the Prophet selected Hyrum Smith. He was the man. Together with Reynolds Cahoon and Jared Carter, he was appointed on the building committee to gather means for the Temple and to superintend its building."*

Again the Lord speaks to them "If you keep not My Commandments, the love of the Father shall not continue with you, therefore, you shall walk in darkness. Yea, verily I say unto you, I gave you a commandment that you should build a House, in which House, I design to endow those whom I have chosen with Power from on High." And they were given the assurance, if obedient, they would have the privilege of seeing His face and receiving knowledge for themselves of His Divine Nature.

May 6, 1833, the Lord, calling the people "My Friends," commands them to commence laying out and preparing a foundation of the City of the Stake of Zion at Kirtland, "beginning at My house, and behold it must be done according to the pattern which I, the Lord have given unto you."

The lot on the south, a house for the Presidency, for work of the ministry and receiving revelations, "wholly dedicated unto the Lord". The second lot on the south, "for printing of the translation of My scriptures." It was on this date the revelations were given regarding the inheritances which Hyrum Smith, Reynolds Cahoon and Jared Carter were to receive.

Utah Genealogical and Historical Magazine, Vol 2, page 53

REYNOLDS GIVEN AN INHERITANCE*

"And on the third lot shall my servant Hyrum Smith receive his inheritance.

"And on the first and second lots on the north shall my servants Reynolds Cahoon and Jared Carter receive their inheritances —

"That they may do the work which I have appointed unto them to be a committee to build mine houses, according to the commandment, which I, the Lord, have given unto you."

Mighty indeed must have been the Prayer of Faith of Hyrum Smith, Reynolds Cahoon and Jared Carter, for Joseph Smith, speaking as a prophet, explains what the Lord says regarding those who shall receive an inheritance from the Lord:

"I (the Lord), say concerning the residue of the elders of My church, the time has not yet come for many years for them to receive their inheritance in this land, except they desire it through the prayer of faith, only as it shall be appointed unto them of the Lord."

Note the Lord's promises to Reynolds — he should have an inheritance in Zion and possess it again in eternity and be appointed to build himself a kingdom that should never have an end; that angels would have charge over him and he would converse with them face to face; that he would stand on the earth with his companion and children; that he would sit in council with the Ancients of Days with his fathers. These with other glorious blessings were "sealed upon him and his posterity forever".**

These inheritances were certain land grants and if the Saints had remained there in Kirtland, the descendants of Hyrum, Reynolds and Jared would have been legal heirs to that property to this day. This is what the Church intended, but the Lord knew that they could never become a great people in the East so they had to leave all and flee to the mountains. Recorded is the following prophecy:

"Yet your children may possess them, but not until many years shall pass away and then I will send forth and build up Kirtland and it shall be polished and refined according to My word."

It is a remarkable but little-known prophecy. At the present time we are asking ourselves the question, "Are we now

---

*Doctrine and Covenants, Section 94, Verses 13, 14, 15
**Patriarchal Blessings, Vol 7, p 295

entering the second phase of Hyrum Smith's prophecy? . . .
Yet your children may possess them . . ."*

The trustees had planned to sell all Church property, but
realizing that the Saints had been driven from their private
dwellings, these temples at Kirtland and Nauvoo would be of
no benefit to them, and when the time should come that they
should return and redeem their inheritances, they would secure them from injust claims, mobs, fire, etc., more effectually
than for the Church to retain them in their own hands.

Today the membership in that region is growing rapidly,
having more than doubled in the past five years. Ten branches
have been organized thus far, and others are contemplated
for the not-far-distant future. In Akron, a chapel has been
acquired and one in Cleveland. The Latter-day Saints are
well received in their communities. They are successful and
highly esteemed

In 1954, the Saints throughout the region were thrilled
by President David O. McKay's dedication of a new chapel
in Cleveland. Many prominent men throughout the nation —
the Governor of Ohio, Governor of Utah and Mayor of Cleveland sent telegrams of congratulations This beautiful chapel,
built almost entirely by the labors of the members, served
as a reminder of the sacrifices of the earlier Kirtland Saints.

The following editorial appeared in the Cleveland Press,
Monday, June 8, 1953:

> If Joseph Smith, the dedicated and courageous founder of
> the Mormon Church, were living today, he would take special
> pride in the news that a new Mormon Chapel shortly will be
> built on Lake Ave. near Edgewater Park The building would,
> for him, undoubtedly be confirmation of his own faith once
> shared by too few in northern Ohio, that the Church had spiritual
> strength and economic substance to live and grow.
> It was the religious forebearers of the builders of this chapel,
> first in Cleveland, who constructed a Mormon Temple more
> than 120 years ago in nearby Kirtland. . . And it must be with
> great pride that Cleveland Mormons can now note that their
> Church strength is sufficient to push the frontier back above the
> route of their once tragic march, and that they can build a
> chapel so close to the historic spot in Kirtland where their
> early temple stood

SIGNIFICANCE OF REYNOLDS' INHERITANCE

The special significance of this inheritance to the descendants of Reynolds Cahoon is that it indicates to us the high
esteem in which he was held by the leaders of the Church,

*See Excerpts of Hyrum Smith's Letter to Saints in Kirtland, *History of
Church* — Vol IV, p 443

not only because of his faith and obedience but because he
devoted his entire life to the work of the Church.

Let us recall his tremendous responsibilities at this time,
December 1831. He has the fantastically difficult job of directing the building of the Kirtland Temple and is also chosen,
with Hyrum Smith, to act as the Counselor to Bishop Whitney, the first Bishop at Kirtland. Many were his responsibilities:

> (a) To keep the Lord's storehouse and received funds of
> the Church, that is to look after the needy and pre-
> side over the temporal affairs of the Church.
>
> (b) To keep account of property consecrated for public
> use and administer needs of the Elders.
>
> (c) To furnish every Elder entitled to it, a certificate by
> which he is entitled to have a right to receive an in-
> heritance in Zion.
>
> (d) To keep account of the labors of every Bishop.
>
> (e) To aid, financially the "Stewards" appointed to look
> after the literary interests of the Church.

Bishop Whitney traveled around among all the churches
searching after the poor, administering to their wants and
Elders Pratt and Cahoon visited the different branches in
Ohio. On January 13th the Elders Marsh and Cahoon traveled
to branches west of Kirtland, holding meetings in Warrens-
ville, Alherst and other places. It was at that time that Mr.
Palmer listened to the preaching of these Elders and joined
the Church. He remarked:

"For the first time I saw the Book of Mormon, and after
reading some letters published, altho' they did not prove
the Book was not true, yet they gave the whole work such
a coloring or appearance of falsehood the feeling was 'that
Mormonism was overthrown,' however we afterwards received preaching from Brother Reynolds Cahoon and others
which made an impression on the minds of many that was
not easily eradicated . . . the way was thus prepared . . . and
many were baptized."

When the Kirtland Temple was commenced, the membership was few. The Church met in a school house 16 by 24 feet,
which was large enough to hold all the Saints, spectators and
visitors; they then undertook to build this temple They did
not have much fine flour bread to eat, not always molasses
for their johnny-cake. Sometimes they had shoes, sometimes

THREE MORMON TEMPLES
Significant in the lives of Reynolds and his sons.

KIRTLAND TEMPLE   NAUVOO TEMPLE

TEMPLE SQUARE IN SALT LAKE CITY
owing the Salt Lake Temple, famous Mormon Tabernacle and the Assembly Hall

July 17th 1832

Met in Conferance & ordained
Br Zebedee Coltrin a highpriest
and from the 17th I labored
with my family both spiri-
naly & temporaly and
with the Church frequen
-tly being Caled to visit
the sick & to lay hands on
them & to put them in
mind of their duty
up to the present

Aug 19th 1832
Therefore these are the
acts of Reynolds up to
August 19th 1832

Attest   R Cahoon

PAGE FROM REYNOLDS CAHOON'S JOURNAL

not, sometimes pants, sometimes very ragged ones. The families underwent great privations and persecutions during this period; not all the stories of privation and hardship can be told.

The temple must be guarded day and night Six months had passed and even in spite of these great privations and hardships, the Lord is not pleased with their efforts. He severely rebukes them for their tardiness and characterizes their delay as a "grievous sin".

The people knew that they were to remain in Kirtland but a short time. Word had been given them "to make Kirtland a stronghold for the space of five years and to prepare everything needful for the building of the House of God, a palace where His presence would be made manifest." We can understand why, when the adversary was marshalling his forces against the church, our Lord urged the Saints to build the Temple speedily. We can understand why the evil one planned to have them scattered before they could rear that sacred edifice.

COMMITTEE PREPARES TO BUILD KIRTLAND TEMPLE

On June 1, 1833, a Circular Letter was prepared by the building committee, who went to work to gather the means by subscription. Thus the building was under way. The following are the words penned by Reynolds Cahoon and his associates:

CIRCULAR*

Kirtland, June 1, 1833

TO THE CHURCH OF CHRIST In (   )

We feel under obligations to write to you as well as to all the brethren of the different branches; and we do this, that you, with us, may exert yourselves to bring about the fulfilment of the command of the Lord . . And unless we fulfil this command, viz; establish an house, and prepare all things whereby the elders may gather into a school, called the School of the Prophets, . . we may all despair of obtaining the great blessing that God has promised to the faithful of the Church of Christ, therefore it is as important, as our salvation, that we obey this above-mentioned command, as well as all the commandments of the Lord.

Therefore, brethren, we write this epistle to you, to stir up your minds to make that exertion which the Lord requires of you, to lend a temporal aid in these things above written, and in order that you may know how to conduct the business, we will relate what we have done and are doing here

*History of the Church — Vol I, p 349

We have met in Conference, and agreed to form a subscription, and circulate it through the churches. The conference also appointed Hyrum Smith, Reynolds Cahoon and Jared Carter, a committee to superintend this business . The subscriptions are now in circulation among us, and our Heavenly Father is opening the hearts of our brethren beyond expectation of many; and not one brother among us, as yet, refuses to exert himself to do something in a temporal way . . and may our Heavenly Father open your hearts also, that you with us, may gather together something to aid as a temporal benefit . .

These considerations we have written to you, knowing it to be our duty to do, and may the Lord help you to exert yourselves with us, in raising the means to bring about the glorious work of the Lord; and may we all be kept by the grace of God unto eternal life Amen.

> Hyrum Smith
> Reynolds Cahoon
> Jared Carter
> Committee

Such energetic attack could not fail to bring response and within a remarkably short time all preparations were made. "On June 5th, 1833, George Albert Smith hauled the first load of stone for the Temple, and Hyrum Smith and Reynolds Cahoon commenced digging the trench for the walls of the Lord's house, and finished the same with their own hands." Others also volunteered and by these means the work progressed.

Brigham Young and the Cahoon Family

It was in the year 1833, that Brigham Young came to Kirtland. He had at the age of twenty-four, joined the Methodist Church, of which church, his brother Joseph Young was a Minister. Upon hearing the Gospel of Jesus Christ as explained by the Latter-day Saint missionaries, both he and his brother Joseph joined the Church of Jesus Christ of Latter-day Saints or the "Mormon Church". Brigham was baptized April 14, 1832, was confirmed and ordained an Elder the evening of the same day. He was called on a mission to Canada, using all his means.

In September, 1833, he came to Kirtland, absolutely destitute, a widower with two children. He had borrowed a pair of shoes and some other articles of clothing as he had spent every dollar he had on missionary labors Many of the members of the Church left Kirtland to go in search of work during the winter. Of the thirty or forty Elders who came to Kirtland that fall, he was the only one who remained there during the winter. The others went wherever they could obtain higher wages than in Kirtland. Brigham Young went to work for Brother Cahoon, one of the trustees of the Temple. "I will stay here and work if I do not receive a farthing for my labors and have to beg bread," said Brigham. "I will stay here and assist to build the temple . . ."

As for wages, Brother Cahoon divided what little he had with Brigham. When the work was done and the balance due was paid, it was subsequently found that none of those who had left Kirtland for higher wages had been able to save as much as had he. He stayed in Kirtland till the year 1837 and then he practically abandoned property valued at $5,000. In Nauvoo he also left houses, and came to Utah without a farthing, except a span of horses, a carriage and harness, all of which had been given him in payment for a house in Nauvoo.*

REYNOLDS HELPS BUILD SCHOOL HOUSE

The temple committee was appointed, not only to obtain subscriptions for the building of the "Houses of the Lord," but were to be managers of the store in Kirtland, through which much of the business connected with its construction was accomplished. Hyrum, Reynolds and Jared also were to raise money and superintend the construction of a school building in Zion. This school was "the first educational movement of the church, the value of which cannot be fully appreciated even yet."

In this school, instruction was given to all who were called into the ministry for the expounding of all scriptures. Parley P. Pratt presided. Hebrew, Greek and Latin were taught. "Seek ye diligently, teach one another words of wisdom; Yea, seek ye out of the best books words of wisdom; seek learning even by study, and also by faith" were the teachings of the Church. Mental and physical health were also stressed. The Mormons were among the first to build schools and universities where ever they settled and this was, probably, the first formal program for adult education in America. William F. Cahoon, son of Reynolds, tells us he attended this school.

They had been told, however, that great blessings were to come "after much tribulation" and history reveals that in Kirtland, only a short time after they had begun to use the

*Journal of Discourses, Vol. XI, pp 295-6

building, persecution (the bitter fruits of religious intolerance) was lifted against them and their leaders were falsely accused Reynolds remarked that the way to heal those wounds would be that the accusers make a public confession which should be printed in the "Star."

REYNOLDS CAHOON AS MODERATOR*

That we as the descendants of Reynolds Cahoon, may appreciate the innermost feelings of Reynolds and those men who loved their prophet, some of the words of the "Resolution of Vindication" for which Reynolds acted as moderator are recopied herein:

RESOLVED That after hearing from the mouths of some, that a suspicion rested upon their minds relative to the conduct of our President as regards his honesty and Godly walk, we have investigated his whole proceedings and we are happy to have in our power to say to our brethren, one and all, that we are satisfied with his conduct, having learned from the clearest evidence, that he has acted in every respect worthy of his high and responsible station in this Church, and has prudently and cautiously preserved the good of this society at large, and is still worthy of our esteem and fellowship, and that those reports could have originated in minds of none except such as either from a natural misunderstanding, or a natural jealousy, are easily led to conceive of evils where none exists

RESOLVED That we say to our brethren that while we are surrounded by thousands eager to grasp at a shadow if they have a hope of turning it into falsehood for the injury of the Gospel, we exhort them to be steadfast and immovable in the truth, resting assured that while they continue to walk in the Holy Covenant you have professed to embrace, that nothing can operate against their good; and that while wickedness abounds, as in days of old, the characters of those seeking the greatest good for their fellow men will be shamefully traduced and every act of their lives misrepresented, and a false shade thrown over their worthy deeds, all this is calculated to create an evil prejudice in the minds of the community, to prevent, if possible, the increase of light; the better to effect evil purposes and keep men in error. We say, dear brethren, may peace and the blessings of our Lord Jesus Christ be multiplied unto you through the knowledge of truth, forever

RESOLVED: That the minutes be signed by the moderator and clerk, and published to the churches in the Evening and Morning Star

Reynolds Cahoon, Moderator
Oliver Cowdery, Clerk

NAME OF THE BROTHER OF JARED IS REVEALED

Before leaving the year 1834, let us relate a certain incident which is of special significance to us as a family and also

*History of the Church, Vol II, page 147.

important in the history of the Book of Mormon. It is pertaining to the christening of an infant son, the seventh child of Reynolds and Thirza Stiles Cahoon.

Among the many questions asked regarding the truths of the Book of Mormon, the following were these:

"Is the name of the brother of Jared known? If so, what is it, and when was it made known? How did the Prophet Joseph Smith get to know definitely the name of the brother of Jared?"

In a note on an article of the Jaredites, Elder George Reynolds in the Juvenile Instructor, Vol. 27, page 282, says concerning the revealing of the name which is not found in the Book of Mormon:

"While residing in Kirtland, Elder Reynolds Cahoon had a son born to him. One day when President Joseph Smith was passing his door he called the Prophet in to bless and name the baby. Joseph did so and gave the boy the name of Mahonri Moriancumer. When he had finished the blessing he laid the child on the bed and turning to Elder Cahoon said, 'The name I have given your son is the name of the brother of Jared; the Lord has just shown (or revealed) it to me.'

"Elder William F. Cahoon, who was standing near heard the prophet make this statement to his father; and this was the first time the name of the Brother Of Jared was known in the Church in this dispensation."

In his document in the Historian's Office, William F. states "Mahonri Moriancumer Cahoon, son of Reynolds and Thirza was named and blessed by the prophet Joseph Smith, who said that 'Mahonri Moriancumer' was the name of the Brother of Jared."

As the posterity of Reynolds and Thirza Cahoon, we are honored that the Cahoon name has thus found favor in the sight of the Lord and that in this humble home "all things were in order" that it was so chosen for the unfolding of one of these hidden truths.

First Public Marriage in the Mormon Church

In this family and home another event of much importance occurred. It is "The First Public Marriage in the Mormon Church." Let us visit with the Cahoon family on this joyful day, a day of happiness, unique in its nature. It is Sunday, January 17, 1836 and all members are especially groomed for the occasion. Yes, it is the wedding of William Farrington Cahoon to Nancy Miranda Gibbs, Lerona Eliza Cahoon to Harvey Stanley and Tunis Rapley to Louisa Cutler.

Thirza Cahoon, the mother of Lerona Eliza and William F, had been promised by the Patriarch — "thou shalt partake of all the blessings . . . sealed upon the head of thy companion . . . for in common with him thou shalt enjoy all the blessings that Heaven and Earth can afford; thou shalt have power to heal thy children and preserve them from the destroyer to be a comfort to thee . . . and also to do any miracle that wisdom will dictate for the health and happiness of thy family . . . Thy heart shall be made to rejoice and thou shalt have riches in abundance; Thou shalt be able to set a table to feed a thousand with as much ease as thou canst now feed ten; . . ."

Surely this promise was put to the test at the marriage of her eldest son and daughter Thirza prepared the wedding feast and there were about three-thousand in attendance.

The Kirtland Temple Dedicated

"Although there are in the world many temples, cathedrals, and churches of architectural and historical interest, yet of all these there is none more unique architecturally or more interesting historically than the 'Temple' which these Latter-day Saints built in the village of Kirtland," says Mr. Thomas O'Donnell, A I A. assistant professor of architecture at the University of Illinois.

Elder George A. Smith said, "The temple was considered a very large building. Some nine-hundred sixty could be seated, and at the dedication, over a thousand persons were together.

"The cost was between sixty and seventy thousand dollars. The size was fifty and five feet in width and sixty and five feet in length in the inner court and built after the manner 'Shown Unto Three' There were two stories or courts, the lower for sacrament meetings, preaching and praying, and the upper one for the School of the Apostles There were four pulpits, one rising above the other like terraces Each of these pulpits could be separated from the others by means of veils, which could be let down or rolled up at pleasure. There were two stands, one on the west end and one on the east end, each consisting of the four pulpits mentioned above.

The Melchizedek on the west, the Aaronic on the east. The benches in pews were movable."

On the building was inscribed, "Holiness To The Lord."

The corner stone was laid July 23, 1833, at which time Reynolds Cahoon was chosen one of the officiating Elders, and on March 27, 1836, their beautiful Temple was dedicated.

An Angel, John The Beloved and the Lord Appear

On the day of the dedication, an angel appeared and sat near Joseph Smith Sr., and Frederick G. Williams. He was tall, had black eyes and white hair, wore a garment extending to near his ankles, and had sandals on his feet. "He was sent as a messenger to accept the dedication" says Heber Kimball. A few days afterwards, a solemn assembly was held in accordance with a commandment received, and blessings were given. "While these things were being attended to, the beloved disciple John, was seen in our midst by the Prophet Joseph, Oliver Cowdery and others "

The three members of the building committee were given a special blessing, "the blessing of heaven and a right in the House of the Lord." Reynolds Cahoon was the only one of the committee present, however, the rights of Hyrum Smith and Jared Carter in the House were preserved.

On Sunday, April 3, 1836, in the afternoon after Sacrament, the Prophet Joseph and Oliver Cowdery retired to the pulpit to engage in silent prayer. The vision surpassing all other glorious manifestations appeared before their eyes — Our Lord Appears, suddenly!

The joy, the satisfaction that came to these Latter-day Saints — "the heavenly manifestations," says an eye-witness (Eliza R. Snow), "no mortal language can describe." It was truly a day of Pentecost. Probably the most glorious spiritual blessings of the entire history of the Latter-day Saints were the events surrounding the dedication of the Kirtland Temple.

The committee had successfully performed its labors and the Kirtland Temple stands, even today, a monument to the indefatigable zeal of Hyrum Smith and his fellow workers on the building committee.

Sometimes the impression is given that because our pioneers went through untold hardship incidental to frontier life that this is the only life they knew. This is as far from the truth as anything could be. The majority of the pioneers were people of refinement and culture. They appreciated the finer things. To prove this, one has only to go back over the trail and see it expressed in the architecture of their homes and church buildings, especially the Kirtland Temple. In these architectural achievements their character was revealed.

Listed among the descendants of Reynolds Cahoon are sons, grandsons and great grandsons outstanding as architects, engineers, builders and designers of beautiful homes and noteworthy edifices. Undoubtedly, they have been endowed with a portion of that gift from him. Imagine their surprise, if after completing a beautiful building, the Lord should appear and speak to them the words He spoke to Reynolds and those fine Saints in this House in Kirtland, Ohio:

"Behold, I have accepted this house . . . I will manifest myself in mercy in this house . . . I will speak unto them with mine own voice if my people will keep my commandments . . Let the hearts of all my people rejoice who have with their might, built this house to My name . . . the fame of this house shall spread to foreign lands . . I am the First and Last; I am He who liveth, I am He who was slain; I am your advocate with the Father."*

To the Kirtland Temple came Jehovah, the Lord, who had spoken these words to them, and the Latter-day Saints were not the only ones who were aware of these supernatural manifestations, for the people of the neighborhood, "hearing an unusual sound like that of a rushing wind and seeing a bright pillar of light resting upon the temple, came running together and were astonished at what was taking place." This continued until the meeting closed at 11 p.m.

"We Saw the Lord"

The pulpit veil had been lowered, the record continues, so that Joseph and Oliver Cowdery were by themselves, but to their mind's eye the veil was removed, and the eyes of their understanding were opened. "We saw the Lord," they exclaimed, "He was standing upon the breast-work of the pulpit, before us, and under his feet was a paved work of pure gold in color like amber. His eyes were as a flame of fire, the hair of his head was white like pure snow, his countenance shone above the brightness of the sun, and his voice

---

*Doctrine and Covenants, Sec. 110.

was as the sound of rushing of great waters, even the voice
of Jehovah — at once majestic, awe-inspiring and sweet."

After this vision closed, according to church records, the
heavens were again opened and Moses appeared and committed unto them the keys of the gathering of Israel and the
leading of the ten tribes from the land of the north. After
this, Elias appeared and committed the dispensation of the
Gospel of Abraham, saying that in us, and our seed, all generations after us should be blessed After this vision had
closed another great and glorious vision burst upon them, for
Elijah the prophet, who was taken to heaven without tasting
death, stood before them to "turn the hearts of the fathers
to the children and the children to the fathers, lest the whole
earth be smitten with a curse" Elijah had again appeared as
was spoken by Malachi before the great and dreadful day of
the Lord Elijah's mission was to restore again the "Work for
the Dead" and "Celestial Marriages" in the temples.

Comparable with these wonderful visions and manifestations, the Lord gave them the joyful assurance which alone
can bring peace to a human heart — "Your sins are forgiven
. . your names are written in the heavens "

Not long, however, could the Mormon people rejoice in
their labors in their temple at Kirtland, for its erection seemed
to increase the hostile opposition to which the church had
been subjected since its organization, and persecution soon
became so violent that all who could dispose of their property and leave, did so and joined their fellow religionist in
Missouri. The preceeding year 1835, found exiles from Jackson County scattered mostly in Clay County, then in 1836,
they gathered at Shoal Creek, Missouri and incorporated the
new County, Calwell

At this time the spirit of speculation in lands and property
throughout the whole nation was also taking deep root in
the Church, the results of which oftimes were evil surmising,
fault-finding, disunion, dissension and apostasy. This was the
condition of the Saints at Kirtland. The United States was
passing through a financial crisis, brought on by over-specu-
lation and other causes, and the people, of the Church who
had been drawn into the maelstrom suffered with the rest
of the victims.

"The spirit of the Lord withdrew from their hearts and
they were filled with pride and hatred towards those who
maintained their integrity. Many of Joseph's friends went

astray in every direction; they boasted of talents at their command and what they would do. The spirit of apostasy continued rampant, and outsiders joined them in their contention against the Church.

"They were affected by the failure of the bank that the Church had set up, this failure being caused, in part, because one of the trusted men of the bank proved to be a traitor. This bank was only one of the hundreds, however, to go down in the panic of 1837. All over the country banking institutions failed. The money of the Kirtland Bank had been invested in land which at this time depreciated greatly in value. Brigham Young, because he had exposed the villainy of some men in connection with the bank failure, became an object of their rage."

Although these Mormon people were enduring all these great afflictions, and had pledged all they had — property, money, credit and reputation to accomplish the building of their great Temple, it was necessary that they should expand their lands, and build more chapels of worship because of their crowded, overflowing condition, the Church record reveals.

REYNOLDS APPEALS FOR THE PAYMENT OF TITHING*
(Kirtland, Ohio, Sept. 18, 1837)

Therefore, a memorial to go forth in the name and by authority of the Church, was issued by Newel Whitney, Reynolds Cahoon and Vinson Knight, the Bishopric in charge of the church at Kirtland.

"To the Saints Scattered Abroad, the Bishop and his Counselors Send Greeting:

"Whereas, the Church in Kirtland has taken into consideration the affairs of the Latter-day Saints in general . . . it has been deemed of great importance to the prosperity of the cause of truth in general, that the Bishop and his counselors send abroad this their memorial to all the Saints throughout the land, as well as to all well wishers to the cause of Zion in this our most happy country.

"It is a fact well known that the Saints have been called to endure great affliction, to bear a heavy burden . . . and besides all this there have been a large number of poor who had to receive assistance . . . and now so numerous are the Saints grown that it is impracticable for them all to gather

---

*History of the Church, Vol II, p 515 to 518

to the places which are appointed for this purpose . . . All these things will be attended with expense.

"It is a fixed purpose of our Lord, and has been so from the beginning, as appears by the ancient prophets, that the great work of the last days was to be accomplished by the tithing of His Saints. The Saints were required to bring their tithes into the store house and after that, not before, they were to look for a blessing that there should not be room enough to receive it. (Malachi 3rd Chapter 10th Verse.)

"Every Saint has an equal interest in building up Zion of our God . . . We all look for the appearing of the great God and our Savior Jesus Christ, but we shall look in vain until Zion is built, for Zion is to be His dwelling place . . . How then is the Lord to dwell in Zion, if Zion be not built up? This question we leave to the Saint to answer . . .

"Whatever is glorious, whatever is desirable, whatever pertains to salvation, either temporal or spiritual, our hopes, our expectations, our glory and reward all depend on our building up Zion . . . Let every Saint consider well . . . the great responsibility which rests on him or her . . .

"We send this memorial in the name of our Master, Jesus, believing that this appeal will be received with great kindness . . . and may God of all grace pour out His richest blessings on your heads and crown you with abundance . . . is the prayer of your brethren in Jesus Christ."

> Newel K. Whitney
> Reynolds Cahoon
> Vinson Knight

Toward the close of the year 1837, many of the leaders and most of the Saints had gone to Missouri. The temple in Kirtland, they now left for good and all. At the very time when men were leaving the Church in considerable numbers, the first foreign mission was organized, and many more joined the Church during this year than left it, as the organization rolled westward to its destiny. Upper Missouri being sparsely inhabited, lent itself admirably to occupation by the Mormon people.

Reynolds Cahoon, with John Smith and Elder Marks, presided over the stake at Kirtland until Reynolds' departure to Missouri in the Spring of 1838. Business was at a low-ebb, spiritual conditions very gloomy, the printing press had been attacked and the people were harrassed and persecuted They took their journey, selling their property for a trifle, but they were composed and listened to the voice of their leaders in Kirtland when they said, "Leave here, get out of the place." Those who ignored this warning met with hardship and apostasy.

REYNOLDS LEAVES FOR MISSOURI

In the Spring of 1838 Reynolds, his wife and family travel to Missouri. They were compelled to leave behind them everything they possessed. "We turned the key and locked the door of our homes, leaving our property and all we possessed in the hands of enemies and strangers, never receiving a cent for anything we owned," says William F., son of Reynolds.

Joseph Smith writes·

"Monday, June 7, 1838. I visited with Elders Reynolds Cahoon and Parley P. Pratt who had this day arrived in Far West, the former from Kirtland and the latter from New York where he had been preaching for some time and our hearts were made glad with the pleasing intelligence of the gathering of the Saints from all parts of the earth.

"Tuesday 8th — I spent day with Elder Rigdon in visiting Elder Cahoon at the place he had selected for his residence and in attending to some of our private, personal affairs.

"Sunday 13th — Elder Reynolds Cahoon preached in the forenoon.

"June 28th — A conference of Elders and members of the Church was held in this place this day for the purpose of organizing this Stake, called Adam-ondi-Ahman."*

MINUTES OF MEETING ORGANIZING STAKE

The meeting convened at 10 o'clock a m in the grove near the house of Lyman Wight President Joseph Smith Jr was called to the chair. He explained the object of the meeting which was to organize a Presidency and High Council to preside over this Stake of Zion and attend to the affairs of the Church in Daviess County

It was then moved, seconded and carried by the unanimous voice of the assembly, that John Smith should act as President of the Stake Reynolds Cahoon was unanimously chosen first counselor and Lyman Wight, second counselor   . President John Smith, Reynolds Cahoon and Lyman Wight then made some remarks   . After singing the well known hymn 'Adam-ondi-Ahman,' the meeting closed by prayer by Pres Cahoon

*History of the Church, Vol III, p 38.

Adam-ondi-Ahman is located immediately on the north side of Grand River, Davies County, Missouri, about twenty-five miles north of Far West and about eighty miles north of Independence. It is an elevated spot of ground which makes the place as healthful as any part of the United States Overlooking the river and country round about, it is certainly a beautiful location. It is here the Mormons gathered by the hundreds; it sprung up over night. Originally, it was called Spring Hill but Joseph named it Adam-ondi-Ahman as instructed by the Lord, "Because," he said, "It is the place where Adam shall come to visit his people or the Ancient of Days shall sit, as spoken of by Daniel, the prophet."

This town was making rapid progress when the Saints saw forming again, those elements which threatened their peace. It is small wonder that righteous anger flushed their cheeks and led them instinctively to form the resolution, "that they would submit no more to such acts of despoilation, injustice and outrage."

It was this sense of outraged injustice and inhumanity which led to the deliverance of the noted oration by Sidney Rigdon at Far West on Wednesday, July 4, 1838 in the course of which, there was expressed a strong determination to no more submit quietly to mob violence and acts of pillage. This outburst against injustice was probably unwise at this time, but it was the natural thing to do. Had the Prophet Joseph Smith, spoken on this occasion, his feelings respecting the repeated acts of injustice heaped upon himself and the Saints in Missouri, would have been more temperately expressed than were those of Sidney Rigdon on the July 4, 1838.

TEMPLE SITE AT FAR WEST DEDICATED

A procession which comprised the infantry (militia), the Patriarchs, the President, Vice-President, Orator, Twelve Apostles, other officers and L. D S. members commenced their march at 10 o'clock a.m. They formed a circle around the excavation and this day, July 4, 1838, the Site for the Temple at Far West was dedicated.

Thus, the Saints spent the day celebrating the Declaration of Independence Joseph Smith was president of the day, Hyrum Smith, vice-president, and Reynolds Cahoon, acted as Chief Marshal

The oration given by Sidney Rigdon proved to be very damaging and a potent factor against the Saints in the subsequent movements of their enemies.

This event was but a minor pretext for the persecutions.
The real cause was that "the religious tenets of this people
were so different from the churches of the age . . . the eccen-
tricity of the religious opinions of the Mormons." A latter-
day prophet had announced a revelation from God and the
gospel had again been restored . . . These statements, the
enemies of the church would not accept.*

REYNOLDS REPRESENTS THE SAINTS IN SOLEMN PLEDGE

In August 1838, the appalling mob crusade began which
finally resulted in the exile of the Mormons from the state
of Missouri The enemies on August 6th, organized with a
determination to prevent the Mormons from voting — the
most sacred right of American citizenship. The Mormons
fought with desperate courage but at last, overpowered by
numbers, they withdrew to their homes.

Some of the leading citizens called upon the Prophet and
together they agreed to hold a conference at Adam-ondi-
Ahman on August 9th. Both parties met in friendly council
and entered into a covenant of peace to preserve each other's
rights and to stand in each other's defense. For the Saints,
such men as Lyman Wight, Reynolds Cahoon, and others gave
their pledge. The settlers were well represented and made
their solemn promise.**

"ORDER OF EXTERMINATION" — OCTOBER 27, 1838

These following events are retold, not to revive incidents
which, for the credit of the country had best be forgotten,
but because they are so closely linked to the lives of our
ancestors and because in these experiences, their emotions
and feelings are so vividly portrayed.

In spite of the "pledge of peace," Governor Boggs issued
an "Order of Extermination" of the Mormons and an armed
mob came upon them which resulted in that terrible massacre
of Haun's Mill. Without any notice of this order to the Mormons, this mob tore down and destroyed their homes, shot
their animals, killed their men, women and children.

Had they committed crimes that merited this treatment?
No! The court records do not show a single instance of our
people having broken the laws Such sorrowful scenes! They
died with these words on their lips, "Whatever you do, O!
do not deny the faith."

*Church Chronology, Printed 1899.
**Joseph, The Prophet, by George Q Cannon

Joseph Smith who had been taken a prisoner, asked General Wilson, "Why am I thus treated? I am not aware of ever having done anything worthy of such treatment. I have always been a supporter of the Constitution of the Democracy." The general answered, "I know it and that is the reason why I want to kill you, or have you killed." That, then was the answer and that was the story! There was no justice.

The inflamed state of public opinion finally reached such a pitch that during the winter months of 1838, Governor Lilburn W. Boggs pledged himself to treat the Mormons "as enemies" and declared that they "must be exterminated or driven from the State." This "extermination" order was issued to the State Militia without any official investigation being conducted. The troups poured in before the Mormons could make an appeal or state their case

At Haun's Mill many were massacred. At Far West and other settlements they were forced to move out on the snow-covered prairies. They appealed to the Missouri legislature for protection but it was a futile gesture. Their unexpected haste in leaving, the lack of preparation and the inclement weather soon resulted in widespread suffering with epidemics and a considerable loss of life. Property valued at two million dollars was destroyed or confiscated. This was the beginning of the story of the trek of our ancestors, the Mormon Pioneers.

REYNOLDS TELLS OF INHUMANITY

Reynolds Cahoon and his son William F. tell us of the inhumanity to them and the outrages that "shock all nature and defy all description." Realizing that it is contrary to the Gospel for man to take vengeance into his own hands, they resigned themselves to whatever should follow, and it was not until a more positive and official testimony was wanted by the authorities at Washington, that their leader, Joseph Smith, advised the Saints to defend themselves by "gathering together knowledge of all the facts, sufferings and abuses put upon them by the people of Missouri" and submit them to the highest tribunal.

The falsehoods promulgated against the Saints had blinded many honest men and women and for their sakes, the truth should be made known and then people of Missouri will some day be glad to make whatever amends they can for the wrongs suffered in that state, not because anybody will en-

deavor to compel them to do so, but because they will esteem
it a privilege to obliverate these mistakes of the past. Then
the facts will be considered important and should be on record. William F. Cahoon made an affidavit of the "Missouri
Wrongs " (See his autobiography on page 86)

MORMONS MOVE OUT OF MISSOURI

A torrential stream of wagons, carts, livestock and people
moved out of the Mormon settlements in western Missouri.
Those of the Mormon leaders who had escaped imprisonment
or death struck a course back across the state of Illinois.
Welcome word came that food, clothing, friendship and shelter
awaited the refugees at Quincy. Word also came that Governor Robert Lucas of the territory of Iowa would offer the
Mormons hospitality and cheap lands In fact some suggested
that the Mormons were more likely to receive fair treatment
in a Federal territory than in one of the states. The Mormon
leaders were appreciative but they chose Illinois. Somewhere
in Illinois they hoped to lay out new farms, find sites for
new cities and build their commonwealth all over again. At
Quincy, however, the charity and warmheartedness of the
inhabitants permitted them to rest and take counsel.

NAUVOO THEIR CITY IN THE WILDERNESS

Fifty miles up the Mississippi River from Quincy, Illinois
a beautiful, green rolling ridge overlooked the mile-wide Father of Waters At the foot of the ridge lay a low, level swampland. This boggy, black-soiled peninsula pushed westward two
miles into the path of the oncoming river. This forced the
Mississippi to make a long, lazy hairpin detour thereby surrounding the peninsula on three sides with its swirling, silt-
laden waters. The Mormons learned that this swampland was
for sale and the terms were good Obviously, it was not a
likely site on which to build a city but because of the people's
poverty there was scarcely no alternative. Joseph Smith
arrived from Missouri after six months of abuse as a political
prisoner. He looked over the marshland and decided that
"with a little hard work" they would make it both healthful
and habitable They gave it the name of Nauvoo, a Hebrew
term meaning "Beautiful Place."

NAUVOO "THE BEAUTIFUL"

Here at Nauvoo, Hancock County, Illinois, our Mormon
Pioneers settled and out of this swamp in that horseshoe

WINTER QUARTERS (Left)
This Memorial represents the Pioneer Saints who lost their lives in the great Western Trek.

CHIMNEY ROCK, NEBRASKA
(Below)
A famous landmark along the pioneer trail, significant to the **Andrew Cahoon Family.**

**FORT MOORE PIONEER
MEMORIAL** (Below)
Los Angeles, California. Depicts Mormon Battalion Flag-Raising Ceremonies July 4, 1847.

**WOMEN OF MORMON
BATTALION
(Right below)
San Diego, California**

THE MORMON PIONEER MEMORIAL BRIDGE
Spanning the Missouri River where the Mormon pioneers ferried their

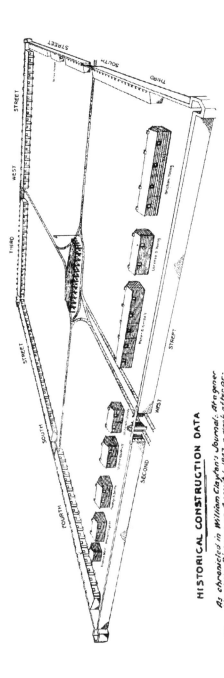

THE OLD FORT
GREAT SALT LAKE CITY
GREAT BASIN
NORTH AMERICA

As constructed by the Pioneers upon their
arrival in the Salt Lake Valley in 1847.

HISTORICAL CONSTRUCTION DATA

As chronicled in William Clayton's Journal: At a general assembly of the Pioneers on August 1, 1847, a week after arrival in the Salt Lake Valley, it was agreed that the various
"companies form into one camp and labor together; that the officers be a committee to form a corral and that the corral be
formed temporary;... that we build houses instead of living in
wagons this winter; that we go to work immediately putting up
houses; that we work unitedly, that the houses form a stockade or
fort to keep out the Indians. Discussion ensued as to relative mer-
its of adobe bricks and logs for building purposes. As shown on
the drawing herewith, homes of the leaders, along the east side
of the square, were log structures. The balance, backed up against
the other three walls, were of adobe construction. The following
accepts from various historical writings of the period cover.
the available material relating with construction of the Old Fort,
the site of which is now known as Pioneer Park or Pioneer Square.
together with extracts from Eliza R. Snow's diary which give an insight into living conditions the first winter there.

bend of the Mississippi sprang up the largest city in the State of Illinois It was a beautiful city with wide, straight streets, houses of brick, lumber or stone; some were large, commodious and stylish. A fine hotel, university, school, stores and churches were built. In five years its population was 20,000, almost as large as Washington, D C and three times larger than Chicago at that time. Across the river in Iowa were ten thousand more Saints and coming from the British Isles and Europe were additional converts

Nothing like this had happened before in the United States The result of the building of these cities was a political miracle and Joseph Smith, the man who planned it, was looked upon in certain circles as a mighty genius. The New York Times called him one of the great men of his age "whose history will rank with those who, in one way or another, have stamped their impress strongly on society" Others said, "he is an extraordinary character, a prophet-hero."

Joseph, however, would take no credit for it He gave all credit to God and insisted that the Church would continue whether he was the President or someone else took his place. He considered himself merely an "instrument" along with the other members of the church in spreading the Restored Gospel among the nations of the earth.

"Build A House Unto Me"

On January 19, 1841, came a command from the Lord ". . . I command you, all ye My Saints, to build a house unto Me . For a baptismal font there is not upon the earth, that they, My Saints, may be baptized for those who are dead — for this ordinance belongeth to My house, and cannot be acceptable to Me, only in days of your poverty wherein ye are not able to build a house unto Me."

Reynolds Chosen To Build Nauvoo Temple

On the eastern plateau overlooking the Mississippi river was to be erected a "large and splendid edifice of grandeur and magnificence" — another Temple.

Reynolds Cahoon who had been officiating as a counselor over the Branch in Iowa, was called to Nauvoo in October, 1840 to assist in the superintendency of building a second great "House of the Lord." The same revelation that directed the Saints to build the Nauvoo House also commanded that they should build a temple. Less than four months after

this revelation was received, the corner stones were laid for
the temple (April 6, 1841). The site of the Nauvoo Temple
was twelve blocks from the residence of the Prophet and
was located an equal distance from the river on three sides.
His home stood near the river bank and the Temple was
erected on the bluffs to the north.

The log house into which Joseph moved is now known
as the "Old Homestead." It was the first Indian trading post
in Illinois. Joseph remained there with his family until the
Mansion House was completed.

Reynolds Cahoon assisted in building the Mansion House.
It was built to accommodate visitors and also to serve as
a residence of the Prophet. The family was living there at
the time of the martyrdom of the Prophet. The Nauvoo House
was also built. This was to be for the boarding of strangers
who came from afar "that the weary traveler may find
health and safety while he shall contemplate the word of the
Lord. . . ."

First Endowment House in this Dispensation

On the second floor of a two-story structure belonging
to the Prophet Joseph Smith was an office, a lodge room
which was also used as the first Endowment House in this
dispensation. It was a brick store and Joseph carried on a
retail merchandising business on the lower floor.

May 4, 1842, the Prophet recorded in his journal that he
spent the day instructing certain men "in the principles
and order of the Priesthood, attending to washings, annoint-
ing, endowments, and the communication of keys pertaining
to the Aaronic Priesthood, and so on, to the highest order of
the Melchizedek Priesthood; setting forth the order pertaining to the Ancient of Days, and all those plans and principles
by which anyone is enabled to secure the fullness of those
blessings which have been prepared for the Church of the
First Born, and come up and abide in the presence of Eloheim,
in the eternal worlds."

"How vain," said their leaders, "are the imaginations of
the children of men to presume for a moment that the slaughter of one, two or a hundred leaders of this church, could
destroy an organization so perfect in itself, and so harmoniously arranged that it will stand while one member of
it is left upon the earth."

THREE APPOINTED TO BUILD NAUVOO TEMPLE

"Before the church was comfortably settled," said William Clayton, "The authorities began to talk on the subject of building a temple. A committee of three was appointed, Reynolds Cahoon, Alpheus Cutler and Elias Higbee. In February, Elder Cutler laid out the foundation of the building, assisted by Elder Cahoon and others, and on the 18th, the brethren commenced to dig the cellar, and notwithstanding the extreme poverty of the church everything moved on and the prospects looked "cheering and pleasing"."*

NAUVOO TEMPLE BAPTISMAL FONT DEDICATED

The font was situated in the center of the basement room under the main hall of the temple. It was constructed of pine timber put together of staves, tongued and grooved, oval-shaped, sixteen feet long east and west and twelve feet wide, seven feet from the foundation, the basin four feet deep. The moulding of the cap and base were formed of beautiful carved work. It stood upon twelve oxen, four on each side and two at each end; their heads, shoulders and forelegs, beautifully carved, projected out from under the font.

The font was dedicated November 8, 1841 by Brigham Young and on Sunday, 21st of the same month, the first baptisms for the dead were performed in the Lord's House. Forty persons were baptized for their dead and from this time, as long as the Saints remained in Nauvoo, baptisms were performed in the Temple.

As may be supposed, the efforts in executing the great task placed upon the building committee did not always meet with the individual likes and dislikes of the people of Nauvoo. The burden was heavy and the difficulties, many. We find complaints at times, such as: "Pulaski Cahoon was never appointed boss over the stone cutters shop . . . not all of the sons of Reynolds Cahoon have paid their tithing . . . William F. Cahoon has paid all his tithing, but some of the others have not . . ." etc.

A case of the stone-cutters against the temple committee was debated on Friday, April 7, 1843. The following is recorded:

"Alpheus Cutler of the building committee said that he

---

*Private Journal of William Clayton, April 8, 1841.

did not know of any wrong he had done. Reynolds Cahoon
said, 'This is not an unexpected matter for me to be called
up. I do not want you to think that I am perfect Somehow
or other, since Elder Cutler went up into the Pine Country,
I have, from some cause, been placed in peculiar circumstances I think I have never been placed in so critical a
position since I was born When President Smith had goods
last summer we had better property, goods would not buy
corn without some cash, instead of horses, we took store
pay I have dealt out meal and flour to the hands to the last
ounce, when I had not a morsel of meal, flour or bread left
in my house If the trustee, brother Hyrum or the Twelve
or any of them will examine and see if I have too much, it
shall go freely I call upon the brethren, if they have anything
against me, to bring it forward and have it adjusted.' "*

HYRUM SMITH DEFENDS TEMPLE COMMITTEE

Patriarch Hyrum Smith, after hearing the testimony of
these brethren, explained the many difficulties of this committee, saying in conclusion, "I feel it my duty to defend the
committee as far as I can for I would as soon go to hell
as be a committee man."

The conference records state that on this date all the
committee men were voted clear of the accusations and the
report was that the Temple Committee had shown no par-
tiality to themselves or any members of the Church; and
that during the last six months, very little means had been
brought into the Temple Committee.

Our history tells us that the architect was to select men
in whom he had confidence, men who were well qualified to
do the work that was wanted. Among the men selected for
the carpenter shop were Truman O. Angell and William F. Cahoon. They were also appointed to attend the Saw-Mill. William F. was foreman over the raisers and timekeeper for the
shop He was second assistant foreman over the framers. Daniel S. Cahoon and Andrew Cahoon were among the first who
commenced cutting stone for the Temple and continued until
it was finished Pulaski Cahoon commenced but did not continue long. He was also the one requested to keep an account
of the labor in the Stone-Cutter's Shop.

---

*History of the Church — Vol V, page 338.

Great was the undertaking of building that structure. It was not like building one today. The Saints could not order their timber from the lumberyard in a state of preparation. There were no iron foundries from which they could obtain the required metal properly prepared But on the contrary, every detail had to be performed by the Saints The timber had to be hewed in the far off forests of Wisconsin, carried to Nauvoo and cut into boards for the various uses of the Temple. It was a stone structure of original design. The stone had to be cut and polished from the quarries and the whole work had to be supplied out of the tithing of the people The builders of these Temples were more than mere men, they were Master Builders

REYNOLDS APPEALS FOR ASSISTANCE

On Friday, April 9, 1841 the General Conference met in Nauvoo . . . the building committee appointed was called upon to address the assembly. Elder Cahoon spoke at length on the importance of building the Temple and called upon the Saints to assist them in their great undertaking. These faithful people labored diligently with sublime self-abnegation. However, now, as had been the case in Kirtland, the spirit of apostasy was possessed by many of the leading men This must have been a severe trial to those of the building committee The work could not progress as it otherwise would have done In their hours of disappointment, comes the comforting truth — "The Lord accepts the will for the deed when His children endeavor with all diligence to obey but are prevented from doing so by the enemy." On that ground their offerings were accepted.

That they were diligent in their efforts, is amply attested by history which tells us that this structure cost more than one million dollars. The Saints were poor and much of the time during its course of construction, they were harassed by their enemies. On many occasions, the members of the committee were called from their labors to the defense of their Prophet and at times they traveled day and night protecting themselves from the mobs Quoting the words of President Brigham Young: "This edifice was raised by the aid of a sword in one hand, trowel and hammer in the other, firearms at hand, a strong band of police, and the blessings of heaven."

CAHOON BROTHERS JOIN NAUVOO BRASS BAND

The Latter-day Saints were a happy people and welcomed their days of rejoicing together. There were many occasions of thanksgiving, feasting and prayer as well as fasting and gratitude. They were lovers of music, and organized a band in which several sons of Reynolds Cahoon were members. They were religious with a keen love for fun and encouraged their children to sing and play harmless games. This side of their lives kept them from the "Slough of Despondency" and brightened their otherwise strenuous and perilous existence. They also possessed strong dramatic instincts, due no doubt to the strenuous life and stirring scenes of those early days.

Upon inquiry it was found that there were several men in the ranks who were or had been at some time, performers on brass and reed instruments. At the call of Joseph Smith, a meeting was held in the house of J. W. Cooledge sometime during the year 1842. In all probability, there were about fourteen members present, including William Cahoon who played the bass drum and Andrew Cahoon who played the piccolo. Although there was no mention of Daniel Stiles Cahoon nor Rais Bell Cahoon attending this meeting, we do know that Daniel S. played the piccolo and Rais B. played the snare drum. They probably enrolled later.

THE FAMOUS BUTTERFIELD PUN

In those eventful days, the Mormon people experienced joy one day and sorrow the next. In Illinois, Joseph particularly had a varied fortune. Among such prominent men as Judge Pope, Stephen A. Douglas and others, Joseph was held in esteem. Among the rougher classes, he was hated. He was arrested many times and acquitted In the year 1842 his attorney, Justin Butterfield, coined his famous pun. Let us relate it here —

"The Governor of the State issued a warrant for the arrest of Joseph Smith. Smith retained Justin Butterfield as Counsel. Butterfield sued out a writ of Habeas-Corpus from Judge Pope of the U S. District Court. Because of the parties involved, the case aroused great interest. Present were Joseph Smith, his Twelve Apostles and leading men of the State. So crowded was the Court Room that some ladies, among them Mrs. Lincoln and one of Judge Pope's daughters, were seated on either side of the Judge."

Amid great silence, Butterfield, dressed in a long blue coat with brass buttons and buff-colored waist-coat, rose slowly. Pausing, he surveyed the row of fashionably dressed women before him and then he spoke:

"May it please the Court:—

"I appear before you today under circumstances most novel and peculiar. I am to address the Pope (bowing to the Judge) surrounded by angels (with a very low bow) in the presence of Holy Apostles, on behalf of the Prophet of the Lord."

Judge Pope discharged the Mormon leaders and it was at this hearing that Butterfield coined a pun so famous that it still lives in legal lore of Illinois.

Time will not permit a description of the violence perpetrated against the Mormon people and the many petitions which were sent to the authorities of the United States. Joseph Smith appeals to his own native state, Vermont. He writes personal letters to John C. Calhoun and other presidential candidates, soliciting their candid replies and rule of action. Joseph relates to them, the sufferings of the people in Missouri, telling them that many had lost their lives and many had been robbed of an immense amount of property, and that in vain, they have sought redress by all constitutional, legal and honorable means

Reynolds Cahoon Appointed on Committee
To Draft Resolutions*

At 11 o'clock a.m., December 7, 1843, a meeting of the citizens of Nauvoo was held near the Temple. Alpheus Cutler was called as chairman and Willard Richards appointed secretary. After the object of the meeting was announced, three able men were appointed to draft the preamble and resolutions. The men appointed were W. W. Phelps, Reynolds Cahoon and Hosea Stout.

These resolutions were to be directed to the Governor of Missouri and to various authorities of the states of the United States, reciting the persecutions of the people of Nauvoo relative to the demanding of the body of Joseph Smith, as well as the common, cruel practice of kidnapping

*Journal History, Dec. 7, 1843.

citizens of Illinois and forcing them across the Mississippi River and incarcerating them in dungeons or prisons in Missouri

Reynolds Cahoon and the other two committeemen left the meeting and returned later with the following:

Whereas the State of Missouri with the Governor at the head, continues to make demands upon the executive of Illinois for the body of Joseph Smith, as we verily believe, to keep up a system of persecution against the Church of Jesus Christ of Latter-day Saints, for the purpose of justifying said State of Missouri to her diabolical, unheard of, cruel and unconstitutional warfare against said Church, and which she has practiced during the last twelve years, whereby many have been murdered, mobbed and ravished, and the whole community expelled from the State

And also to heave dust in the eyes of the nation and the world, while she, as a State, with the Government to back her, continues to slip over the river and steal the property of the Latter-day Saints, and kidnap the members of said church to glut her vengeance, malice, revenge and avarice, and to make slaves of the said captives or murder them
Therefore—

Resolved unanimously, as we do know that Joseph Smith is not guilty of any charge made against him by the said State of Missouri, but is a good, industrious, well meaning, and worthy citizen of Illinois, and an officer that does faithfully and impartially administer the laws of the State; we as citizens of Illinois crave the protection of the Constitution and laws of the country as an aegis to shield him, the said General Joseph Smith, from such cruel persecutions, beseeching the Governor of Illinois not to issue any more writs against the said General, or other Latter-day Saints (unless they are guilty) but to let the Latter-day Saints 'breathe awhile like other men' and enjoy the liberty guaranteed to every honest citizen by the magna charta of our common country.

Resolved, That as citizens of the State of Illinois, we solicit the attention of the Governor and officers generally of the State, to take some lawful means and measures to regain the citizens that have been kidnapped by the Missourians, and to prevent the said Missourians and said government from committing further violence upon the citizens of Illinois

Resolved, as the sense of this meeting, that according to the true meaning of the law, that those citizens of any section of the country, who do not rise up as virtuous, free men, (when any portion of the inhabitants congregate or combine to injure, slander or deprive another portion of their rights) and magnify the law, to clear themselves from such unhallowed attempts to subvert order and law, they by their silence make themselves accessories of the crime of such unlawful assemblage. . . .

Resolved unanimously, That we solicit the Governor, by all honorable means, to grant us peace, For We Will Have It.

Alpheus Cutler, Chairman
Willard Richards, Secretary

Appeals to Governor Brings No Relief

*"An extra ordinance for the extra case of Joseph Smith and others" was passed by the city council of Nauvoo on December 8th, 1843 "whereas, that hereafter if any person or persons shall come with process, demand or requisition, founded upon the aforesaid Missouri difficulties, to arrest said Joseph Smith, he or they shall be subject to be arrested by any officer of the city with or without process . . . and be imprisoned in city jail . . ."

The enactment of such ordinances, however, did not affect the unlawful treatment of Mormons in Nauvoo. The appeals to the Governor only brought the following statement·

"Thus far I persume that the whole community feels a deep interest for that which is the case of 'Mormons' today, may be the case of the Catholics tomorrow.

"Your case is certainly a very emergent one and the consequences as important to Your Society as if the war had been waged against the whole state, yet the public has no other interest in it than that the laws be faithfully executed."

After reading one of the letters from Governor Ford, Joseph writes.

"It appears from this letter that Gov. Ford has never taken pains to examine the evidences placed in his hands, and probably never will He evidently has taken little pains to examine the Constitution of the United States or even reflect upon the ordinary principles of human rights."

Then Joseph Smith continues, "A union of executive, judicial, and military powers have exterminated 15,000 of its innocent inhabitants who were not even charged with any crime; they have robbed them of all they possess on earth, murdering hundreds of men, women and children and expelling all the others from the State among strangers in midwinter, destitute of everything upon the face of the earth that could possibly have a tendency to make life desirable. — Oh! humanity where has thou hidden thyself Oh! reason, where art thou fled? Patriots of '76, has your blood been spilt in vain that in 1843 the executive of a great republican State, can with coolness say, 'I have not yet read them, and probably never will.' Is liberty only a name; is protection of person

---

*Journal History, December 14, 1843 History of the Church, Vol. VI, pages 101-2.

and property fled from free America? Let those answer who can."

JOSEPH SMITH CANDIDATE FOR PRESIDENT OF UNITED STATES

In 1844 Nauvoo had become the largest city in the State and additional converts were coming in from the British Isles and Europe. This was the election year. Joseph's friends desired to nominate him as a Presidential candidate to run against Clay, Calhoun and Van Buren. They agreed he had the leadership, capacity, and qualifications for the office.

Joseph at first discountenanced this proposal but later permitted his name to be entered as a nominee at the Illinois Convention. There were two reasons:

First, he could get no assurance from the other candidates that they would take any positive steps to protect religious minorities. Secondly, the Mormon people discovered that they could not vote for either Whigs or Democrats in Illinois without making serious political enemies among defeated candidates . . . and thinking to allay resentment against his people, Joseph Smith permitted his name to be used on an independent ticket, "thus offending no party."*

On January 29th, 1844, Joseph was nominated as a candidate for the President of the United States, the nomination being sustained by the State Convention May 17th, that year. The announcement was made to the world. The Iowa Democrat printed the following:

"A New Candidate in the Field"

"We see from the Nauvoo Neighbor that General Joseph Smith, the great Mormon Prophet, has become a candidate for the next presidency We do not know whether he intends to submit his claims to the National Convention or not, but judging from the language of his own organ, we conclude that he considers himself a full team for all of them

"All that we have to say on this point is, that if superior talent, genius and intelligence, combined with virtue, integrity and enlarged views are any guarantee to General Smith's being elected, we think that he will be a full team of himself"

The enemies of Joseph now marshalled all their strength against him and in the same year of his nomination for the Presidency of the United States, Joseph and Hyrum Smith were murdered while in jail, committed upon an illegal mit-

---

*Story of the Mormon Pioneers, by W. Cleon Skousen.

timus by Robert F. Smith, Justice of the Peace and Captain of the Company stationed at the jail.

Because of the intimate association of Reynolds Cahoon and his family with Joseph and Hyrum at this time and because of the active part Reynolds took during their last days on earth, it is essential that this part of our story be related somewhat in detail.

EXCERPTS FROM JOSEPH SMITH'S JOURNAL

One of the last entries written by Joseph Smith in his own journal while in Nauvoo was that of Saturday, June 22nd 1844, just five days before his death. It was regarding a letter written by him to "His Excellency, Thomas Ford, Governor" and signed "Your obedient servant Joseph Smith." It contained Joseph's pleadings for justice. Regarding the governor's answer, Joseph writes:

"I had a consultation for a little while with my brother Hyrum, Dr. Richards, John Taylor and J. M. Bernhisel and determined to go to Washington and lay the matter before President Tyler. About 7 p.m. I requested Reynolds Cahoon and Alpheus Cutler to stand guard at the Mansion, and not admit any stranger inside the house. I asked O. P. Rockwell if he would go with me a short journey and he replied he would . . ."

Soon after dark, Joseph called Hyrum, Willard Richards and some others into his upper room and said: "Brethren, here is a letter from the Governor, which I wish to have read." After it was read, Joseph remarked, "There is no mercy, no mercy here." Hyrum said, "No, just as sure as we fall into their hands, we are dead men." Joseph replied "What shall we do, brother Hyrum?" Hyrum replied, "I don't know " . . . All at once Joseph's countenance brightened and he said, "The way is open, it is clear to my mind what to do, all they want is myself and Hyrum, then tell everybody to go about their business, not to collect in groups, but scatter about, there is no doubt that they will come here and search for us. Let them search, for they will not harm you or your property, not even a hair of your head. We will cross the river tonight and go away to the West."

He then went out of the house, told brothers Butler and Hodge to take the Maid of Iowa* to the upper landing and put his family and the family of Hyrum, his brother, upon the boat to go down the Mississippi and up the Ohio to Portsmouth where they should hear from them. He then took brother Hodge by the hand and said, "Now, brother Hodge, let what come, don't deny the faith and all will be well. I told Stephen Markham that if I and Hyrum were ever taken again, we should be massacred, or I was not a prophet of God. I want Hyrum to live and avenge my blood, but he is determined not to leave me."

About 9 p m Hyrum came out of the Mansion House and gave his hand to Reynolds Cahoon saying, "A company of men are seeking to kill my brother Joseph and the Lord has warned him to flee to the Rocky Mountains to save his life. Good-by, Brother Cahoon, we shall see you again." In a few minutes Joseph came from his family, his tears were flowing fast He held his handkerchief to his face and followed his brother Hyrum without uttering a word.

O P. Rockwell rowed the skiff which was so leaky that it kept Joseph, Hyrum and Doctor Richards busy bailing out the water with their boots and shoes to prevent it from sinking. Sunday 23rd, they arrived on the Iowa side of the river. They sent Rockwell to Nauvoo with instructions to return the next night with horses for Joseph and Hyrum and pass them over the river and they would be ready to start for the Great Basin in the Rocky Mountains.

About 9 o'clock, brother Bernheisel crossed over the river and Reynolds Cahoon also went to visit Joseph to explain to him as requested, regarding the Governor's letter A posse had arrived in Nauvoo to arrest Joseph, but as they did not find him, they started back. In a letter written by Joseph to Emma Smith, his wife, he calls the place "Safety".

At 1 o'clock p m Emma sent Rockwell to Joseph, requesting him to entreat Joseph to come back Reynolds Cahoon accompanied him with a letter which Emma had written to

---

*The *Maid of Iowa* was owned by the Church or some member of the Church It was used for transporting provisions for the Mormon people, also for their own transportation at different times Under the date of June 4, 1844 is recorded that Pulaski Cahoon and A Morrison wished to obtain this vessel They proposed to give $100 a month for its use They made their own bonds with their own security, but they were not received by Joseph Smith

the same effect. Emma insisted that Joseph should come back.
She also insisted that Reynolds Cahoon use every persuasion
with Joseph to come back and give himself up L D. Wasson
and Hiram Kimball were likewise pursuaded by Emma to in-
duce Joseph and Hyrum to start back to Nauvoo These men
went to Joseph as true friends to explain to him the Governor's letter and to deliver the message to him from his wife,
Emma

History records· "When they went over they found Joseph,
Hyrum and Willard (Richards) in a room by themselves having provisions on the floor ready for packing. Reynolds Cahoon informed Joseph what the troops intended to do and
urged him to give himself up in-as-much as the Governor
had pledged his faith and the faith of the State to protect him
while he underwent a legal and fair trial. After much persuasion, Joseph decided to return to Nauvoo, saying — "If my
life is of no value to my friends it is of none to myself"   .
and after studying a few moments Joseph said to Hyrum,
"If you go back I will go with you, but we shall be butchered"
. . . then after a short pause, Joseph told Cahoon to request
Capt. Davis to have his boat ready at half-past five to cross
them over the river.

June 24, Joseph and Hyrum and thirteen others went to
Carthage and gave themselves up No trial had been held, but
they were thrust into Carthage jail the evening of their arrest
When Joseph went to Carthage to deliver himself to the pre-
tended requirements of the law, two or three days previous
to his assassination, he said, "I am going like a lamb to the
slaughter; but I am calm as a summer's morning; I have
a conscience void of offense towards God and towards all
men. I shall die innocent, and it shall yet be said of me —
He was murdered in cold blood."

Reynolds Cahoon at Carthage With Joseph Smith

We must conclude that Reynolds Cahoon was in Carthage
with Joseph and Hyrum as the record states: "Joseph instructed Cahoon to return to Nauvoo with all haste and fetch
a number of documents for the promised trial"* and to
further substantiate this fact, we are told that "Elder Cahoon
returned (to Nauvoo) from Carthage for some papers.** It

---

*History of the Church, Vol VI — page 599
**History of the Church, Vol VII — page 130

appears that Reynolds did not go back to Carthage again this time, he sent these papers out by O. P. Rockwell.

On June 27th 1844, the jail was surrounded by an armed mob of from 150 to 200 men. The guard of the jail was prostrated, Hyrum was shot in the throat, nose, back and breast. He fell saying "I am a dead man." Joseph leaped to the window, four bullets entered his body, one in the right shoulder, one in his breast and two others in his left leg and hand He fell outward, dead. John Taylor rushed to the window, a ball entered his leg, one struck his watch and struck his left hip as he lay on the floor. Dr. Richards remained unharmed.

The effect of this butchery was like the bursting of a hellish tornado. The murderers ran for their lives, lest the Mormons should turn and kill them suddenly. "The wicked flee when no man pursueth." The villages seemed without inhabitants as in an instant. The excitement had been great, but the indignation more terrible. A reaction took place and men of influence came from abroad to learn the facts and went away satisfied that the Mormons were not the transgressors.

Friday June 28, 1844 at 2.30, the corpses arrived guarded by a few men from Carthage. They followed the bodies of Joseph and Hyrum to the Mansion House where addresses were made, exhorting the people to be peaceable and calm and use no threats. There were fourteen men who were the Prophet's bodyguard, among them were Alpheus Cutler, Capt., Reynolds Cahoon and Samuel H. Smith.

Sheriff J. B. Backenstos mailed a list of names of officers, guards and those active in the massacre at Carthage. He condemned these assassins and said in part, "I most cheerfully give you any information in my power in reference to this matter, the only thing I regret about is that these things, I am fearful, will be put off so long that I will not live to see or hear of the awful vengeance which will in the end overtake the Hancock assassins."

Volumes could be written quoting expressions of censure regarding the acts of the assassins. Many newspapers of the United States, termed these acts — "unprovoked murder;" "lynched while under guise of protection;" "bloody deed;" "premeditated murder." Quoting the words from one publication: "From all the facts now before us, we regard these homicides as nothing else than murder in cold blood, murder against the plighted faith of the chief magistrate of Illinois — murder of a character so atrocious and so unjustifiable as to leave the blackest stain on all its perpetrators, their aiders, abettors and defenders." — The O. S. Democrat.

ILLEGAL ARREST OF REYNOLDS CAHOON

Just three months after the death of Joseph and Hyrum, Reynolds and several other Latter-day Saint men were "illegally arrested for treason" and forced to go to trial at Carthage. Can one imagine the emotions in the hearts of these brave men? Carthage, the same city and the same jail where their beloved friends were so recently murdered.

The date was Wednesday, Sept. 24, 1845. Since the Court was not ready for trial, the company proceeded to the jail where Joseph and Hyrum were martyred. The blood of Hyrum still stained the floor where he fell. The walls were marked with bullet holes. Elders Taylor and Richards showed the others the position which the brethren stood to defend themselves at the time of the martyrdom. How desolate Carthage looked!

Reynolds returned to the Court House where, with Daniel Spencer, Orson Spencer, brothers Richards, Taylor, Phelps, Rich, Cutler, Scott, Hunter and Clayton, they were put under arrest and taken to Justice Barnes' office. Here they were put under examination and asked if they wanted witnesses subpoenaed. They replied, "No."

DeBackman, the person who made the affidavit on which the writ was issued, made his appearance. Upon being sworn and asked if he personally knew the defendants or any of them, he answered that he did not and stated that he made the affidavit upon the strength of the rumors which he heard at the time and because of his great prejudice against the Mormons. He believed these reports and did think that the Mormon leaders were guilty of treason.

The examination was held before Justice Barnes, assisted by Justice Bedell. The court, according to law, dismissed the case and at 3 p .m. Reynolds and his friends started on their return home from Carthage.

At Malcomb, the people were under considerable excitement. No friendly hand was offered them; only threats were used against them in the most lawless manner. Reynolds tells the following:

"We found it altogether imprudent to let ourselves be seen, those people threatened us saying, they would 'butt us out of town'. After dinner we returned to a private room upstairs where we witnessed the increased state of excitement. We were waited upon by a committee sent to confer with us and this committee expressed in unqualified terms their entire disapprobation of the annoyance and pledged themselves to see us protected . . . their pledge was kept and we arrived home safely."

The Mormon people wished peace above all other earthly blessings. A communication was written Sept 24th in which they made an appeal to be permitted to transact their business honorably and without interference and they proposed to leave for their new home in the mountains the next Spring. They were willing to sell their property at a fair price, and would accept merchandise, groceries, cows, mules, sheep, wagons, harnesses and such things in payment. They were prepared also to receive any proposition in case the citizens preferred to sell their own property to the Saints and leave the Saints in quiet possession of the country They had broken no laws and wished only to worship God according to the dictates of their conscience, a right guaranteed by the Constitution of the United States

Joseph died a martyr of Religious Freedom; he died for all men Before we close the recital of these events, let us quote Joseph's own words: "The Saints can testify whether I am willing to lay down my life for my brethren . . . I have been willing to die for a Mormon, I am bold to declare before heaven that I am just as ready to die in defending the rights of a Presbyterian, a Baptist or any good man of any other denomination; for the same principle which would trample upon the rights of the Latter-day Saints would trample upon the rights of the Roman Catholics, or of any other denomination who may be unpopular and too weak to defend themselves."

The death of the Prophet and his brother had stunned both the Latter-day Saints and their enemies everywhere. "Bear It," whispered a voice from within, and then came the glorious promise to those Mormon people "Fear not, wait patiently, your prayers are heard and the promise is that all things shall work together for your good and to My Name's Glory."

NAUVOO TEMPLE COMPLETED

Obedient to the commandment, the Temple was completed. Joseph and Hyrum did not live to see the Nauvoo Temple. It was dedicated quietly on April 30, 1846 by Joseph Young, brother of Brigham Young, and publicly on May 1, 1846 by Orson Hyde. Their zeal and sacrifices had not gone unrewarded, for from the date of December 10, 1845, when the first endowments were given until February 7, 1846, when the Temple was closed for Ordinance work, more than 5,500 endowments had been given in the Nauvoo Temple. On December 10th and 11th, 1845, Thirza and Reynolds Cahoon received their endowments

REYNOLDS AND THIRZA SEALED IN CELESTIAL MARRIAGE

Reynolds and Thirza were sealed in "Celestial Marriage" in the Nauvoo Temple at 7:10 p.m., January 16, 1846 by President Brigham Young. They believed in this marriage covenant, that it was the covenant, now revealed, which would make valid their marriage for both time and eternity It was new, yet old as the Gospel, as old as the plan of salvation adopted in the Council in Heaven, that only the covenants that are sealed by the Holy Spirit of Promise, through one who holds divine authority, remain in force after death. And that the marriage covenants, as performed by man-made governments and religions, social customs and habits were valid only "till death doth us part."

This Celestial Law now explains to them that marriage is destined for eternity as well as for time and that God appoints and ordains His Elders holding the keys of authority, to seal on earth that it may be sealed in heaven and that those who do not enter their family relations under the Celestial law, remain single in eternity, for "they neither marry, nor are given in marriage." With the restoration of the Holy Priesthood, the church asserts that this power to seal marriages for time and all eternity is given to God's chosen men, and in the temple, the contract is made everlasting. This was a promise the Savior gave to His Apostles while on earth — "And I will give unto thee the keys of the kingdom of heaven, and whatsoever thou shalt bind on earth shall be bound in heaven; and whatsoever thou shalt loose on earth shall be loosed in heaven."

There had been only a few short months for the Saints to perform this glorious work In their Temple they had received of the "Power from High," which blessings they had need of to help them on their perilous journey to the West.

All during the summer of 1846 as they were moving away, they heard threats of incendiarism In Nauvoo, some of the Saints' homes had been burned and there was constant fear that their Temple would share the same fate. It was now in the possession of the mobs and the once hallowed structure stood as an abandoned building.

TEMPLE DESTROYED BY FIRE

After the Mormons had evacuated Nauvoo and their trek from Illinois to Utah was near completion, the news came to them that the Temple had been destroyed. Telegraphic dispatches were sent — "This magnificent temple was observed to be on fire this morning, nothing left but the naked and blackened walls." The catastrophe occurred early Monday morning, October 9, 1848.

Public opinion condemned the act as one of incendiary origin, "the work of some nefarious incendiary." One publisher felt that the temple "should have stood for ages and that none but the most depraved heart could have applied the torch to effect its destruction."

A demand to fix the responsibility was made immediately. Forty-four representative citizens signed the announcement to ferret out, arrest and legally convict such guilty person or persons. The total reward amounted to about $640. There were several suspects The most likely person seemed to be Joseph B. Agnew who was an ardent hater of the Mormon people, and took part in many violent activities. Accusations against Agnew came from several individuals, among whom was Major Bidamon, husband of Joseph Smith's widow. Bidamon stated that Agnew was paid $500 for burning the Temple. This money came from some jealous inhabitants of Carthage.

Among the Saints in the Rocky Mountains the final downfall of the Temple produced only a mild reaction. They felt sad, but Brigham Young consoled them by saying he "would rather it should thus be destroyed than remain in the hands of the wicked. If it be the Will of the Lord that the Temple be burned instead of being defiled by the Gentiles — Amen to it."

From such a narrative as this, one might expect the

Nauvoo Temple to be a thing of the dead past, however, this is not the case. These events were not merely facts about a physical building of stone and wood; they were vital experiences in the lives of many people, as builders and as makers of history.

Citizens of Illinois and other states visited this "Shrine In The Wilderness." Its imposing sight gave rise to mixed feelings according to the viewpoint of the particular spectator. John R. Smith, the artist, painted this great Mormon Temple and exhibited it over the country as part of his "Leviathan Panorama of the Mississippi River." We may be sure that increasing interest among the descendants of the Builders of the Temple, will prove Nauvoo to ever remain a most historic spot.

ALL THAT REMAINS

In a city of twenty-thousand Saints, where once echoed the laughter of children and voices of prayer, now reside less than two-thousand people, and all that remains of the old Temple site is a pump in the well which furnished water for the Baptismal Font.

The Nauvoo House, the Mansion House and the "Old Homestead" of Joseph Smith still remain and are owned by the Reorganized Church. These buildings are located near the intersection of Main and Water Streets near the bank of the Mississippi River and in this same vicinity are the graves of Emma, Joseph and Hyrum Smith.

The Old Court House, the City Hall still remain. The building known as Carthage Jail remains and reminds the traveler of the foul deeds committed there. It was purchased by President Joseph F. Smith.

Part of the temple site is owned by the Reorganized Church and the other part by the Church of Jesus Christ of Latter-day Saints. The burned walls remained standing until May 27, 1850. Stones from the temple may be found in many buildings in Nauvoo and it is claimed they may be found in nearly all states in the Union and in Europe.

Reynolds Cahoon was one of the twenty Elders who went with President Brigham Young to the attic of the Temple in Nauvoo early that Sunday morning of November 30, 1845 and prayed that the Lord would hear their prayers and deliver them from their enemies until they had accomplished His Will in His House. They asked for blessings on their families and that the Lord would lead them to a land of peace

THE EVACUATION OF NAUVOO

Hurriedly, the Mormons were making every preparation for the evacuation of their city. Thanksgiving Day in Nauvoo found the bellows blowing and the whole city alive with activity. Stores, houses and public buildings had been converted into machine shops The mobs were anxiously awaiting the spoils incident to the departure of the Mormons.

Brigham Young ordered the evacuation of Nauvoo and the month of February, 1846 found the Mormons in full flight across the frozen crust of the Mississippi River headed toward the unknown west and the setting sun. Behind them lay their ravaged city; before them, prairies, deserts, mountains, sagebrush and savages of America's unconquered West If civilization would not proffer them a haven of safety, the wilderness would.

Many curiosity seekers came to witness their departure and when they heard the Gospel as related by those Mormon Saints, they too, were converted to the truthfulness of the Church of Jesus Christ of Latter-day Saints Enoch Bartlett Tripp, father of Naamah Tripp Cahoon and grandfather of the compilers of this book, was among those who visited Nauvoo at that time, accepted their teachings, became a member, defended their Temple and joined them on their trek to Utah

Although the flight from Nauvoo was a retreat in disorder, Brigham Young rallied the pioneers at Sugar Creek, seven miles west of the Mississippi River It was here on February 5th, that Brigham organized them into "the Camps of Israel," in captains of tens, fifties and hundreds.

That bitter, cold night, nine wives became mothers; nine children were born in tents and wagons in the wintry camps. How those tender babes, those sick and delicate women were cared for under such conditions, is left to the imagination of the sensitive reader How those aged, infirm and helpless exiles crossed those desolate plains, rivers and prairies is a tale which has never fully been told.

Sugar Creek was no place for the pioneers to tarry. They prepared to lay roads across Iowa, which took months. The first companies acted as trail blazers and set up a chain of supply depots. They would break the sod and plant grain, build bridges and rafts.

REYNOLDS AND HIS FAMILY LEAVE NAUVOO

On March 9, 1846, the Cahoon family left their beautiful City. Reynolds and brother Cutler were given instruction to "roll out their companies as quick as possible." During the journey of March 14th, Reynolds was thrown from his wagon, dislocating his shoulder. William F and Daniel S. Cahoon, sons of Reynolds, left with their wives and families. They were members of the Nauvoo Brass Band and traveled with this band, playing numerous concerts throughout the various settlements of the Middle West to earn funds to help the great migration.

William Clayton tells of the part music played in the lives of the tired pioneers when at the end of the day's journey, the musicians would strike up a tune and the group would join in the dance and song Because of their love of good music, the pioneers built, purchased and played the best band instruments of the time They were encouraged by their leaders to organize orchestras, bands and musical societies Brigham Young desired to lay a foundation of great music for the Mormon people and their bands and orchestras have added greatly to the art and culture of the West.

THE MORMON BATTALION

It was on June 14, 1846 that Brigham Young and the advanced company of the fleeing Saints reached the Missouri River, not far from Council Bluffs. They had intended to send a pioneer party of men into the mountains to prepare their trail, but the "Call of the Mormon Battalion" prevented this, for scarcely had they arrived, when into the Camp rode a United States Officer, Capt. James Allen. He bore an urgent request from President Polk for five hundred Mormon volunteers. The object was to recruit a battalion for service in the Mexican War to be marched to California. Term of the enlistment was for one year, regular infantry pay, with discharge from service on the Pacific Coast.

Did they go? Yes, five-hundred men strong and true, known as the "Mormon Battalion," left their loved ones in the wilderness. "But," you say, "Look at the treatment they had received at the hands of the United States Government and the people generally." Regardless of this, their beloved country needed aid They had embraced the Gospel of Jesus Christ. "Return not evil for evil, but overcome evil with good."

"You shall have the battalion," Brigham Young promptly replied and within a few days its muster rolls were complete. Brigham told them that it was their duty to go and promised them that, if they lived rightly before the Lord, they would not have to do any fighting. This prophecy was literally fulfilled. On July 16th, just one month later, they marched to Ft. Leavenworth, commencing the longest infantry march in recorded history.

To take five hundred of the ablest men at such a time was to bleed the Mormon people of manpower when the need was most desperate. At the call of Brigham Young, teamsters relinquished their posts — the wagons and stock to be driven by wives, children and aged grandparents, across an unchartered continent. No more heroic chapter had ever been written than this example of loyalty and obedience from the toil-hardened men who made up the Mormon Battalion.

The Battalion marched to the Pacific Coast, completing their Infantry march from Council Bluffs, Iowa to Warner's Ranch in Southern California, a distance of about 1,100 miles. Their commanding officer, Lt. Col Phillip St. George Cooke, now became Commander of the Military District of Southern California, and was ordered to re-deploy his battalion to Los Angeles.

On March 17th 1847, the Battalion arrived in Los Angeles from their encampment at Mission San Luis Rey and on July 4, 1847, on the site of historic Fort Moore, came the dramatic moment when the United States flag was first raised above the Mexican Pueblo de Los Angeles. This was seven months before California became United States Territory. The flag was smartly saluted by the entire military establishment of Los Angeles, including troops of the First U. S. Dragoons, the New York Volunteers and the Mormon Battalion as a thirteen gun salute was fired and the first United States flag was hoisted to symbolize the advent of the American era in California.

FORT MOORE PIONEER MEMORIAL

(A Tribute To Los Angeles Pioneers)

Looming boldly against the skyline to the north of Los Angeles Civic Center, the magnificent sweep of the Fort Moore Pioneer Memorial wall now stands as an inspiring tribute "To the Brave Men and Women Who, With Trust in

God, Faced Privation and Death in Extending the Frontiers of our Country to Include This Land of Promise." Those are the words of the inscription on the 68-foot pylon that rises in front of the memorial wall.

On July 3, 1958, this magnificent monument was dedicated. Our reader is invited to commemorate with us, this inspiring event. Our home is not far from Fort Moore in Los Angeles We were honored by motoring with Ora Pate Stewart to this historic spot to celebrate the dedication. Ora, as she is known by her dearest friends, is the wife of Colonel Robert W Stewart. She is a beloved author, lecturer and teacher Of these dedicatory services, she writes as follows:

"We gathered together and parked our cars on a strip of near-free way at a place where the hill has been trimmed back . . . They call it Hill Street. Why should we stop? Why should we remember? It is a long story — one hundred eleven years long.

"On this hill on the Fourth of July 1847, assembled U. S. soldiers, raised the American flag, commemorating for posterity, a march, a cause, and a new frontier of freedom. A broadened America stretched beneath that flag."

MORE STARS IN THE FLAG

"A new flag was raised on July 3, 1958 made new with the addition of new stars. In all other ways this new flag is the same flag we have loved through all our years. May God preserve its supremacy in all our years to come!

"Honored guests and committeemen were acknowledged and awarded. The Mormon Choir of Southern California sang and the 72nd Army Band rendered stirring music. Leo J. Muir, son of Wm. S. Muir, the young soldier who helped to raise that earlier flag, unfolded the new emblem and guided it to its presiding place at the top of the memorial pole. Elder Hugh B. Brown, grandson of James S. Brown, who was a 19-year-old youth when the former flag was raised, offered the dedicatory prayer asking God to keep this flag aloft. Mayor Norris Poulson, Dr. Hugh C. Willett, Hon. Eugene W. Biscailus, Hon. John Anson Ford, Mrs. Moses Cozzens who conceived this idea of the monument, and many other commemorators paid respect and appreciation to the pioneers.

"We stopped because we want always to remember. We are glad that we stopped; and we hope always to remember."

And now we return to the story of our Utah Pioneers —
Reynolds Cahoon and his family in their camp at Garden
Grove and at Mt. Pisgah in 1846.

WINTER QUARTERS

On May 8, the Cahoon family arrived at Garden Grove,
where they met their brother, Andrew He had been carrying mail for the pioneers between Nauvoo and Garden Grove.
The ferry boat was completed June 29th and the next day
Brigham Young and others of the advancing party crossed
the Missouri River. On July 6th, the Camps of A. Cutler
and Reynolds Cahoon were about three miles from Mt. Pisgah
and not until about three weeks later do we find them, "On
the flats wanting to cross the Missouri, several are sickly.
The hill on the west side of the river being very abrupt and
steep, it required the doubling of teams and every man is
requested to turn out with teams and help these people "

Bridges had been washed out, they had encountered great
rains, and the progress very much retarded It required the
entire spring, summer and fall of 1846 for the main camps
to cross Iowa and reach the river, and Brigham Young concluded they must make a temporary haven It was in September that site was selected on the west side of the river and
named Winter Quarters.

ANDREW CAHOON APPOINTED ON HIGH COUNCIL

Andrew Cahoon was appointed on the Municipal High
Council to superintend the affairs of the brethren on the
West Side of the Missouri River where it was decided they
should settle together. He assisted in building the first Anglo-
Saxon settlement in what is now known as the State of
Nebraska Here he remained until November when he was
sent on a foreign mission.

In December, Winter Quarters consisted of 3,483 people
living in 548 log houses, 83 sod houses or dugouts. During the
first severe winter one of every six persons died of exposure
or disease occasioned by privation and want and some 600
were buried in the cemetery at Winter Quarters The compilers' own great grandfather, George Eddins, father of Jessie Eddins Tripp and grandfather of Naamah Tripp Cahoon,
was one of these pioneers who died in a dugout at Winter
Quarters. George Eddins and wife joined the L D S Church
in England She died there. He made caskets for many

pioneers before he died, leaving three orphan children, Louisa, John and Jessie Eddins. These children were placed in the homes of different families, and did not see each other again until sometime after they arrived in Salt Lake Valley.

The Violin That Came Across the Plains

The story of young John Eddins and his "violin that crossed the plains" reads like a romance. John had sailed with his father's family from England to America to join the Latter-day Saints. On the ship was a German boy who owned the marvelously sweet-toned instrument. This German boy took ill and upon arrival was taken to a hospital. He kissed his violin, hugged it to his breast and appealed to John to buy it from him with the promise, that it never would leave the Eddins family. John purchased it and carried it across the plains to Utah. John played the violin and many a campfire was enlivened by its beautiful music.

His granddaughter Dixie DeVere was given the violin. She became an accomplished violinist and performed in many famous musicals. She was offered a Stradivarius worth $1500 in trade for it, but she refused saying, "The promise of my grandfather to the young German boy is still binding." The priceless violin was never more than a few feet away from her side. She played in many performances in Salt Lake City and throughout the country in the early days.

Where Once Persecution Raged

On June 1st, 1953, one hundred and six years after the arrival of the pioneers at Winter Quarters, an important ceremony marked the dedication of a bridge, honoring these brave Mormon Pioneers* — a majestic steel bridge, spanning the Missouri River at Omaha at almost the exact location of the Old Ferry Crossing. The North Omaha Bridge Commission officially named this bridge, the Mormon Pioneer Memorial Bridge. Dr. Karren, chairman of the commission wrote: "The commission and people of Omaha feel they have been greatly honored by the Church of Jesus Christ of Latter-day Saints in giving approval to the name."

They selected the name with the realization, "the Mormon Pioneers who have crossed the river at this site were a brave and fearless lot, having a firm belief in the right to worship their God in their own way, and were willing to make whatever sacrifices necessary to obtain their objective."

---

*The bridge was dedicated on the 152nd birthday anniversary of Brigham Young

The day previous, May 31, 1953, Memorial Services were also held in the cemetery. President David O. McKay in his dedicatory address remarked:

"This bridge becomes another memorial to the faith and undaunted heroism of the Utah Pioneers. It is erected not alone in honor to individuals, but in commemoration of the ideal, virtues and faith for which they sacrificed their lives." This impressive ceremony symbolized the advance of religious understanding. And a review of the progress of the previous 106 years gives us renewed hope in the possibility of peace and understanding for all mankind.

ARCHITECT, BUILDER AND BUSINESS MAN

Reynolds proved himself to be not only a great architect and builder but also indeed, a shrewd business man capable of engineering many complex problems. This is evidenced by the numerous financial difficulties he assisted in solving for his church and people. For instance, in the year 1846, it is recorded that he was "appointed to borrow money from certain individuals which is necessary to be paid on corn contract. He is instructed to build a bridge, the contract to be paid in corn," and again, "the Council in December voted that he be placed on a committee of three to build a House for the Omaha's."

Again let us refer to the Patriarchal blessing given Reynolds on January 24, 1845 when he is blessed by the Lord with "strength more than common for man in order to do his labors," and further that the Lord had given him "skill to transact business with prudence and judgment, and that "angels had been given charge over him to defend his cause." Reynolds could not and did not fail.

ACCEPTS "WORD AND WILL" AS DIVINE GUIDANCE

On January 14, 1847 a revelation known as the "Word and Will" of the Lord was given to Brigham Young. It was instruction to the Saints; how they were to organize the migration so as to preserve unity and harmony; how to protect the companies from enemies and to guide their conduct for their Western Migration. Our record tells us that when this revelation was read at the meeting of the High Council in Winter Quarters, Reynolds Cahoon was present and "moved that it be received by the people, saying it was the Voice of Righteousness." The following was its creed:

"Keep all your pledges one with another; Covet not that which is thy brother's. Keep yourselves from evil and take not the name of the Lord in vain. Cease contention, backbiting, drunkedness, and borrowing without paying back. Be honest, restoring that which is found belonging to another. If any man seek to build up himself and seeketh not God's counsel, he shall have no power and his folly shall be made manifest . . . If thou are merry, praise the Lord with singing, music, with dancing and with a prayer of praise and thanksgiving. If thou are sorrowful, call on the Lord, thy God, with supplication, that your souls may be joyful."

Organization For The Western Trek

January 25, 1847, Brigham Young organized his company. I. Morley was nominated president with Reynolds Cahoon and John Young as counselors, each as Captains of one hundred. Winter Quarters was to be stockaded, guards to be kept and the women, whose husbands were in the army, were not to be emigrated until after the pioneers. It was necessary for Brigham to further organize his companies, and on Thursday June 1st, the company voted that Brigham Young should act as General Supt. of the emigrating companies. D. H. Wells was sustained as aid-de-camp, I. Morley as president with Reynolds Cahoon and Wm. M. Major as his counselors. H. S. Eldredge was chosen Marshal.

May 19th, 1848 was probably the happiest day in many, many long months for the family of Reynolds Cahoon, for on this day, into their camp at Winter Quarters their son Andrew arrived from a foreign mission and with him were the Saints from Scotland. Andrew had been on this European mission since November 1846, almost a year and a half. This must have been a joyful occasion.

Andrew and one hundred twenty new Mormon emigrants left their native land in Scotland, in Feb. 1848 on the ship "Carnatic"; had crossed the great Atlantic Ocean, landed at New Orleans and after a most tedious journey, arrived at Winter Quarters. It was in Scotland that Andrew met the Carruth family where he and Mary Carruth were married. Margaret and Janet were sisters of Mary, and Margaret tells us in her autobiography that from Winter Quarters the Carruth family traveled to Utah with the pioneers.

The travels and activities of the Carruth and Cahoon families were from that time on, the same as their Pioneer

Companies: sometimes fording streams in which their wagons over turned; sometimes encountering storms so severe that thunder and lightning tore their equipment to pieces; and then always came the orders: "Stop! Unhitch the teams." There was always sunshine in a day or two and all were happy again. Certain days were washdays in the camp. Other days the men would hunt buffalo and the ladies would dry the meat. Meetings were held and numerous were the occasions when Reynolds preached the sermons. Yes, they were truly a spiritual people, but it was not prayer and religion alone that sustained them; it was a song or a dance and the music of the band.

It was that same brass band, led by Capt. William Pitts, that had cheered the people in Nauvoo and of which Col. T. L Kane said, "The orchestra in service on the occasion of the departure from Winter Quarters astonished one by its numbers and fine drill." It now had a stranger effect as its sweet music re-echoed through the uninhabited country. It might be, when the Pioneers were fording the Platte, the dreariest of all wild rivers, or on the plains when the whistling wind would bring the first faint thought of a melody — perhaps a home-loved theme, perhaps Mendelssohn's strains, away out there in those Indian marches.

GREETINGS TO ANDREW CAHOON FROM BRIGHAM YOUNG
The Date • The Place • The Event

After a meeting on the prairies July 16, 1848, when many had retired for the night, a message was received by Reynolds Cahoon that President Brigham Young, who was journeying to Chimney Rock, Nebraska, desired Andrew and Reynolds go to meet him; that he had some important instructions for Andrew. And what were these instructions? We, the descendants of Andrew may well ask this question — it is most interesting to us.

The compiler recalls the story told many times by her father Daniel F. Cahoon. Let his words explain this incident: "President Brigham asked my father Andrew and my grandfather Reynolds to go to meet him; he had a message for them. They went as was requested and when they met Brigham he said, 'Brother Andrew, I wish to tell you that I believe the finest thing that you can do is to marry those two other Carruth sisters, Margaret and Janet. That is my advice to you.' "

Mary Carruth, the one sister had married Andrew in
Scotland November 9th, 1847, just eight months previous.
What a honeymoon! A husband with three brides! Well,
together these three Scottish lassies debated the issue and
decided in the affirmative. Grandmother Margaret, a young
lady sixteen years old at the time of the marriage, writes in
her autobiography: "On the evening of 17th July 1848, when
the company had camped for the night, Janet and I were
married to Andrew Cahoon by President Young." (See Historical Sketch of Andrew Cahoon, Pages 117 to 121.)

The history of the Cahoon and Carruth families from this
time until they arrived in the valley of Salt Lake, is without
particular event Reynolds is speaker at the meeting July
21st. Many times they have difficulty with their cattle, mixing
in various herds; many times their wagons are held fast in
the rugged mountain passes. At such times, "the boys put
their shoulders to the wheels and helped each other out" . . .
Aug. 3rd, Capt. Cahoon crosses the ravine up the Platte Valley. Aug. 8th, Cahoon's company ascended the hill and journeyed through the valley of the Sweetwater.

A letter was received from Elder Pratt, addressed to
Brigham Young and the Saints now journeying to "Salt
Lake". He had dated it Aug 8th and tells them of the gardens
in wheat and corn, squash, melons, beans and good wheat,
grown without irrigation in the Salt Lake Valley. "Some,"
he says, "have lost crops but we are greatly blessed. We have
four saw mills; plenty of timber."

Aug. 8th, Cahoon's company ascended the hill and journeyed toward Mineral Springs. Aug. 9th, a very cold morning, Capt. Cahoon gathered his cattle and resumed the journey through the long valley of the Sweetwater. Sept 12th
President Young is about two miles in advance and President
Kimball is at Fort Bridger. In a number of the references,
Cahoon is spelled "Calhoun". This is probably a misspelling.

They continue to journey through the long vale, over hard
roads and through barren sagebrush Sept. 13th, Morley's
Camp started first . . . Cahoon's next; they crossed the
Muddy Fork. The mountains in the distance are covered with
snow.

Margaret Carruth Cahoon says, "We arrived in Salt Lake
Valley in the evening of Sept. 23, 1848, which was about one
year later than the first pioneers of July 24, 1847." The

families of William F. and Daniel S. Cahoon did not arrive
in Salt Lake Valley until Sept. 24, 1849.

It is difficult for one, now traveling over the same route
with his family in a parlor car, to realize the hardships endured by a whole community in which were the aged, the in-
valids and infants; camping with a scant store of provisions
or medicines; crossing unbridged streams and usually walking most of the way, but this was accomplished more than
one hundred years ago.

LIFE IN SALT LAKE VALLEY WITH CAHOON FAMILY

The following stories pertain to certain activities in the
life of Reynolds from the time he entered Salt Lake Valley
until his death in 1861. He continued to occupy many important positions in his Church and country; ever loyal to
his convictions of the truthfulness of the Gospel principles
of the Latter-day Saints Church. He was affectionately called
"Father Cahoon" and truly loved by all who knew him. He
mingled with his people in all their political, religious and
social affairs. In their festivities, he was honored on all
occasions. He occupied the position of Counselor of the High
Priest Quorum until his death. He gave counsel, instructed,
led and guided his family, friends and loved ones, whenever
the occasion presented itself.

The particular events of the next few months are briefly
related — Reynolds taking a leading discussion in many
problems such as keeping canyons and roads in repair, man-
aging the Church Farm, acting as judge or counter of game
for the extermination of ravens, hawks, wolves, foxes, etc.
He is also appointed on the committee to erect a building
for an "armory." He is speaker at the general conference
and at each conference is sustained as First Council to the
High Priest Quorum.

CHRISTMAS DAY — 1851 IN SALT LAKE VALLEY

We can be sure there was supreme happiness during this
year; let us rejoice with them on this Christmas Day. Our
picnic party is in the Carpenter's Shop on Temple Block which
is cleared and decorated for the occasion. Great grandfather
Reynolds, great grandmother Thirza, Uncles William F., Daniel S., Andrew, Mahonri M., Rais B. and the wives of these
Cahoon sons are all in attendance. Oh yes, probably Truman
Carlos, the baby just one year old is there, and we can be

sure our cousin, Thirza Stanley and all our relatives and friends are at the party. In fact, several hundred guests attend this celebration.

From midnight until daylight of Christmas morning the band serenaded the city. It is quite a treat for Uncle William F., Uncle Daniel S., Uncle Rais B. and Grandfather Andrew to play their musical instruments again. Like magic, their music makes the sleeping mountains echo with the sound of rejoicing. Our attention is drawn more particularly to the Governor's Mansion, in front of which a troop of horsemen is drawn up in military order. This was the Brass Band, mounted on their horses, giving His Excellency, Governor Young, good wishes in sweet musical strains.

At 10 o'clock the management is in respectful waiting to receive those who are invited to the party — the merry workmen with their happy wives, smiling daughters and brave-hearted sons At 11 o'clock the house is called to order, the band strikes up a tune, his Excellency, the Governor, Hon. Heber C. Kimball and other distinguished personages lead off the first dance. Ninety-six to one hundred persons are on the floor at one time. There is no confusion, no dissatisfaction, no complaining — each enjoying the blessings of the day with happy merriment. Now refreshments are served, after which Gov. Young and Gen. Wells make addresses.

Our Christmas festivities continue. On Friday, Dec. 26th, Willard Richards gives us an address He tells us of the difference of the evening of June 27th, 1844 and the tragedy at Carthage, Illinois. We dance and celebrate in good cheer until midnight. We applaud with enthusiasm, the beautiful vocal and instrumental numbers. A vote of thanks is moved for the managers, and our guests, now numbering five hundred, respond in one voice. Our great grandparent Reynolds Cahoon offers the benediction. We now bid our friends and loved ones, "good-night" and retire with gratification for the best Christmas Festival we have ever witnessed.

FOURTH OF JULY 1852 IN UTAH

Again, let us look into the mirror of the past. It is July 4th and "as the first beams of the dawn appeared, the thunder of the cannons from the artillery roared out a Federal Salute, followed by sweet strains of music." A meeting is held in the Bowery. This being Sunday, the Fourth was celebrated on Monday, July 5th when an escort composed of thirty-one

Silver-Grey Veterans (aged men) representing the thirty-one different states, gathered at the State House.

The Mormon Battalion hailed the reveille by gathering on the Temple Block to prepare for the duties of the day, while the splendid bands were driven in carriages through the city diffusing joy and happiness. The escort was formed at the tabernacle at 8:30 a.m. with the Silver-Grey Veterans taking the front, followed by the Mormon Battalion and a company of the guard, each preceded by a band "They marched to the house of His Excellency the Governor, here his suite were in waiting in the following order. Mr. Kimball, Richards, Pratt, Smith, Woodruff, Rich, Wells, Applby, Bullock, Stout, D. Spencer, O. Spencer, Phelps, Fullmer, Reynolds Cahoon and others." These men were received into rank between the aged veterans and the Battalion.

The National Flag was unfurled on the flagstaff receiving a National Salute from the cannon's mouth, followed by a Territorial Salute. They then marched to the Tabernacle. After the escorted party was seated on the stand, the escort entered by the south doors, while the "Star Spangled Banner" was played. All doors were thrown open; the anxious crowds rushed in and soon the spacious hall was filled. After prayer, music and the reading of the "Declaration of Independence," an appropriate speech was given in behalf of the thirty-one aged veterans, then "the band played on."

Yes, the Mormon pioneers had come 1400 miles into the heart of a generous wilderness, but president Brigham Young could see more than isolation in this land. His eyes, like the prophet Joseph's, burned with images of the future. He saw the desert yield up the walls and roofs of another great city, the seat of an empire.

"THIS IS THE PLACE"

(By Elizabeth Cannon Porter in The Desert Magazine)

"This Is The Place," said Brigham Young, but at first the brethren were not sure. Again he exclaimed "It is enough. This is the right place. Drive On." This was a place which brought them close to God and the most skeptical of the Saints could sense that there was a nobility in the vast horizons and the wind that smelled of juniper and thunderstorms, and the soaring rock temples carved by eternity from the same rock that would blunt plows. So in 1847 to a land

ORIGINAL SALT LAKE THEATRE

MEMORIAL SALT LAKE THEATRE

DEEDS ON LAND AND OLD THEATRE

QUIT CLAIM DEED

REYNOLDS CAHOON

-to-

BRIGHAM YOUNG SENIOR

Book B   Page 171
Recorded   Apr. 26, 1860
Dated: April 23, 1860
Consideration: $1,000.00

QUIT CLAIMS·

All his right of claim, interest and possession of the following described land in Salt Lake County, Territory of Utah, to-wit·

Part of Lot 1 in Block 75 to-wit: Commencing at a point upon the Southern boundary of said lot which is 225 feet East from the South West corner of said lot and running East 105 feet or to the Southeast corner of said lot, thence running North along the Eastern boundary of said Lot 10 rods; thence running West to a point directly North of the place of beginning, thence South to the place of beginning, containing 105/264ths of an acre as platted in the Plat A, Great Salt Lake City Survey.

Two Witnesses   Reynolds Cahoon

Ack'd April 24, 1860 by the signer of the above transfer before John T. Caine, Notary Public, residing at Salt Lake County, Utah Territory.

WARRANTY DEED

BRIGHAM YOUNG SEN. and MARY ANN YOUNG, his wife

-to-

W.B. CLAWSON, JOS. A. YOUNG, THOMAS WILLIAMS, LEGRANDE YOUNG, JOHN T. CAINE and JOHN W. YOUNG

Book 4   Pages 402-3
Recorded: Aug. 19, 1873
Dated: July 29, 1873
Consideration· $100,000.00·

CONVEY AND CONFIRM:

All that certain piece or parcel of land known and described as follows:

Parts of Lots 1 and 8 in Block 75, commencing at the Southeast corner of said lot 1, thence running North 178 feet, thence West 105 feet, thence South 178 feet, thence East 105 feet to the place of beginning, containing 18,690 square feet of ground as plotted in Plot A, Salt Lake City Survey, and known as the Salt Lake Theatre including scenery, costumes, properties and musical instruments unto the said grantees, their heirs and assigns as tenants in common.

Two Witnesses   Brigham Young Sen.
                          Mary A. Young

Ack'd July 29, 187_ by Brigham Young Sen. and Mary Ann Young, his wife, before James Jack, Notary Public, residing at Salt Lake County, Utah Territory. SEAL.

both splendid and forbidding came a people visionary and practical.

"Ten years after that day when the first wagons groaned to a halt, an empire was taking shape. The pioneers had pushed their little colonies north into Idaho, west to California, south to the rim of the Grand Canyon; and near Zion Park in Southern Utah, lived the grandchildren of pioneers from London and tidy New England farms in a land they called Zion."

A monument commemorating the arrival of Brigham Young and the Mormon Pioneers was erected at the historical spot at the mouth of Emigration Canyon, east of Salt Lake City. Beautifully landscaped, it is set like a jewel in the midst of a five hundred-seventy acre mountain park. On July 24, 1947, a celebration was held marking a century since the pioneers entered the valley.

Ground Broken For Salt Lake Temple

Since the day Brigham Young said, "Here is the spot where we shall build a temple," this thought had been uppermost in the minds of the Mormon Pioneers. On April 6th in the year 1851 at the general conference, a motion was read and carried by acclamation. Yes, it was "A motion to build a Temple to the Name of The Lord Our God, in Salt Lake City, Utah." D. H. Wells was to superintend the building of the Temple and the public works.

Ground was broken in Great Salt Lake, preparatory to excavating for the Temple foundation on Feb. 14th 1853. The people assembled on the Temple block at 10 o'clock President Young witnessed the surveying of the site by J W Fox under the supervision of Truman O. Angell, Architect. President Young gave a thrilling speech; the earth was loosed about six inches deep and the ground was declared broken for the Temple. Work was begun for the laying of the foundation, and on April 6th the South-East corner was dedicated.

No definite information is given us as to the exact part Reynolds took in the building of the Salt Lake Temple. We know that he did labor many years here; that he was present at all conferences discussing plans for its erection and with the same energetic fervor he manifested in the infant days of the Church when he was one of the committee for the construction of the former temples, he now appealed to the Saints in Salt Lake to assist in building this Temple. He delivered many sermons in the Tabernacle and when the Utah Legislature met Dec. 12th 1853, the House of Representatives appointed him Sergeant-at-Arms.

Truman O. Angell was the Temple Architect. Two granddaughters of Reynolds had married into the Angell family;* therefore, there is a closer association between them, not only because of the mutual interest in the building of the Temple, but also in the ties of family relationship. This magnificent structure was not completed until 1893, many years after the death of Reynolds. However, our records tell us that during the first years of its building and planning, he took an active part and was on the temple grounds whenever he was able.

LAST WRITTEN MESSAGE OF REYNOLDS CAHOON

We re-copy to the memory of our ancestor Reynolds Cahoon, an epistle which he and his fellow-officers formulated March 2nd, 1856. This glorious message was written just five years previous to his death. It is one of his last printed messages. If he were with us today, would he not speak these same words to us?

An Epistle to Members of the High Priest Quorum**

"We feel constrained to write you a few words of Council in the Lord. May peace, grace and the Holy Ghost be and abound with you and yours, is the desire of your servants in the Lord. That these blessings may be with you, we write to you to encourage you to diligence and perseverance in well doing and to be up and doing, for the time draweth nigh, when you with us, will be called upon to render an account to Him who has called us to this high and holy calling, who will award every man according to his works; and the works required of us, no man can know, unless he has the light of the Spirit of God dwelling in him; and if he has that, he will not be barren nor unfruitful in the knowledge of his duties to his brethren and his God. That man will know the voice of the Good Shepherd, whose voice will be full of music and charms to his ears, whom he will follow as sheep follow their shepherd into green pasture beside cooling brooks, to feed and quench their thirsty souls. So will it be with the man of God, whose heart is always open to the whisperings

---

*See Addenda, p 167, Cahoon-Angell Family
***Deseret News,* March 2, 1856, Vol. 6 4

of the Spirit of the Lord. The counsel of the man of God is to him the word of the Lord, the mind and will of God. He goes to him with all his might to carry out his counsel, and the Lord works with him and he is able to accomplish all the Lord requires at his hands.

"If it is the building of forts, he is on hand to build them; to plow or sow, to reap or mow, or to go to the nations and teach them that the Lord has raised up a prophet and through him, brought to light the sacred records of the Prophets of Old, and in short, to do all things which are required of him to do; not for the sake of property, which is after the manner of the world, but for the sake of glorifying God, in helping to build up Zion, and establishing His Kingdom upon earth; and also for the love of Truth, which has come forth from God, which is testified of by the Holy Ghost, which dwells in him and is a light to his feet, and shines around him so he can hold to the light and life of God.

"Brethren, that you may possess that spirit, live and walk in the light of it and know the voice of the Good Shepherd, we give unto you a few words of counsel. Seek earnestly to know the mind and will of God concerning yourselves by prayer and faith, and be humble and contrite before Him, even of a broken heart and a contrite spirit; administering unto thy brethren, the words of life, and withhold not thy substance from the poor and needy, the widow and the orphan, that their cries may not ascend to God against you, but administer of thy substance unto them, lest God proves you to be unworthy of the blessings which he has bestowed upon you, and takes them from you and gives them to another and you be found wanting.

"Be a peacemaker among thy brethren, 'for blessed are the peace-makers, for they shall be called the children of God.' Assist the Bishops in carrying out the counsels of the Lord, and be teachers of righteousness in the midst of the people of God, both by precept and example in your own houses, be exact and regenerate those that are given you in the Lord. Remember to teach thy children according to the covenants which you have made in the House of the Lord, which, if you do, they will not be found cursing and swearing, nor fishing and skating on the Sabbath, but will be at the house of worship with you, or at home reading the word of God which has come through the Prophets; or being taught by their mothers the words of the Lord, and the object of their creation that they may grow up to honor and glorify God upon the earth.

"Do you read the Book of Mormon, Doctrine and Covenants, Bible, the sermons, and the counsels of the men of God, and understand the words of the Lord which are for us who live in this the eleventh hour? We believe there are many High Priests who do not own that sacred record, the Book of Mormon and not many who do own it who do read it nor the Book of Doctrine and Covenants; for we have traveled among you, in many houses we have not found them, neither in your places of worship, and it proves to us that you are not interested in them as you are in your flocks and herds and your houses and lands. It is well for you to look after those blessings which God has given you but not place them first in your affections and worship them instead of Him who has created them, and given them to you. Those blessings are given you to use, and you are accountable for how you use them.

"Brethren, do you search those books that you may know the kind of God concerning the dispensation in which we live? Then you will know some things that the Lord is about to do in the midst of the House of Jacob and Israel. We feel, brethren, that we should be up and doing for it is the last — the eleventh hour — and if we expect to receive our penny, we must labor and earn it, lest we be found naked, not having on the wedding garment in the day of our Lord, and we will be compelled to hear these unwelcome words, 'Depart from me, I know you not.'

"Brethren, look at these things before it is too late, and see that you labor as though you must learn as much in one hour as those who have gone before us did in ten. Attend your quorum meetings that you may receive instructions or instruct others in the ways of the Lord, for there are many who come and are ordained and then disappear, and are known no more unless a committee is sent to hunt them up. We want such to attend the meetings for unless you abide in the vine you will wither and die, and be ready for the burning, for we shall prune the vine as any of the branches become dry or unfruitful, as far as we are made responsible; and to carry out this, we have appointed men in most of the settlements in this Territory to watch over you, and teach you in your duties as God's High Priests, and to report to us from time to time.

"It is not expected that those who are called to take the Presidency of the meeting in the different settlements, should set apart counselors, and organize as an independent quorum, or ordain men to the high and holy priesthood, but simply to preside at their meetings, and see that they meet often and report to the President of the Quorum from time to time. If a bishop of a Ward or settlement cuts off a member belonging to the Quorum, report the name to us, also the cause, or what he was cut off for, that we may blot out his name from the record.

"Brethren, receive this counsel and word of admonition in the spirit in which we give it, and God will pour out His Spirit upon you that you will not be barren nor unfruitful in the knowledge of the Lord.

> David Pettigrew, Pres.
> Reynolds Cahoon,
> D. Page Jr., Clerk
> George B. Wallace Counselors"

REYNOLDS RECEIVED HIGH PRAISE

Reynolds Cahoon received the highest praise from those who knew him best, especially from Hyrum Smith and the Prophet Joseph Smith while they were alive. So also did President Brigham Young pay tribute to Reynolds at the general conferences of 1857, 59 and 60 Brigham Young refers to his association with Reynolds, of brother Cahoon conveying his (Young's) family out to his house and helping them while Young was on a mission. Let us refer particularly, to the remarks of President Young in the Tabernacle June 3rd 1860. He is speaking of the early days and his acquaintance with the Cahoon family. These are his words:

"You have frequently heard me refer to my poverty when I moved to Kirtland in the Fall of 1833. Not a man ever gathered with the Saints so far as I have known but had more property than I had. When I came into the Church, I distributed my substance and went preaching and when I gathered with the Saints, I had nothing. I then said I would not build up a gentile city. Other mechanics went from Kirt-

land to different cities to get employment, I said to them,
'I will work here if I do not receive one farthing for my labor
and have to beg for my bread. I will assist in building up this
place and I will make many dollars to your one by so doing.'

"I did, for when I started to the West on 5th of following
May, I could have bought what almost the whole of them
had made during the winter. They told me that it often cost
them more to get twenty dollars they had earned than it
did to earn it

"I went to work for brother Cahoon, one of the Kirtland
Temple Committee. He had little or no means, and only a
shell of a house. I helped him and the Lord threw things in
his path and he paid me for my labor. I had more in my
possession for my labor than any who had gone out in search
of work during the past winter."

THE FAMOUS SALT LAKE THEATRE

"Like a great castle of mystery and dreams," rose the
pillars and walls of the Salt Lake Theatre; a castle indeed,
which stood as an historic monument to Drama, Music and
Art in Utah "But", we ask, "Why include this in Our Cahoon Story?"

First, because many of the children of Reynolds feel that
their pioneer ancestor did play an important part in the
building of this famous "Play House" and they are inspired
in the thought that Reynolds was so closely connected with
its history.

Second, because some of the descendants of Reynolds actually performed on its stage and too, because William F., son
of Reynolds, had the honor of raising the first curtain for its
opening performance. This position of "Fly-man," William F.
held until the time of his death. Here is the story:

Reynolds Cahoon was the first and only private owner
of the lots where the Great Salt Lake Theatre was built The
location was the corner of First South and State Street, com-
prising a large portion of that block. One day Brigham Young
came to Reynolds and said, "Brother Cahoon we need your
lots, we must build a theatre."

No doubt there were mingled thoughts in the minds of
Reynolds and Thirza. These lots were probably the only property they now owned They were very valuable lots in the
heart of Salt Lake City. Reynolds and Thirza had given every-

thing of worldly value they had ever possessed to their
Church. They had dedicated every moment of their lives for
the Gospel's sake When they left their beautiful cities of
Kirtland and Nauvoo, their homes and property were left
behind and many times they had said "We have Given All
To God".

Now they were aged and could no longer do hard, labori-
ous work for their own maintenance nor for their Church.
Reynolds could not now go out traveling as a church missionary. He could not go out through the church to "gather
subscriptions" to build another temple and then superintend
its construction. He could not go and make "appeals to the
Saints for funds" and then build another great school house
for the education of their missionaries, nor could he erect
another "fine hotel," another "Nauvoo Mansion".

No doubt they remembered the past and recalled the days
of happiness and peace in Nauvoo when Joseph, their Prophet,
had organized a dramatic company for classical plays where
Joseph himself, had fostered the drama and where the sons
of Reynolds and Thirza had played in the band Again their
inspired leader Brigham Young said, "We wish to build a
theatre".

No, there were many things Thirza and Reynolds could
not do to help build a city of Zion in the Desert, but they
did own this fine property just where this majestic "Play
House" could be erected, where drama of such magnitude as
had never yet been dreamed of, would respond to spiritual
tutorship under inspired leaders.
"Yes", they reasoned, "these lots can perform a mission
for us, and 'Give or Sell', our Church shall have them." So
on April 23, 1860, history tells us, Reynolds Cahoon con-
veyed this property to Brigham Young for the purpose of
erecting the Salt Lake Theatre.   ,

Romance of the Old Play House

The first rock was hauled onto the lots June 20, 1861
and in July, the following month, construction was commenced. Just eight months later on March 6, 1862, the great
building was dedicated for its formal opening by Daniel H.
Wells. March 8, 1862, two dramatic performances initiated
the new "Play House."

This majestic building, the "Cathedral in the Desert" as it was called, with its galleries, its elaborate ceilings, boxes with their filigree, scenes and curtains painted by great artists, was by far the largest structure yet built by the Latter-day Saints.

"Its fame was known far and wide, every actor was a brother and every actress, a sister. In fact, it was elevated to the cast of a dramatic temple and all entertainments were opened with prayer. It was made a high school to the public and not in the entire history of the stage, ancient or modern, was ever a theatre before, thus endowed as a Sacred Dramatic Temple for the people."

There were many serious and many very humorous incidents in its history. When the pioneers had no money, the tickets were purchased with eggs, chickens, turkeys, vegetables, fruit, etc. Patrons took their lunch and visited and talked of all the late happenings. One lady was wearing her new dentures for the first time and as that was really something to tell about, she passed them through the audience to show the skilled workmanship.

President Brigham Young made the decisions as to the type of entertainment and the type of performers. All must meet with his approval. The young ladies should always wear ankle-length dresses, the young men, must always appear in gentlemanly attire.

"On one occasion, President Young gave explicit instructions that the curtain should not go up for the play until certain requirements were obeyed. The stage manager, with wilful intent to disobey, rang the curtain. Brigham, the modern Joshua, so the story goes, commanded the curtain — 'Stand Still'. And it stood still. The fly-man pulled and struggled, he called others to his assistance, but the stubborn curtain didn't budge until Pres. Young's instructions had been fulfilled, and then it glided up as quietly as a piece of silk."

Reynolds died one year before the completion of the Salt Lake Theatre. Although he never lived to see the magnificent structure, it can now be said of him, "He truly gave all to his church".

The famous old "Play House" has since been torn down. The property was sold to the Mountain States Telephone Company and a metal plaque on the wall of their building marks the spot where the theatre once stood.

When we ponder on the value of this piece of property today, we may well remark, "sold or gave". However, let us relate the incident as grandmother Margaret Cahoon, one of Andrew's lovely wives, has written it:

"During the year 1860-61, Andrew's father, Reynolds sold his lots to Pres. Young to build a theatre on. For his payment he received a number of oxen, wagon, cows and merchandise, etc. He also had a debt paid he owned in the tithing office which was several hundred dollars. He was well satisfied with the pay as he thought he got a big price for it."

After the sale of the property, Reynolds and Thirza moved to South Cottonwood (now Murray), Salt Lake County, Utah. Here they lived with their son, Andrew, who provided and cared for them until the time of their death.

On the University of Utah campus, is to be erected the Pioneer Memorial Theatre in memory of the famous old Salt Lake Theatre. The building is under the direction of the National Society of the Sons of the Utah Pioneers On the front and back of each of the 1,022 seats will be placed a plaque honoring a Utah pioneer. To the memory of Reynolds Cahoon, a plaque will be placed by Chester Pulaski Cahoon, a family representative and great grandson of Reynolds.*

Death of Reynolds Cahoon
(From The Deseret News)

"Reynolds Cahoon died at 12 o'clock noon, Monday April 29th 1861 of dropsy at his residence in South Cottonwood Ward. He was the son of William Cahoon and Mehitable Hodge, born Cambridge, Washington County, New York April 30th 1790. He was among the early settlers in northern Ohio. Was in the service of his country during the War of 1812. He was among the first that embraced the Gospel in Kirtland. Was baptized by Elder Parley P Pratt, October 12th 1830 and ordained High Priest, June Conference held in Kirtland 1831. He was one of the first Elders that visited Jackson County, Mo.

"He was one of the building committee for the Temple in Kirtland and was among those that were driven from home in dead of winter and exterminated from Missouri. He was one of the building committee for the Temple in Nauvoo and his voice nerved the arm and put life in the workman upon its walls. He crossed the plains the first season after the

*See Ground-breaking Ceremonies of Memorial Theatre page 160

pioneers. He has labored several years here about the Salt Lake Temple.

"He never listened to the voice of the 'Stranger' but followed the true shepherd. He was always found in the midst of the Saints as a cheerful partaker in all tribulation, privation and persecution. He was an active member, a faithful servant and a true friend to the Prophet of God while he was living; full of integrity and love for the truth and always acted cheerfully the part assigned him in the great work of the 'Last Days'. He has fought the good fight; he has kept the Faith, and has died in hope of a glorious resurrection."

In a beautiful lot in the Salt Lake City Cemetery lies the remains of these noble ancestors, Reynolds and Thirza Cahoon. At this time (1960), not even a wooden marker designates the graves of these immortal pioneers. May we, their descendants, erect a monument to pay honor to their names.

THE WIVES OF REYNOLDS CAHOON

Reynolds Cahoon married three times. His first wife was Thirza Stiles, his second, Lucina Roberts (Johnson) and his third, Mary Hildrath. The celestial marriages of Thirza, Lucina and Mary to Reynolds Cahoon are recorded in the Microfilm department of the Utah Genealogical Library in Salt Lake City, Utah. The date was January 16th 1846 and the film is known as "Nauvoo Sealings". These marriages were performed by Brigham Young.

THIRZA STILES, REYNOLDS' FIRST WIFE

Thirza Stiles, first wife of Reynolds Cahoon, was the daughter of Daniel Olds Stiles and Abigail Farrington. According to the church records, Thirza (sometimes spelled Thurza) was born October 18, 1789 at Sanesborough, Connecticut. (At the present time, there is no such city.)

It appears that the Stiles family resided in various places: in Brandon, Rutland, Vermont; in Herkimer, New York and in cities of Connecticut. The Cahoon Family Records state that Thirza was born in Lansingburg or Rensselaer, New York, (or probably in Rensselaer County.)

She had two brothers, Farrington and John and one sister Abigail. Her mother died September of 1793, leaving four

*Abigail Stiles married John Patten, brother of Apostle David W. Patten.

small children, the eldest being six years old and the youngest, an infant of one month. Her father married a second wife, Sarah Buckland, and to them were born seven children.

Daniel Olds Stiles was a Revolutionary soldier at the age of seventeen years. He was a Baptist, "fine presence and agreeable manner." He was a tailor and while at one town, he traveled and studied under an Indian Doctor, hence the tradition that he was partly of "Indian birth." Daniel O. was the son of John Stiles and Betsey Olds.

Thirza and Reynolds Cahoon were married December 11, 1810, by Honorable John Stiles, probably in Newport, New York. They were members of the Church of Jesus Christ of Latter-day Saints and according to the manner of their church, their celestial marriage was performed January 16, 1846, in the Nauvoo Temple, the temple they helped to build.

She had lived in the more highly developed communities of the eastern United States. She came from a comfortable home and had she chosen to remain there, could have spent all her days on earth without want or privation However, she endured extreme hardships and sacrificed all for the Gospel's sake. She united with the women in Kirtland and Nauvoo amid scenes of persecution to help forward the building of the temples there. Probably she very often recalled the words spoken by their Prophet when the ladies were working on the temple veils, "Well, sisters," he said, "You are always on hand. Mary was first at the 'Resurrection', and the sisters now are the first to work on the inside of the temple."

Thirza, Charter Member of Relief Society

Great was their joy when on March 17, 1842, Joseph Smith organized the Relief Society in Nauvoo. The place was the lodge-room above his store. Its object was not only to relieve the poor but to teach the gospel and to save souls. Twenty-six women formed this first membership. Thirza was a charter member but was unable to be present. Emma Smith, the wife of Joseph Smith was the first President chosen. They deprived themselves of many necessities in order to feed the workmen of the temple.

They would churn butter for them, reserving none for their own tables. At one time they had saved enough money to buy glass for the temple and when the church was indebted for lands, these women gave this money to liquidate

that debt On one occasion, Reynolds Cahoon was sent by
the prophet to address the members of the Relief Society
and at this time he promised them many great blessings

The Relief Society is one of the oldest Women's Organizations in America Its prosaic name is retained because of
its historical significance.

Like their sisters of ancient Hebrew days, they took over
primary social tasks that have become submerged and forgotten in our modern existence. They shared with those more
needy, sustained and encouraged their husbands, cared for
the sick and distressed, comforted the dying and laid away
the dead; those were woman's tasks in the classic, age-old
division of labor among the Hebrew and Christian peoples.

On January 24, 1845, Reynolds and Thirza Stiles Cahoon
went hand in hand to seek a "Patriarchal Blessing" from the
Patriarch of their church Reynolds was told he was a descendant of Ephraim, son of Joseph who was sold into Egypt;
Thirza was told she was of the house and lineage of Judah.

We, the descendants of Reynolds and Thirza are endowed,
not only with the great blessings of the "Priesthood" through
the line of Ephraim, but also the distinctive blessing of
"Ruling Power" through the lineage of the "Royal Blood of
Judah." These two lines are our great heritage. May we,
the descendants of this wonderful mother, pay tribute to her
name.

LINEAGE OF JUDAH*

"The Jews are still a part of the major House of Glory,
altho of the separate House of Judah Be it carefully and distinctly noted here, however, that there are two kinds of Jews
in the world today One, the Sephardim Jew who is of the ancient
and eminent stock of old and is really of the ancient royal line
of Judah, and of which the noble mostly came, none less than
Jesus of Nazareth. Some of the very greatest scientists of the
world of today as in all centuries past, are Sephardim Jews

"The other is the Ashkenazim Jew who is Jewish by religion
only, but has very little, if indeed any at all, of the blood or
talents of ancient Judah He is not a Jew at all in reality This
Ashkenazim Jew is vastly inferior to the Sephardim Jew to
whom he is of no blood relation, and in most cases, inferior in
stock, mentality, spirituality and works

" 'Israel', says Worth Smith, 'was to lose all trace of her distinguished lineage for centuries It has been revealed that this
is a tragic fact. But from this generation forward, the true awareness of her identity will penetrate more and more into the

---

*Lineage of Judah by Worth Smith

consciousness of Israel's peoples until in due season all of them shall know it'

"Judah was the son of Jacob and was given the blessing of 'Ruling Power' or to hold the 'Scepter and Power' of Earthly Rule until 'Shilah' (Christ) should come It was Judah who pleaded for the life of Joseph who was sold into Egypt Ephraim, a descendant of this Joseph, was given the greater blessing, that of the 'Priesthood'."

DEATH OF THIRZA STILES CAHOON
(From The Deseret News)

"At Bishop (Andrew) Cahoon's home at South Cottonwood, on November 20, 1866, Thirza Stiles, wife of Reynolds Cahoon, died The deceased was born in Sanesborough, October 18, 1789. She embraced the Gospel in the winter of 1830, since which time she has been with the Church and shared all the hardships and persecutions of the Saints. She was the mother of seven children, had fifty-two grandchildren and fifteen great grandchildren to imitate her virtues and call her blessed.

> *Deck'd with the garland of integrity,*
> *She lived for God and immortality,*
> *Faithful 'till death — she mingles with the blest*
> *And with the just will share a glorious rest.*

LUCINA ROBERTS, REYNOLDS' SECOND WIFE

Lucina Roberts, the second wife of Reynolds Cahoon, was born in March 1806, at Lincoln, Addison, Vermont. She was the daughter of Elisha Roberts and Mary (or) Dolly Murphy. Lucina was the widow of Peter Johnson. Peter and Lucina had a son, Jarvis Johnson, born July 6, 1829 at Lincoln, Addison, Vermont.

Lucina received her patriarchal blessing January 24th, 1845 and was told that she was of the "House of Joseph through Manassah". She was endowed December 31st 1845 as Lucina Roberts.

MARY HILDRATH, REYNOLDS' THIRD WIFE

There is very little known about Reynolds' third wife, Mary Hildrath, where and when she was born or where or when she died. As previously mentioned, we do know she was sealed to Reynolds January 16, 1846, in the Nauvoo Temple, Nauvoo, Hancock County, Illinois. Mary and Reynolds had no children.

CHILDREN OF REYNOLDS CAHOON

Reynolds Cahoon and his first wife, Thirza Stiles had seven children. The first five children were born in Harpersfield, Ashtubula County, Ohio; the last two were born in Kirtland, Geauga County, Ohio.

William Farrington Cahoon, born November 7th 1813, died April 4th 1893.

Lerona Eliza Cahoon, born October 25th 1817, died June 18th 1840.

Pulaski Stephen Cahoon, born September 18th (or) 20th, 1819 (or) 1820, died February 1892.

Daniel Stiles Cahoon, born April 7th 1822, died November 13th 1903.

Andrew Cahoon, born August 4th 1824, died December 13th 1900.

Julia Amina Cahoon, born September 24th 1830, died September 1st 1831.

Mahonri Moriancumer Cahoon, born July 26th 1834, died January 24th 1888.

Reynolds Cahoon and his second wife, Lucina Roberts had three children.

Lucina Johnson Cahoon, born about 1843, probably Nauvoo, Hancock County, Illinois, died as child.

Rais Bell Cassen Reynolds Cahoon, born October 13th 1845, Nauvoo, Hancock County, Illinois, died February 11th, or 27th, 1911.

Truman Carlos Cahoon, born January 18th 1850, Salt Lake City, Salt Lake County, Utah, died February 4th 1911.

WILLIAM
FARRINGTON
CAHOON

DANIEL
STILES
CAHOON

MARY WILSON DUGDALE CAHOON
Second wife of William F. Cahoon

JANE AMANDA SPENCER CAHOON
First wife of Daniel Stiles Cahoon

MARTHA SPENCER AND DANIEL STILES CAHOON
Martha was the second wife of Daniel Stiles Cahoon

WILLIAM FARRINGTON CAHOON
(From his Autobiography and Historical Records)

✦

The Power that guides large masses of men, and shapes the channels in which the energies of a great people flow, is something more than a mere aggregate of derivative forces. It is a compound product, in which the genius of the man is one element, and the sphere opened to him by the character of his age and the institutions of his country, is another — G S Hillard

✦

"I, William F. Cahoon, was the first born and oldest son of Reynolds Cahoon and Thirza Stiles. I was born in Harpersfield, Ashtabula Co., Ohio on the 7th day of November, 1813. When I was about 17 years old, I was baptized & confirmed a member of the Church of Jesus Christ of Latter Days by Elder Parley P. Pratt, on 16th day of October 1830, and I was ordained a Priest under the hands of Oliver Cowdery at a Conference of Elders held at the town of Orange, Ohio on the 25th October 1831. On 2nd Feb. 1835 was selected as a Seventy."

At age seventeen, William F. was appointed a Ward Teacher. His duty like all Ward Teachers was to visit the members of the Church, ask them certain designated questions and report back to the officers of his Quorum. The following humorous incident is told by William F. upon the occasion of bearing his testimony. He is speaking of the Prophet Joseph Smith. It is entitled—

A Humble Ward Teacher*

"Before I close my testimony concerning this good man (Joseph Smith), I wish to mention one circumstance which I shall never forget. I was called and ordained to act as a Ward teacher to visit the families of the Saints. I got along very well 'til I was obliged to pay a visit to the Prophet. Being young, only 17 years of age, I felt my weakness in the capacity of a teacher. I almost felt like shrinking from my duty.

---

*This story was furnished by Lernoa A. Liddle, daughter of James W. Cahoon, son of Andrew It was recorded in the *Deseret News* (Church Section; *Juvenile Instructor*, Vol 27, page 492; also in "Recollections of the Prophet Joseph Smith" by George Q Cannon

"Finally, I went to the door and knocked and in a minute the Prophet came to the door. I stood there trembling and said to him; 'Brother Joseph, I have come to visit you in the capacity of a Ward teacher, if it is convenient for you.'

"He said, 'Brother William, come right in. I am glad to see you. Sit down in that chair there and I will go and call my family in.'

"They soon came in and took seats. The Prophet said, 'Brother William, I submit myself and family into your hands', and took his seat.

" 'Now, Brother William', said he, 'Ask all the questions you feel like.'

"By this time my fears and trembling had ceased and I said, 'Brother Joseph, are you trying to live your religion?' He answered, 'Yes'.

"I then said, 'Do you pray in your family?' He answered 'Yes'.

" 'Do you teach your family the principles of the Gospel?' He replied, 'Yes, I am trying to do it'.

" 'Do you ask a blessing on your food?' He said he did.

" 'Are you trying to live in peace and harmony with all your family?' He said that he was

"I turned to Sister Emma, his wife, and said, 'Sister Emma, are you trying to live your religion? Do you teach your children to obey their parents? Do you try to teach them to pray?'

"To all these questions she answered, 'Yes, I am trying to do so'.

"I then turned to Joseph and said, 'I am now through with my questions as a teacher and now if you have any instructions to give, I shall be happy to receive them.'

"He said, 'God bless you brother William, and if you are humble and faithful you shall have power to settle all difficulties that may come before you in the capacity of a teacher.

"I then left my parting blessing upon him and his family, as a teacher, and departed."

WILLIAM GOES ON TWO MISSIONS

"From October 1831, during the next twelve months, I was occupied laboring with my hands making boots and shoes gratis for the Elders who were starting out to preach and for the support of my father's family, occasionally holding meetings and bearing my testimony to the truth of the work of God in the last days, also in visiting the churches exhorting the Saints to faithfulness and obedience to the commandments of God.

"On the 19th of November I started on a mission to the East in company with Zebedee Colton and John Boynton with whom I traveled for a few days and then was appointed to travel with Father (Reynolds) Cahoon and David Patten. With the last, I traveled as far East as Silver Creek in the State of New York, preaching and baptizing in several places The Lord accepted our labors and we were greatly blessed laboring in God's work.

"I arrived home from my mission February 27, 1833 and remained until March 21st, when I was then appointed to travel and preach the Gospel in company with Elder A. Lyman. We traveled through the east of Ohio, through Pennsylvania and part of New York preaching and baptizing with great success. While with Elder Lyman, I was called by the voice of the Church and ordained an Elder. The spirit of the living God was with us.

"The last part of August I returned home and labored with my hands until May 5, 1834. I then enlisted to go to the land of Zion in Jackson County and started with the Volunteer Company under the Prophet Joseph Smith for the delivery of the brethren who had been driven from their homes by a ruthless band of mobocrats.

"On May 5, 1834 the Camp left Missouri. It was truly a solemn morning, we left our wives, children and friends, not knowing whether we would see them again as we were threatened by enemies that would destroy and exterminate us from the land. We were facing the 'lion in his den'.

"Joseph Smith had made this pledge to us, 'If you will go with me to Missouri and keep my counsel, I pledge that I will lead you there and back and not a hair of your head shall be hurt'. 'This camp', said William F., 'marched through a population of tens of thousands of people like lambs among wolves, but no man among them opened his mouth to say, 'Why do you do so?' On we marched singing our favorite song, 'Hark listen to the Trumpeters'.

A MIRACLE ON THE PRAIRIE*
(As told by Wm F and Father Cole)

"While traveling across the vast prairie, treeless and waterless, they camped at night after a long and wearisome day's march. They had been without water since early morning, and men and animals suffered greatly from thirst, for it had been one of the hottest days of June Joseph sat at his tent looking out upon the scene. All at once he called for a spade. When it was brought, he looked about him and selected a spot, the most convenient in the Camp for men and teams to get water. Then he dug a shallow well, and immediately the water came bubbling up into it and filled it, so that the horses and mules could stand and drink from it. While the camp stayed there, the well remained full, despite the fact that about two hundred men and scores of horses and mules were supplied from it."

This incident was related to Elder O. B. Huntington by William F Cahoon. It was also told to Elder Huntington by Father Zera Cole while Elder Huntington and Father Cole were working for the dead in the Logan Temple Zera Cole was with the "Camp of Zion" and when it went to Missouri in 1834, Wm F's brother-in-law, Harvey Stanley, also went with them.

The Autobiography continues:

"We journeyed, pitching our tents by the way, and arrived in Missouri in the latter part of June. We then numbered two-hundred and five. A council was held to determine what steps to take when the Word of the Lord came to the Prophet Joseph saying the time had not come to 'take the sword in hand to redeem Zion.'

"Many in the Camp murmured because we were not permitted at this time to restore our brethren at all hazards, which greatly displeased the Lord, who a few days afterwards sent a scourge amongst us; the cholera which took from us sixteen or more of our number. This caused great sorrow and mourning in our Camp. It is a fearful thing to fall under the displeasure of the living God and to openly rebel against Him and murmur at the counsel of His servant, the Prophet.

"Shortly after our Camp broke up. Some returned to the Churches in the East and some were required to tarry and

---

*See *Joseph the Prophet,* page 499, by George Q Cannon

aid in defending the new homes they had chosen. It fell my
lot to remain until the fall. I labored with my hands until
I was taken sick with the fever and ague.

"In the latter part of October I received my discharge
and in company with Elder H Riggs, I started for home by
way of the rivers for we were not able to travel by land.
I arrived home 17th day of November, 1834. This was a day
of rejoicing for both parents and children and we felt to thank
God for preserving our lives and bringing us together again.
As soon as my health permitted I commenced going to school
and I attended all the Church Meetings as far as I was
able to."

"Twelve Apostles" and "Seventies" Organized

"On the 14th day of February 1835, a conference was
called which lasted several days. On the 14th of the month,
the Quorum of The Twelve Apostles was organized for the
first time in this dispensation. At this conference, there was
also organized the First Quorum of Seventies. I was called
as a member of the First Quorum of Seventies and was ordained to this office, 28th Feb , 1835 "

During a journey of a thousand miles, with trials and
hardships innumerable, the sterling character of these men
surely was put to the test. They became leaders at a later
period, their early leadership being manifest through these
experiences. Brigham Young too, the great Moses of the
Latter Day, here received his first lessons under the eyes
of Joseph Smith, the Prophet.*

Referring to this period of Latter-day Saint History and
Zion's Camp, Church historians say:

"God, it appears was about to choose His Foreign Ministry,
His Special Witnesses to The World — the Twelve Apostles
and the Quorum of Seventies — and from these men of
'Zion's Camp', who had offered their all in sacrifice — even
life itself, for the Work's Sake — God chose His worthy witnesses, His tried and tested leaders. Their duty was to go
into all the world, whither-so-ever the Twelve Apostles should
call them This Quorum, in other words, constituted the Foreign Ministry of the Church in connection with the Twelve
Apostles under whose direction they labored."

---

*Whitney's *Life of Heber C. Kimball.*

"Some of the men of this Camp who went down with
Joseph" comments George Q. Cannon "were among the no-
blest. They adhered to the Lord's commands and to His
Prophet with all the fidelity of their souls. They were of such
exalted faith and courage that their righteous fame stands
with that of the greatest disciples of old."

William F. continues in his autobiography, "The next season, after I had been ordained a Seventy, I went and labored
on the Lord's House and continued so to labor until the
temple was finished and dedicated April 6, 1836. I received
my washing and annointings and remained in Kirtland.

First Public Marriage in a Mormon Church*

"On January 17, 1836, I married Nancy Miranda Gibbs.
We were married before a concourse of people. Several hundred witnessed the ceremony. It was done to establish prece-
dent of Public Marriage by the Church instead of taking out
a license from the County Court, marriage notice being published several times previously in the Church, which custom
was allowed by the laws of the state. About three thousand
assembled both inside and outside the Church when we were
married. Nancy was only 17 years old when we were married."

Form of Marriage Certificate

I hereby certify, that, agreeable to the rules and regulations
of the Church of Jesus Christ of Latter-day Saints, on matrimony, Mr. William F Cahoon and Miss Nancy M Gibbs, both
of this place, were joined in marriage, on Sabbath, the 17th,
instant

Kirtland, Ohio, January 19th 1836

Joseph Smith, Jun

Of these very interesting marriages, Joseph Smith writes
the following· "Sunday 17th Jan. 1836 I attended meeting
at the school house at the usual hour, a large congregation
assembled . . . In the afternoon I joined three couples in
matrimony in public congregation, viz; William F. Cahoon
and Maranda Gibbs, Harvey Stanley and Lerona Cahoon,
Tunis Rapley and Louisa Cutler. We then administered the
Sacrament and dismissed the congregation which was so
large that it was very unpleasant for all We were then invited to a feast at Elder Cahoon's which was prepared for
the occasion, and had a good time while partaking of the
rich repast; and I verily realized that it was good for brethren

*History of the Church — Vol. II, pages 376-377.

to dwell together in unity, like dew upon the mountains of Israel where the Lord commanded blessings, even life forevermore."

SACRIFICES HOME IN KIRTLAND

"In the Spring of 1838," William F. continues, "I with my family and my father, Reynolds and his family went from Kirtland to Missouri. My family consisted of wife and daughter we had named Nancy Ermina, born 23 Feb. 1837. I left behind me a good lot all paid for, for which I labored very hard to get, also a good seven-room house well furnished and owned by myself . . I could not dispose of it, so I turned the key and locked the door and left it, and from that day to this, I have not received anything for my property which is in the hands of strangers. However, we left it and went on our journey, pitching tents for a house. After a long and tiresome journey we arrived at Far West 5 May 1838, and we rejoiced to find the Saints prospering and in good spirits. I remained here until the Fall of the year, laboring for the support of my family.

"I then moved to Adam-Ondi-Ahman where I commenced to build for myself, a log house but was compelled to stop on account of the mobbers who came upon us. This was a time of grief and trouble to us, the mob who infested this beautiful region of country, were constantly creating excitement after excitement adding rumor to rumor until we were forced to watch them by night, as well as by day We were so harrassed that we were not able to build houses or even spare time to procure food for our families and we lived in peril. Our fare was also poor as we could not get our corn ground and we had to punch holes in pieces of tin and take ears of corn and grate them on the tin to get or make meal for our bread, and we had to live on this kind of food for six months.

SAINTS KILLED OR BANISHED FROM MISSOURI

"After a great deal of excitement and some skirmishing, the governor of the State of Missouri, Lilburn W. Boggs sent his blood-thirsty minions, who surrounded us, his ever-to-be remembered and execrated inhuman order, for the extermination of the Latter-day Saints or their eternal banishment from their homes, their houses and land, and from the State. In pursuance of which order, all the surrounding branches of the Church, were either butchered in cold blood, old and young included in one indiscriminate slaughter or else they were driven into Far West. I and my family went into Far West and the mob at length concluded to strip us of all we possessed and then banish us from the State . . .

"I was at Far West at the time of the arrival of the main body of Bogg's cut-throat minions. It was like opening the gates of hell, for such creatures as they were, could come from no other place, or at least they were inspired by the fiends of hell to accomplish the devilish designs of the infamous scoundrel who sent them, Lilburn W. Boggs. I expect the Lord will reward him according to his works and give him his portion with his master, the devil, Amen.

"I, in company with all the rest of the church there, was arrested and put under guard. We were forced to sign a deed of trust of all we possessed. I passed an examination of seven consecutive days, after which I was permitted to return to my family at Adam-Ondi-Ahman. I found my wife in deep sorrow and weeping, for she knew not what had become of me or whether I was alive or dead.

AFFIDAVIT OF WM. F. CAHOON

MISSOURI WRONGS*

I hereby certify that in the year 1838, I was residing in Daviess County, Missouri, and while from home I was taken a prisoner in Far West by the Militia, and kept under guard for six or eight days, in which time I was forced to sign a Deed of Trust, after which I was permitted to return home to my family in Daviess County, and found them surrounded by an armed force, with the rest of my neighbors, who were much frightened. The order from the Militia was to leave the county within ten days, in which time my house was broken open and many goods taken out by the militia.. We were not permitted to go from place to place without a pass from the general, and on leaving the county, I received a pass as follows:

"I permit Wm. F. Cahoon to pass from Daviess to Caldwell County, and there remain during the winter, and thence to pass out of the State of Missouri.

—Signed Nov. 10, 1838
Reeves, a Brigadier General."

During this time, both myself and my family suffered much on account of cold and hunger because we were not permitted to go outside of the guard to obtain wood and provisions; and according to orders of the Militia, in the Spring following, I took my family and left the State with the loss of much property.

WILLIAM F. CAHOON

Territory of Iowa, Lee county. Subscribed and Sworn Before D. W. Kilbourn, J. P.

---

*History of the Church, Period I, Vol. IV, page 52.

"My father (Reynolds), was also made prisoner at the same time and was under arrest several days. As soon as he gained his liberty, we and our families moved to Far West with many more families of the saints and remained there until the 4th February, when the time was nearly up for us poor exiles to leave the State and seek other homes somewhere in the wide world.

"We started and arrived at Quincy in the State of Illinois where we found a people who treated us with the greatest degree of hospitality and kindness, assisting the Saints with food and giving them houses to live in. After stopping at Quincy about five weeks, I went to live with a man by the name of Travis who gave me employment and towards whom my bosom burns with gratitude. May the God of Abraham, Isaac and Jacob reward him and his family for their kindness to me and my family when we were poor and forlorn without a home and shelter. I remained with this man until the next Fall. I then moved to Montrose in Lee County, Iowa.

SAINTS GATHER AT NAUVOO

"During this time, the Prophet Joseph had purchased a small location for the Saints to gather, which he laid off in squares and named Nauvoo. I remained in Montrose until the Spring of 1842. I then moved to Nauvoo and commenced working on the temple of the Lord as a carpenter and joiner. The Lord prospered me in my labors so that I was enabled to build a small house for a home among the Saints. I was appointed time-keeper of the carpenters and joiners who worked on the Temple.

"Soon after I moved to Nauvoo, the Saints began to gather from all parts of the world and from the surrounding States in great numbers. Houses began to be built in all directions and the city of Nauvoo constantly increased in number and enlarged her boundaries and under the wisdom and direction of God's Prophet Joseph Smith, Zion was greatly blessed and the Saints rejoiced in the Truth and in seeing His purposes and plans carried out as they were revealed through His Servant Joseph.

"At length the storm burst forth and it seemed as if the devil with all his forces was arrayed against the Saints of the Most High and he found plenty of help for the Prophet Joseph was harrassed from all sides, — from foes without and traitors within the Church. Those, at least some of those, whom he had blessed, turned and stung him; some under the 'garb of sanctity', but whose deeds were as black as hell, — faithless, rotten-hearted wretches who would sell their father's soul for 'filthy lucre'. For they did sell him, who was a father to the people, the Prophet of God, the brave, true-hearted man among men; Joseph Smith and his noble and loving brother Hyrum, the Patriarch.

"The same unrelenting, fiendish hatred that possessed the people in Missouri, followed the Church to Nauvoo and robbed the Church of God and the world at large, of two of the most God-like men who have ever lived in any age.

JOSEPH AND HYRUM SMITH MARTYRED

"On the 27th day of June at 5 p.m , Joseph Smith and Hyrum were brutally murdered. The particulars of this cruel and inhuman act are well known and will have to be atoned for by this Nation. The murder of the Prophet seemed for a time to quell the mob spirit of even the actors themselves and Nauvoo increased faster than ever

"In the Spring of 1845, I was appointed to superintend the raising of all the timbers of the temple. We finished raising all the framing part August 23, 1845 When the temple was enclosed, the cowardly wretches again commenced the work of devastation, but the Lord, Himself, interposed in behalf of His people, manifested His power and filled the hearts of the wretches with such fear, that when a few horsemen appeared before them to give battle, they fled out of the State, and then we saw the fulfillment of the words written in the Book of Mormon, that a people who will strictly obey the revelations of God, He will bless and prosper them in the land. Again, on the 9th and 10th of September, the mob began to burn our houses and destroy our property, the property of the Saints, and kept up a continual scene of persecution from this time 'till we left Nauvoo.

JOURNEY INTO THE WILDERNESS

"I continued work on the temple and in the endowment rooms until the 3rd of February 1846. On the 4th of February, I began to repair wagons for our journey into the wilderness, for it was surely one. I worked on wagons 10 days and on the 15th, I and my family left with the Nauvoo Brass band, and my brother Daniel S. was along with us. We bid farewell to the beautiful city of Nauvoo, the city of Joseph, and started for the camp of Israel which was Sugar Creek in Iowa. Here we joined Brigham Young's Camp

"We had a hard time It was very cold weather, wet and snow and frost, but the Lord sustained us and we journeyed west, pitching tents by the way We reached Garden Grove. I was appointed to over-see the house building and keep the roll of workmen.

"We built houses and laid out farms. I remained at this place until the 13th of May. I left my family at this place, took my team and my brother Daniel's family and traveled first in Brother Spencer's company until the 19th and then went back for my family. They were well.

We then started West and the 24th, we camped with Brother Charles C Rich and others and on the 26th, we arrived at the main camp. I remained at this place until the 7th of June. I then started back with my team to meet my father's family. On the 8th, I found them and Father Cutler and family. I remained behind to get some wagons they had left behind a few days before, while they continued their journey.

"On the 12th, we arrived at the main camp at Pisgah. I remained in camp two days and the 14th began to go back to trade for oxen and provisions for our journey On the 15th, my brother Andrew, myself and Father Cutler and some others started back for the settlements. We were kept busy traveling and trading until 6th July. We then started for the camp in the wilderness. On the 12th brother Daniel came back to help us We traveled fast to get back as soon as possible. The Camp had gone on

"The 23rd we overtook Father Cutler's Camp, on 31st, we crossed the Missouri River and on Saturday, 1st August, we reached the main camp. On 5th, we traveled to a place afterwards called Cutler's Park where I remained until 21st day March, 1849, when my brother Daniel and myself started for the Salt Lake Valley where the Church had found a resting place.

"The Pioneers led by Brigham Young entered this valley after a very tiresome journey of 1000 miles from the Missouri River, on the 24th July 1847. They built a Fort and put in seed as soon as they arrived and they laid out the city of Great Salt Lake.

"In the meantime, during the time I remained behind, I was busy all the time, cutting and hauling logs, building houses and sheds, barns, fencing, shoe-making, in fact I was Jack-of-all trades, nothing came amiss I was always on hand either to work on a farm, haul wood, build a mill or attend meeting. During this time, I went back into Missouri to work for provisions for my family and preparing myself for my journey across the mountains into Salt Lake Valley.

Traveled Six Months to Reach Salt Lake

"As stated above, I in company with my brother Daniel and our families, started on the 21st March and camped the first day at Brother Burgess, six miles out At length, we were on the way leaving civilization behind us and glad to get away from it, and as we journeyed across the great plains in the wage of the pioneers, we felt as if the 'God of Joseph' was with us and blessed us and preserved us. On our way we had the usual vicissitudes of the early travelers across the plains, such as fording rivers, and when we could not ford, making rafts and building bridges, killing snakes, burying our dead, guarding our cattle and traveling under difficulties.

"We traveled day after day, for six months and on 24th day September 1849, we entered the valley in company with my father and Andrew's family who came to meet us. Was It Not A Joyful Meeting! Only those separated from their families for a long time, can tell.

Life Spent in Service of the Church

"From the time I entered the valley, most of my time has been spent working on public works and the Church in different capacities. I worked as foreman over the carpenters of the Tabernacle that was pulled down in 1877 to make room for the present rock Tabernacle that was being built in the year 1878. I worked on the Woolen Mills in Canyon Creek, what is now the Paper Mill In fact, my life has been spent generally in the service of the Church.

"I rejoice still in the truths of the Gospel of Christ I am happy in doing the Will of My Father in Heaven. I thank God for preserving me in the Truth and for watchful providence that has been over us, a people. We were driven out from Nauvoo at the point of a bayonet, into the wilderness in the extreme cold weather, homeless and friendless Yes, God was our Friend, He led us by His Almighty Power, and with an outstretched Arm, He has delivered us; Our sorrow, He has turned into Joy. He has sanctified our tribulations to our good

and has blessed and multiplied us as a people until we have
become a Great People. He has made the wilderness we came
to inhabit to "blossom as the rose," and Utah Territory is
prospered and the City of Salt Lake is one of the most beautiful cities on the face of the earth, and the wonder of the
Nation who drove us forth from their midst.

"To God Be All The Praise For It, He that hath done it,
using His Saints as the instruments of His Will."

Thus we have the autobiography of William F Cahoon *
In this, and in the sketch of Reynolds Cahoon, his Life's
Story has been told He was one of the speakers at the dedication of the Temple in Manti, Utah, May 21st 1888 After
the Salt Lake Theatre was built, he raised the first curtain,
and held the position of Curtain Man or Fly Man, until the
time of his death.

Before closing our history, let us refer to the records of
the Church Journal History of Oct. 10, 1865. It is the second
anniversary of Zion's Camp. A festival is being celebrated in
the Social Hall, Salt Lake City Here we find William F. and
his family entering into the true spirit of the occasion He
relates in his jocular "Cahoon Style," the incident of Brother
Woodruff scolding him.

A program was prepared in which William F, Joseph
Young and family sang, "Oh Happy Souls Who Pray". The
favorite song of Zion's Camp, "Hark Listen to the Trumpeters" was also rendered William F. bore his testimony,
referring to Joseph Smith and Brigham Young receiving
revelations from God. He tells about the promise given by
Joseph to the members of Zion's Camp, that if they would
go with him and keep his counsel, they would not be harmed

William Farrington Cahoon was an exemplary citizen, un-
obtrusive in his manner and throughout his life career was
held in high esteem by his associates and acquaintances as a
faithful Latter-day Saint and an upright man. He died April
1893 in his 80th year, at his residence in the 12th Ward in Salt
Lake City, Utah He married four times and had fourteen
children. In his demise, passed away one of the comparatively
few remaining members whose connection with the Church
dated from the days of Kirtland.

---

*The Autobiography of William F Cahoon was given to the John Far-
rington Cahoon Family and through their courtesy and the efforts of
Stella Cahoon Shurtleff, a Micro-film copy of it has been placed
in the Utah Genealogical Library at Salt Lake City, Utah

Resolutions of Respect
(June 5, 1893)

"The members of the Second Quorum of Seventies at their last meeting passed appropriate resolutions of respect to the memory of the late William F. Cahoon, who at the time of his death was Senior President of the Quorum."

NANCY MARANDA GIBBS

Nancy Maranda Gibbs was the first wife of William F. Cahoon. She was born July 27, 1817 or 1818, in Benson, Rutland County, Vermont. She was the daughter of Aaron Gibbs and Prudence Carter. She married William F. Jan. 17, 1836 having joined the Mormon Church in 1831. She moved to Kirtland in 1833 with her widowed mother.

In his autobiography, William F. relates:

"She was a cheerful partaker of the tribulations, privations and persecutions of the Mormon people; a true friend and companion, always energetic in the truth. Nancy died Sunday, Oct. 6, 1867 at her home in the 12th Ward, Salt Lake City."

*Eleven children were born to William F. and Nancy Cahoon: Nancy Ermina, Lerona Eliza, John Farrington, Prudence Sarah Ermina, Thirza Vilate, William Marion, Daniel Coyton, Joseph Mahonri, Henry Reynolds, Stephen Tiffany, and Andrew Carlos Cahoon.

MARY WILSON DUGDALE CASSON

Mary Casson was the second wife of William F. Cahoon. They were married Sept. 23, 1845 in Nauvoo, Hancock County, Illinois. She was a pioneer into Utah in 1849 and suffered the persecutions of the Saints in Nauvoo. She was a devoted wife; a true and benevolent friend. Four children* were born to William F. and Mary: James Cordon Casson Cahoon, Samuel Casson Cahoon, Mary Ellen Casson Cahoon, and George Edward Cahoon. Members of these Utah Pioneers moved into Canada, becoming pioneers of Cardston, Alberta, Canada.

ELVIRA MARSALL JONES

Elvira was the third wife of William F. Cahoon. They were married June 12, 1871, Salt Lake City, Utah. She was

---

*See the life sketches of his children in *The Cahoon Story*.

born Aug 5, 1834 in Boomstick, Howard County, Missouri.
It appears from the records that William F. and Elvira were
divorced Nov. 11, 1878. There were no children by this marriage.

OLEANA OLSEN

Oleana Olsen was the fourth wife of William F. Cahoon.
They were married Feb. 28, 1878 in Salt Lake City, Utah.
She was born Aug 17, 1833 in Sjoberg Molina, Norway.
She died Dec. 21, 1928. Before her marriage to William F.
Cahoon, she had married Nils Neilson by whom she had two
children: August Neilson, born Feb. 22, 1865, Fredricknold,
Norway, and Otilda Georgorine N. Neilson, born May 16,
1859 Fredricknold, Norway. No children were born to Wil-
liam F. and Oleana Cahoon.

LERONA ELIZA CAHOON STANLEY

*The dignity, the grandeur, the tenderness, the everlasting and
divine significance of motherhood*—DEWITT TALMAGE

—DEWITT TALMAGE

Lerona Eliza Cahoon, the second child of Reynolds Cahoon
and Thirza Stiles, was born October 25, 1817, Harpersfield,
Ashtabula County, Ohio. She moved with her parents to
Kirtland, Ohio where, on January 17, 1836, she married Harvey
Stanley.

The details of her marriage have been told in William
F. Cahoon's autobiography. William F was her older brother
and he tells of the marriages which were performed by the
Prophet Joseph Smith when three couples were united in
marriage on the same day at the L D S. Church in Kirtland,
Ohio. There were about three thousand guests who witnessed
this ceremony. It was unique since it was the first "Public
Marriage" performed without the issuance of a license. This,
however, according to law was not necessary, as announcement of marriages had been made public many times previously in the Church.

Lerona Eliza was only nineteen years of age at this time
and Harvey, about twenty-five. They lived in Kirtland then
moved with the Mormon people to Nauvoo, Illinois. Harvey
helped to construct the Nauvoo Temple. The couple then
moved to Lee County, Iowa, where a child was born to them
on Nov. 22, 1839. They named this little girl Thirza Lerona
Stanley. On June 18, 1840, when the baby was only seven

months old, the mother, Lerona Eliza died and was buried at Monroe, Iowa; a young mother scarcely twenty-three years of age and the only living daughter of Reynolds and Thirza, to whose home little Thirza Lerona was taken.

HARVEY STANLEY

Harvey Stanley was a member of the First Quorum of Seventies. He was ordained under the hand of the Prophet Joseph Smith along with his two Counselors, Sidney Rigdon and Oliver Cowdery. On the 28th of February, 1835, the Church in council assembled, commenced selecting certain individuals to be Seventies. From the number of those who went up to Zion's Camp with the Prophet Joseph Smith, Harvey Stanley and William F. Cahoon were among those who were ordained and blessed at that time to begin the organization of the First Quorum of Seventies. "They are to constitute traveling quorums to go into all the earth, whither-so-ever the Twelve Apostles shall call them. They constitute the foreign ministry of the Church."

THIRZA LERONA STANLEY TAYLOR

Thirza Stanley, born Nov. 22, 1839, was the daughter of Lerona Eliza Cahoon and Harvey Stanley. Her mother died when she was seven months old and her grandparents, Reynolds and Thirza Cahoon, took her to their home and cared for her during her life. She went to Utah with them and was the youngest of the Cahoon Pioneers. At seventeen years of age she married Hilliard Burnham Taylor. They were sealed in the Endowment House April 29, 1856, Salt Lake City, Utah.

After her marriage she moved to California, then returned to Utah and later went to LaGrange County, Missouri to reside near the home of her uncle, Pulaski Stephen Cahoon.

Hilliard was born March 20, 1824 in Stockbridge, Windsor, Vermont. He was the son of Paul Taylor and Polly Burnham. Hilliard Taylor's family has not yet been identified. He does not seem to be of the President Taylor Family of Utah. His mother's family has been traced from Polly Burnham, daughter of Wolcott Burnham, son of Appleton; son of Rev. William, son of William, son of Thomas Burnham of Lincoln, Vermont.

Reynolds' history records that Hilliard was endowed as William Burnham Taylor. Temple Records show he was baptized April 16, 1854 and that he married his first wife, Asenath Eleanor Lufkin and was sealed in the Endowment House Nov. 22, 1854.

PULASKI STEPHEN CAHOON

That best portion of a good man's life — His little, nameless,
unremembered acts of kindness and love — IBID

Pulaski Stephen was the third child of Reynolds Cahoon and Thirza Stiles. He was born Sept 18th, 19th or 20th, 1820 at Harpersfield, Astabula County, Ohio. He assisted in the construction of the Temples at Kirtland and Nauvoo

He was married to Louisa Leopold, Feb 9th, 1840. Louisa, daughter of Valentine and Elizabeth Leopold, was born April 1st, 1822. The marriage of Pulaski and Louisa was solemnized Jan 30, 1846 in the Nauvoo Temple by Brigham Young *

Pulaski was a merchant and early history of the Church tells us that at one time Pulaski wished to purchase the ship called the "Maid of Iowa", which belonged to the Church but Joseph Smith did not desire to sell it. Later, it was in this ship that Joseph and Hyrum left for the place called "Safety", previous to their death in the Carthage Jail

John Pulaski Cahoon, son of Andrew Cahoon of Salt Lake City, Utah, visited with the family of Pulaski Stephen and tells us that he had a carpenter and leathershop in Missouri and although blind, was still working at his vocation

Louisa, his wife, died March 17, 1890 and two years following on Feb 15, 1892, Pulaski Stephen passed away Both died in LeGrange, Lewis County, Missouri. Three children were born to them:

George Henry Cahoon — Born July 15, 1841, Nauvoo, Ill. died June 30, 1842, Nauvoo, Ill.

Thurza Elizabeth Cahoon — Born Oct. 2, 1843, Nauvoo, Ill. — Died July 7, 1844, Nauvoo, Ill

Amos Reynolds Cahoon — Born April 30, 1846, Quincy, Ill. was the only child who lived to maturity. He married Emma Agnes Hooper, born Dec. 8, 1849 in Ohio, the daughter of Jacob Hooper and Mary Watson Amos Reynolds and Emma had two children

Charles Wilbur Cahoon — born Feb. 10, 1869 in LaGrange, Mo. (resided in Chicago).

Mary Louisa Cahoon — born Sept. 1, 1870, LaGrange, Mo. Married Charles Conrad Cameron (resided in Ill.). Mary and Charles had one son, Alan B. Cameron.

---

*Micro-film — "Utah Film 1-215"

DANIEL STILES CAHOON

(From the biography by Emma Regene Cahoon Peay)

Something men have that half-gods never know, the
power to sensitize cold, lifeless things; to make
stones breathe, and out of metal grow escarpments
that deny the need of wings. —VIRGINIA MCCORMICK

Daniel Stiles Cahoon was the fourth child of Reynolds Cahoon and Thirza Stiles. He was born April 7, 1822, Harpersfield, Astabula, Ohio. He was married July 27, 1843 to his first wife, Jane Amanda Spencer, by Pres. Brigham Young at Nauvoo, Illinois. While on their pioneer trek to Utah he married his second wife, Martha Spencer at Council Bluffs, Iowa, in 1847. Jane Amanda and Martha were sisters.*

Daniel S. joined the Mormon Church about 1830 and was baptized by Wm. E. McClelland at Harpersfield. He lived in Kirtland, Ohio, later in Nauvoo, Illinois. When a boy, he lived at the home of the Prophet Joseph Smith and worked for him, riding the horse while Joseph cultivated corn and potatoes. Later he carved one of the oxen for the Nauvoo Temple Fountain.

Daniel and his families were driven from Nauvoo in Feb. 1846. They spent the summer passing through Illinois to Winter Quarters and remained there until 1848 then went to Salt Lake Valley with the pioneers. Daniel and his families left Nauvoo Feb. 15, 1846 in company with the Nauvoo Brass Band. His brother William F. who was also with them, writes:

"We bade farewell to the beautiful City of Nauvoo and journeyed to the Camp of Israel which was on Sugar Creek in Iowa, joining there Brigham's Camp. We traveled first in the Brother Spencer's Company. On 23rd July we overtook Father Cutler's Camp and crossed the Missouri River. On 1st August we reached the Main Camp and traveled to Cutler's Park where we remained until 21st day March, 1849, when we started for the Salt Lake Valley. We traveled six months arriving in the valley 24th Sept. 1849 where we met our father Reynolds and our other brothers. They had arrived the year previous. What a happy welcome!"

AN EXPERT STONE CUTTER

Daniel S. was an expert stone-cutter and bricklayer and had the honor of being the second-best stonecutter who worked on the Temple.

---

*Celestial marriages, March 12, 1848 at Cahoon's house, Winter Quarters, Nebr. (Utah F 1 p. 707-21a Nauvoo Sealings.)

He resided in Murray, Salt Lake County, Utah (South Cottonwood) and later moved to Deseret, Millard County, Utah where he and his son, Theron, built the L D.S Meeting House They were pioneers of Deseret, building the big smelter between Drum and Deseret as well as many of the houses there Daniel S. owned a large herd of cattle and a farm. His home was known as the "Corner". He was a member of an orchestra, playing the piccolo for dancing and entertainment.

On Dec. 23, 1844 he was ordained to the First Council of Seventies On Feb 16, 1853 he was chosen President of the Thirty-sixth Quorum of Seventies and from 1855 to 1857 he officiated again as the President of this Quorum On May 20, 1857, he fulfilled an L.D S Mission to Deer Creek, South Eastern Wyoming and Labonta. In 1863 he served on the Grand Jury for the Territory of Utah and again was called on a second mission to the Eastern States.

ILLUSTRIOUS CAREER CLOSED
(Deseret News, Nov 1903)

"Daniel Stiles Cahoon, oldest Church Member and Pioneer laid to Rest, Deseret, Millard County, Utah. Daniel S. Cahoon who is thought to have been the oldest member of the church and one of the sturdy pioneers of Utah, died at his home Nov. 13, 1903. He was the son of Reynolds and Thirza Stiles Cahoon . . . Baptized 1831 by Wm. McClellan, labored on Kirtland and Nauvoo Temples; was driven from home in the dead of winter from Nauvoo, Ill ; crossed the plains with the Saints and suffered all the trying circumstances they passed through. He labored a number of years on the Salt Lake Temple, lived in South Cottonwood until 1877 then moved to Deseret, Utah. Brother Cahoon died firm in the faith. He bore a powerful testimony that Joseph Smith was a true Prophet of God. He had heard Joseph Smith predict things that had come to pass and had attended him from attacks of his enemies.

"On Friday, Oct. 23, 1903, this year, at the gathering of the Utah Indian War Veterans, when so feeble that he could hardly stand up, he said that it might be the last time he would ever speak in public and he bore so strong and feeling a testimony of the Prophet Joseph Smith that the Spirit seemed to thrill the hearts of all present with a knowledge of the truthfulness of what he said . . . He was the father of sixteen children, sixty grandchildren and twenty great grandchildren at the time of his death. A large congregation attended the funeral services held in the Deseret Meeting House. A number of his oldest acquaintances spoke in glowing terms of his honorable and faithful career. Interment was in Oasis Cemetery.

"Thus, one by one of those who lived and assisted the Prophet Joseph Smith are passing away, and only a short time remains until their voices will no longer be heard."

JANE AMANDA AND MARTHA SPENCER

The two wives of Daniel Stiles Cahoon, Jane Amanda Spencer, and Martha Spencer (sisters) were born in Stockbridge, Berkshire County, Mass. — Jane, Dec. 12, 1822 and Martha, Nov. 14, 1831. They both died in Utah.* Their parents were Hyrum Spencer and Martha Spencer and although they had the same name, were not related.

When Jane Amanda, Martha, and their brother, Hyrum Theron were very young, their mother, Martha Spencer died and their father, Hyrum, moved to Nauvoo, Ill. They all knew the Prophet Joseph Smith very well. Hyrum Theron says:

"Our father worked on the Nauvoo Temple; he had charge of Rock Hauling. When we were driven out of Nauvoo, father died on the trail."

**"When the Mormons first fled from Nauvoo, the mobs followed them. Their father, Hyrum, was one in charge with gathering the scattered cattle and herding them safely across Iowa. He rode in the saddle six days and nights with but a night's sleep, and when he collapsed, death whisked him away. His coffin was made from the side-boards of a wagon. His body was brought to Mt. Pisgah or Garden Grove, for burial."

Daniel Stiles Cahoon was the father of sixteen children. Each wife was the mother of eight. The children by his first wife, Jane Amanda, were: Mary Jane, Sarah, Maria, Hyrum Spencer, Daniel S., Theron, Reynolds, who died in infancy, and Anna (or Anne) who died when only three years old.

The children by his second wife, Martha, were: Nancy Amanda, Julia, Charles Henry, Martha Ellen, Margaret, Antoinette who died when she was two years old, Orson Spencer, and Alpha Alonzo.

---

*See Spencer Family, page 153.
**Skousen History.

ANDREW CAHOON

THE THREE WIVES OF ANDREW CAHOON
Margaret Carruth Cahoon
Mary Carruth Cahoon   Janet Carruth Young Cahoon

Oval Insert: Mary Barr Carruth, mother of the Carruth sisters

ANDREW CAHOON AND HIS EIGHT SONS
Back Row: Joseph C., Albert E., Reuben Reynolds, Daniel E.
Front Row: A. Alonzo, Andrew, James W., John P.

ANDREW CAHOON

*Let the record be made of the things of today, lest
they pass out of memory tomorrow and are lost
Then—perpetuate them, not upon wood or stone that
crumbles to dust, but upon paper chronicled in pictures
and words that endure forever* —KIRTLAND

Andrew Cahoon was born August 4th, 1824 at Harpersfield, Ohio. He was the fifth child of Reynolds Cahoon and Thirza Stiles. In 1811 Andrew's father, Reynolds Cahoon moved from New York to Ohio residing in Harpersfield twelve years, in which town Andrew was born.

The family then moved to Kirtland, Ohio where they became quite successful and accumulated considerable property It was here that Andrew's parents heard of the Book of Mormon or "Golden Bible", as it was known then. They became satisfied that the book was of Divine origin, accepted the principles of the Gospel of the Church of Jesus Christ of Latter-day Saints and were baptized in 1830. This was just six months after this Church was organized.

ANDREW'S BOYHOOD

Thus, our first insight into the early life of Andrew, acquaints us with the fact that the home of his parents was a very religious one. Andrew was twelve years old when the Kirtland Temple was dedicated, and a young man of twenty-two years when the Nauvoo Temple was completed. On both these magnificent edifices, his father, chosen by revelation, was a member of the building committee. Our information is definite that the Cahoon boys, William Farrington, Daniel Stiles and Andrew were active with their father in the construction of these temples. Andrew's brother, Pulaski Cahoon commenced work also, but did not continue long William F. tended the saw-mill while Daniel S. and Andrew were among the first stone-cutters for the temple, laboring diligently until it was completed.

FIRST YOUNG GENTLEMEN AND LADIES SOCIETY

The first information recorded in the Journal History pertaining to Andrew Cahoon, refers to the organization in Nauvoo, of a society known as the "Young Gentlemen and Ladies Society."

99

The "Young Ladies Retrenchment Association" was founded by Eliza R. Snow; later it became the "Young Ladies Mutual Improvement Association". The Society to which Andrew belonged, however, was probably the initial organization of the "Young Ladies and Young Men's Mutual Improvement Association."

The first meeting of the girls and boys of the "Young Gentlemen and Ladies Society" was held at Heber C. Kimball's home, and the second, at Elder Farr's school room. The room was filled to over-flowing.

Elder Kimball delivered the addresses, exhorting the young people to study the scriptures, "enable themselves to give reason for the hope within them" and be ready to go on the stage of action when their present instructors and leaders had gone behind the scene; also to keep good company and keep unspotted from the sins of the world; to be obedient and pay strict attention to the advice and commands of their parents who are better calculated to guide the pathway of youth than they themselves

"I advised them", said Elder Kimball, "to organize themselves into a Society for the Relief of the Poor, for the collecting of funds for this purpose and to perform this charitable act as soon as the weather permitted . . . I gave such advice as I deemed to guide their conduct through life and prepare them for a glorious eternity."

"I felt more embarrassed" he continued, "to stand before them than before kings and queens."

Andrew Cahoon was one of the three members chosen by his young friends to draft the constitution or by-laws for their society. It was unanimously adopted.

These young men and women understood the perfect plan for the building of their future cities and they too labored to bring about these conditions. They visualized with admiration the future cities of the world, where "there would be no rich, no poor, no slums, no corrupt politicians, no criminals nor dishonest business methods. Where the farmer could enjoy every advantage of city life and each would assist the other." This was to be the plan for building Nauvoo, the city where Andrew lived.

They labored diligently, as did their parents, to erect their beautiful Nauvoo Temple. Structures were built by contributions and a most united effort was necessary, moreover, it was not like erecting a building today. Every detail had to be performed by the Pioneer Saints. Timber could not be ordered from the lumber yard, it had to be hewed in the far-off forests of Wisconsin, carried to Nauvoo and cut into boards for the various uses. There were no iron foundries from which they could obtain the required metal properly prepared, the stone from the quarries had to be cut and polished and this whole work had to be supplied out of the tithing of the people However, before the Nauvoo Temple was completed their beloved leaders were martyred

Appointed Superintendent of Affairs on West Side

The enemies of the Church thought the death of the leaders would terminate the Church but this was not the case, for there were other fine men holding the Priesthood and their conviction "that this was the Church that God had established with its Gospel in all its fullness," renewed their determination to prosecute the work of building their Temple. After its completion and dedication, their enemies with bitter intolerance, attempted to destroy it and in 1846, drove the Mormon people across the river into the prairies of Iowa and Nebraska. Two temporary points were selected, Garden Grove and Mt. Pisgah. It is at Garden Grove we find Andrew delivering mail consisting of thirty-three letters and again May 11th with twenty-four letters, after which he returns to Nauvoo with mail from Garden Grove.

On Friday, August 7, 1846, a council of the Twelve Apostles decided that the brethren on the west side of the Missouri River should settle together. A municipal High Council consisting of Andrew Cahoon, A Cutler, Jedediah M. Grant and others was appointed to superintend the affairs of the Church here at Winter Quarters It was here that our grandfather Andrew, as one of the High Council, formed the first Anglo Saxon settlement in what is now known as the State of Nebraska.

It was a regular city consisting of 3,483 people living in sod-houses and dug-outs, and was divided into 22 Wards with Bishops. They built a Council House which was used for councils, Sacrament, meetings, dances and other entertainment. During this cold winter 700 Mormons died and some 600 were buried in the cemetery at Winter Quarters

Only such great ideals as God and liberty, faith in God and sublime confidence in inspired leadership caused 15,000 Mormons to seek refuge on the plains between Nauvoo and Winter Quarters in the Fall of 1846. They offered their lives as truly as did former-day Christians who faced death in the Roman Arenas.

In passing, let us quote Bancroft's tribute to the Mormon people:

"There is no parallel in the world's history to this 'Migration Nauvoo'; it is one of the most outstanding feats in the history of colonization."

A majestic steel structure — the Mormon Pioneer Bridge — now commemorates the site of the historic Mormon Crossing of the Missouri River.

ANDREW CALLED ON MISSION TO EUROPE

On October 20, 1846, a letter of appointment was written to Elder Andrew Cahoon and William Mitchell to go to the British Island to preach the Gospel. Three days later the Council retired to the Post Office and chatted with Orson Spencer and Andrew until midnight about their starting on their mission to England. Sincerely believing this to be a command from the Lord, Andrew and his companions accepted this call to preach the Gospel in these foreign lands. The date of their departure is not certain, however we know it was sometime in November of 1846

A letter written by Orson Spencer to Brigham Young substantiates this:

Philadelphia, Nov 26, 1846

President Brigham Young·

I arrived here well on the 23rd inst , in company with Brother Cahoon Tell Father Cahoon that Andrew is well, having gained ten pounds in weight We have not received any aid since we left but have good hope and spirit. We preached here and will leave in the morning car for New York . I will write before I cross the Atlantic

Your brother & humble servant,
Orson Spencer

ARRIVAL IN GREAT BRITAIN

The events of the voyage across the Atlantic Ocean could be related best by these Mormon missionaries themselves. We are told that a great storm arose and the ship was reported lost and that many had perished in the mighty deep. Our first information of their arrival in the British Isles is an address issued to the Saints by Franklin D. Richards, printed Jan. 27, 1847 in a publication called "The Star":

Wednesday, Jan 27, 1847

It now becomes our duty and privilege to address a few words to the Saints in the British Isles through the medium of The Star   On account of the supposed decease of our worthy Brother Orson Spencer we were called from our field of labor in Scotland, but it affords us superlative pleasure to advise our readers that he is alive and in our midst and enjoying excellent health and buoyant spirits, as is our beloved Elder Andrew Cahoon who accompanied Brother Spencer from the camp of the Saints to this land   They landed at Liverpool on Saturday Evening 23, after a protracted voyage of about forty days, encountering storms and gales, but by the kindness of a Father's care, they were preserved from any serious disaster   .

Your brother in Christ, and fellow-servant in the Kingdom of God

F D Richards

Again in January 29, 1847 the following greeting appeared:

TO THE SAINTS IN GREAT BRITAIN

It is with inexpressible satisfaction that we hail Elder Orson Spencer and Elder Cahoon and congratulate the Church on their safe arrival in your midst

They are men of God, worthy of your utmost confidence and well calculated to cooperate with those already in your midst in carrying out and perfecting all those measures for your future prosperity and deliverance as a people of which the foundation had been laid

P P Pratt
John Taylor

ANDREW GOES TO SCOTLAND

Now we shall travel with grandfather Andrew to Scotland, the home of our early ancestors. We attend a conference, the date March 28, 1847 and the place "Odd Fellows Hall, 175 Trongate. The meeting is called to order by Brother Richards, after which the beautiful hymn is sung — "Come Ye That Love The Lord". This is probably one of grandfather's favorite hymns, for he asked that it be rendered. The prayer is offered by Andrew and another hymn is sung. Elder Richards then arises and tells us how happy he is to see so many together and that it is with a feeling of gratitude to his Heavenly Father, that he is able to appear among us. He asks if the conference has accepted his labors and will sustain him as their president   This being put to a vote, was carried unanimously. Well, now, we can't say unanimously, for we notice that Elder Cahoon did not vote — he did not raise his hand. We shall let him tell us about that later.

Brother Richards reports that there are now approximately 1,338 Latter-day Saints holding church offices there and by baptism, 68 members have just been added. Elders Cahoon, Douglas and Drummond are called to retire to the side room where they attend to the ordination of many of the members.

It is now the afternoon and Brother Richards has just delivered a short, impressive discourse explaining the necessity of preaching the Gospel, "whether men receive it or not". Grandfather Andrew is called to speak:

"I feel proud to be present for the first time at a conference in Scotland, especially where there exists so much good order, love and peace," he says, and then continues, "and now I must explain, that when the vote was taken in the forenoon, whether we sustain Elder Richards as our president, I did not hold up my hand. I was reflecting upon the past concerning the Prophet Joseph in the land of America and while I was thus reflecting, the vote was passed. And as I did not hold up my hand at that time — I will now hold up both my hands, and I further move that we sustain Elder Orson Spencer and F. D. Richards as counsellors to the Presidency of the Church of the British Isles . . ."

RICHARDS PAYS TRIBUTE TO ANDREW

Elder Samuel W. Richards then pays tribute to Andrew as follows:

"Elder Andrew Cahoon is a faithful and worthy brother and has come to labour amongst us in this conference and I hope you will all attend to his instructions, as he might sometimes be sent to transact business for me throughout the branches and I hope you will receive him as kindly as you would me."

The evening services convene at six o'clock; a good number of the country gentlemen attend and not one dissenting vote has been heard throughout the day. With the best of feelings, love and good order, our conference adjourns until the last Sunday in June

APPOINTED PRESIDENT OF CLITHEROE CONFERENCE

With admiration, we refer to "The Millennial Star" of Sunday, Aug. 15th, 1847, in which this beautiful tribute is paid to our beloved grandfather

"Elder Andrew Cahoon is appointed to take the Presidency of the Clitheroe Conference. In this appointment the conference will only need become acquainted with Brother Cahoon, to love him . . . He has known the Church and been familiar with the Prophet and the wisest Counsellors from his early youth, both in prosperity and adversity. The conference may safely cherish him in their hearts and uphold him in all his ways as a teacher of righteousness.

"In the Clitheroe Conference, Sunday, Sept. 12, 1847, Elder Cahoon received the vote of support as President of the Conference, following which, he prepared measures for the spread of the Gospel by preaching and circulating the letters and works on the Gospel."

Made President of Edinburgh Conferece

Our journey with Andrew takes us to Edinburgh, Scotland. It is September 17th of the same year, and he is President of this Conference. He opens the afternoon and evening sessions with prayer. The memorials of the "Messiah's Death and Resurrection" were administered and contributions given the poor. There was an ardently attentive audience. Again, the following December 12th, he presides at another Conference, held in the "Saints Meeting Room". He advises the members of the necessity of attending to the letter of the law, as given in the Doctrine and Covenants regarding the "The Order of the Priesthood and Manner of going out into the World". In the afternoon services, he delivers another edifying sermon regarding the "Duties of the Presiding Elders", after which Elder Watts arose and advised the Saints to attend to the instructions of Elder Cahoon. He says, "they are good and I am determined to practice them myself". Commenting on the import and sublimity of the discussions by Elder Richards and these missionaries, the record states — "neither time, nor space, nor death, itself, can efface from their memories, those inspiring themes."

This is the last Conference in the Foreign Mission for Andrew Cahoon. He is released from his mission and history tells us that he left for his home in the U.S.A. just two months later, February 1848.

IN THE LAND OF THE COLQUHOUN CLAN

It is with pride that we refer to the missionary labors performed by Grandfather Andrew Cahoon, however, this is only the half-part. His missionary labors took him into Scotland, the land of our early ancestors, the Colquhouns (Colquhoun was the original spelling of the name Cahoon). Here, in Scotland he met, admired and loved so dearly his Scotch friends, that he chose for his life companions, three of Scotland's finest lassies, Mary, Margaret and Janet, daughters of William and Mary Barr Carruth. Andrew and Mary were married November 9, 1847 at Birkenhead, Renfrewshire, Scotland before their departure to America and Margaret and Janet were married to Andrew during their journey with the Utah Pioneers.

MARGARET CARRUTH CAHOON TELLS A STORY

Margaret's autobiography contains a most complete story about the life of the William Carruth family in Scotland; her journey with her brothers and sisters from Scotland to America; a detailed biography of her husband Andrew Cahoon; and a genealogy of the children of Andrew. In her story, she also includes a brief history of the Church of Jesus Christ of Latter-day Saints or the Mormon Church. To Margaret we are indebted for much valuable information. This autobiography, she gave to her son, Daniel Farrington Cahoon and he cherished it as a most priceless gift. The following is just as grandmother Margaret wrote it or dictated it for others to write:

WILLIAM CARRUTH AND MARY BARR OF SCOTLAND

"Mary Barr Carruth was the mother of nine children. I, Margaret Cahoon, being the youngest child. William Carruth, my father, died of blood poison six weeks before my birth, leaving my mother a widow with four living children. I, when born, making the fifth, they having buried four children before my father's death.

"Father and mother were of the hardy stock of Scotch farmers, and as farmers did in those days, they knew the art of self-preservation and maintenance, raising practically everything in food and producing their own clothing from the farm. Samples of Scotch linen produced from the farm over one hundred years ago are still in our family, souvenirs of their handiwork. Grandmother on my Mother's side was a Stewart, a descendant of Mary Stuart, Queen of Scotland, and father was from the hardy Scotch farmer class.

"After father's death, mother was left in charge of the Birkenhead farm, the farm which had been leased by the Carruth family for generations. It was so large that it required two men, besides my brothers James and William, to do the work and also two women to help with house and dairy work."

BIRKENHEAD FARM

(From the "Carruth Family" by Harold B Carruth)

Birkenhead, which was for so many years the home of this (Carruth) branch, was a part of the old Semple estate of Fulwood which appears in a charter of 1573 Birkenhead farm contains about one hundred acres and lies on the south side of Gryffe Water in the united parishes of Houston and Killellan These parishes were joined in 1760, prior to then the farm was in Killellan Parish We do not know for sure when the (Carruth) family first settled on Birkenhead but it was probably near the 27th of Oct 1765 . . Robert Carruth was succeeded in the tenancy by his son James and Birkenhead was occupied by his descendants until, at least, 1911 at which time the tenant was a Robert Carruth Young.

William 3 (Son of James[2], son of Robert[1] Carruth) was born at Birkenhead, Scotland, Sept 1, 1781 and died there Feb 3, 1832 He married Mary Barr, July 29, 1815, the daughter of John and Janet Barr Mary was born March 14, 1790 and died May 23, 1875

James[4] Carruth, brother of Mary, Margaret and Janet Carruth, was the oldest of nine children in the Carruth family He was born (a twin) June 15, 1816 in Birkenhead The other child died in infancy.

When James was not quite sixteen years of age his father died leaving him with the responsibility of caring for the family. He took over the operation of Birkenhead, and saw that his brother William was educated to the age of fifteen and apprenticed to a Trade.

William[4] commenced the "Carruth Family Journal" originally dated Birkenhead, Jan. 1, 1847. He was a pioneer to Utah and writes: "Mormonism brought me to this place." His great grandson, Blaine William[7], continued to record the family generations and has taken steps to preserve it by having it micro-filmed in the Utah Genealogical Society in Salt Lake City. From William's sister Margaret Carruth Cahoon's Journal, much of our Andrew Cahoon history is taken.

MARGARET CONTINUES CARRUTH STORY

"My father owned quite a lot of money and he also had
property consisting of houses which came into his possession
by holding a mortgage which had not been cleared by the
owners of the houses which were located in the town of Johnson. Before my father died he made a Will leaving all of his
money and property to his children and wife, each of whom
could take possession of his or her share when he or she
was married or became of age.

"About seven years after my father's death, a company
built a railroad over the river Griffe which was along the
border of the Birkenhead Farm. A young man by the name
of James Young Jr. who was a carpenter by trade worked
on the bridge. He boarded at my mother's home and it was
in this way that my sister Janet got acquainted with him.
After their marriage, Janet received her share of father's
money. She and her husband went to Glasgow to live. Her
husband continued to work at his trade.

"My mother took care of the farm for nine years, paid
off all the leases and expenses. She then married a widower
with four children. John Anderson, his oldest son was married. Mother moved to Cambeltown, Argyleshire, to a farm
named Benson, taking Mary and me. He took his three daughters; Elizabeth, Isabell and Jane. The Birkenhead Farm was
left in charge of brother James who was engaged to be married. He got his share of father's money, using part to renew
the old home but his sweetheart changed her mind.

James Young Jr. was born September 27, 1816, Kinross,
Kinross, Scotland and died April 21, 1847, Birkenhead, Ren-
frewshire. He was the son of James Young and Grace Christie.
James Jr. and Janet Carruth Young had three daughters, Mary
Barr Young,* born May 19, 1841 at Cowcadden, Glasgow; Grace
Christie Young, born September 29, 1843, Birkenhead, Scot-
land; and Jannette (or Janet) Carruth Young born September
16, 1845, Birkenhead, Scotland.**

JANET AND HUSBAND HEAR ABOUT MORMONS

The Birkenhead Farm was just west of Paisley and Andrew Cahoon was located at Paisley with the missionary
group there.

"While on the Farm, Janet and her husband heard there
were Mormon Elders in Johnson and Linwood preaching their

*See "The Cahoon Story."
**See Addenda, page 153, Spencer and Covey families.

doctrine," Margaret's story continues. "They went several times to hear them preach. In 1844, they were baptized and James Young jr. was appointed President of Johnson Branch of the Scottish Mission until his death. During James Young's sickness, Elders Andrew Cahoon and Samuel W. Richards went to administer to him. These two Elders had been appointed with a number of others from Nauvoo in 1846 by President Brigham Young to labor in the British Mission.

CARRUTH FAMILY PREPARES FOR AMERICA

"James Young had arranged to leave Birkenhead farm at the expiration of the lease and go to America, but he died before the plans could be carried out. Calling Janet to his bed-side, he asked a pledge, that she take their little girls and go with the missionaries. So when the Carruth brothers and sisters decided to leave in the Spring of 1848, Janet sold her stock, farm implements and house furniture to assist with the expenses. James Young, senior, the aged grandfather decided to go with them. Andrew Cahoon was released from his mission that he might accompany and assist them on their journey.

"When my brothers and sisters were preparing to start on the journey, my mother, who believed all the principles of Mormonism, decided to let me who also believed, go with them and become a member of the Church. Therefore, I packed up my belongings and went back to Birkenhead with mother to bid a last farewell to her children.

"A short time before we left Scotland, my brother William and I got the money out of the bank that had been left to us by father. Mary also got the remainder of hers. The houses that belonged to father could not be sold at this time as the man from whom father got the mortgage was in America and could not be located. So they were left for my Uncle James Lang to sell. He gave part of the money to mother and then sent the rest to my brother James, he being the oldest of father's family.

"After the property matters and everything was arranged, we bade farewell to our dear mother who was a true and beloved woman believing all the principles of the gospel. She would have been baptized and become a member of the Mormon Church, and would have also come to America with us, but her second husband was very bitter against the Mormons and she did not leave him because he was very good and kind to her and did everything to make her happy. He was very kind to all of mother's children and treated them as he did his own."

WEDDING OF WILLIAM CARRUTH JR.

On Feb 12th 1848, William Carruth left Birkenhead and went a distance of about three miles where a wedding convened according to former arrangements. William writes: "On this same day in the evening, I was married to Margaret Ellwood at her parents home, then by command of the Lord, my wife and I, after taking farewell of our aged parents, brethren, friends, home and country traveled to Liverpool where we met my brother James and sisters Mary, Margaret and Janet, and Andrew Cahoon, my brother-in-law. From this time on we were under the guardianship of Elder Cahoon."

CARRUTH CHILDREN LEAVE MOTHER IN SCOTLAND

Margaret tells us that they left their aged mother and old home February 12, 1848, traveled on the train to Greenock, then sailed to Liverpool to join William and his wife, Margaret Ellwood.

"While here," says Margaret, "my brother James and I were baptized in the Atlantic Ocean, Feb. 17th, 1848, and when the ship which was named, 'Carnatic' was ready for the voyage, we were ready to start. Our ship was under the control of Capt. McKenzie, who was a kind and generous man. There were a great many people on board and we had a very long and tedious journey . . . James Young sen. Janet's father-in-law died on the voyage and was buried in the ocean."

ONE HUNDRED TWENTY SAINTS SET SAIL

The following account of the voyage of the ship "Carnatic" and its arrival in America is related in "Journal of The British Mission" — 1848.

"The Ship Carnatic, Capt. McKenzie in charge, obtained its clearance papers 18th Feb. 1848 and sailed on the morning of the 20th with a company of 120 Saints on board, nearly 100 of them adults. This company which was made up on a short notice of Saints 'with cheerful hopes and buoyant feel-

ings,' went out under the superintendency of Elder F. D.
Richards, assisted by C. H. Wheelock and Andrew Cahoon.
Samuel W. Richards acted as clerk.

"For thirteen days the Carnatic was tossed violently about
in the Channel and Irish Sea, during which time all the emigrants suffered more or less from sea-sickness On Sunday,
Feb. 27th, the vessel was beating off Milford, and it was
proposed by the Chaplain, if the weather did not change, to
put to Haven the next day; but she succeeded in clearing
the Cape and standing out to sea. Several times she ran so
close upon the rocks and shoals, the Capt. ordered to put on
all the sails she could bear, which made her roll and wallow
in the sea with apparent madness, but the threatened danger
was thereby avoided. This was the roughest part of entire voyage.

"As soon as the elements and the sea-sickness would permit, the emigrants were organized into such divisions as
equalized the labor of cleaning, building fires, receiving water,
maintaining watch, etc., among the men each day of the
week. Regular hours were also appointed for prayer and meetings held on the Sabbath, when the sacrament was administered. When the Captain saw how diligent the Saints were
in observing good order, he laid aside the rigid formality
of ship-rules, and granted them every comfort and convenience which the vessel afforded. When warmer latitudes were
reached, he also prepared shower baths which were conducive
to health and comfort.

"On the 16th of March, the Carnatic passed between the
Azores and Mainland, and entered into the region influenced
by the trade winds. About this time, one of the passengers
known as Father James Young began to fail daily, not-with-
standing the diligent attention paid him. After being prayed
for, he received immediate relief, but was soon afterwards
seized with renewed attacks. Distressed with cramps, he
passed away on the evening of 13th. After being neatly laid
out, his body was enclosed in canvas; a weight of coal also
put in the canvas, and attached to the feet. At forty minutes
past six o'clock on the morning of the 31st, the remains were
consigned to a watery grave. The water was so still that the
corpse was seen as it sank to a great depth."

ARRIVAL IN AMERICA AFTER 61 DAYS AT SEA

"Sunday April 2nd, 1848 the ship passed into the Caribbean Sea between the islands of Antigua and Guadaloupe. She passed by the Island of Cuba on the 13th and on the 17th in the afternoon, Elder Richards and others first saw Balize, a village at the mouth of the Mississippi River. On the 19th April, the company arrived safe and well at New Orleans. So attached had the kind-hearted captain become to the Saints whom he had brought across the mighty deep, that he parted with them in tears. The Crew bestowed three cheers as the emigrants left the vessel.

"At New Orleans, Elder Scovil, who had been appointed as Church emigration agent, was on hand to receive the company. The baggage was allowed to be landed without opening a single barrel, box or parcel of any kind. The entire company left New Orleans Sunday April 23rd on the Steamboat "Mameluke" and after a pleasant trip arrived at St. Louis, April 30th.

"The Saints were counseled not to remain at St. Louis. All who had means to go to the Pottawattamie lands, Iowa, began at once to make preparations to continue the journey farther up the river and finally a contract was made with Capt Patterson of the Steamboat "Mustang" to take the Carnatic Company as well as other emigrating Saints who had arrived in St. Louis from different parts of the United States, to Winter Quarters at the rate of five dollars for each person over twelve years of age allowing one pound luggage to each. This company which consisted of about one hundred fifty souls, sailed from St. Louis about May 9th 1848 and arrived at Winter Quarters about the middle of the month."*

CAHOON AND CARRUTH FAMILIES MEET

Margaret gives us the story in her own words of their arrival in America and the meeting of the Carruth-Cahoon families.

"We arrived at New Orleans, U.S.A. at the mouth of the Mississippi River after being on the water eight weeks and four days. We stayed at New Orleans a few days, then took

*Millennial Star, Vol X, Pages 74, 169, 203 and 204

a steamer and went up the river to St. Louis. Here we stayed nearly a week. My brothers James and William left us and journeyed by land with some brethren and taking money with them, they bought a great many horses, oxen, cows and wagons for the journey across the plains. The rest of us went on a steamer up the Missouri River to Winter Quarters where we were joined by William and James.

"Here we met Andrew Cahoon's father, mother, brothers and their families. We found them in very destitute circumstances and Andrew took the merchandise and provisions we had purchased at St. Louis and divided them among all his father's family."

WILL MY NEW FRIENDS LIKE AMERICA?

Undoubtedly, Andrew asked himself this and many other questions during the voyage across the ocean. Andrew had left a beautiful city, Nauvoo. "Now, what are the conditions of my folks at home? What has happened to my home? Where shall I find my mother, father, brothers and sisters?"

Andrew was returning with a group of one hundred twenty members of his Church, among them were his wife Mary, her sisters Margaret and Janet, Janet's three young daughters, his brothers-in-law, James and William Carruth. All were his friends and relatives. These were some of the finest people the world had ever known. They had come from wealthy homes where there was ample money for their every convenience and comfort. Now what is to be the greeting in their new country and home? How difficult to explain to his new friends that the leaders of the Church had been driven into a wilderness and were on a long trek to a barren land! What would be the response from these fine friends and loved ones from Scotland?

Janet Maria Woolley Taylor, granddaughter of Andrew and Janet answers this last question in an interesting biography she has written of her mother Rachel Cahoon Woolley, in which she says·

"At Winter Quarters were many Saints who had been destitute from their homes, and among these were Andrew Cahoon's parents and two brothers with their families. Without second thought, the supplies purchased in St. Louis were divided with the needy. The remaining money was then turned

over to Andrew to buy what was needed for the trip . . .
oxen, cows, heavy wagons, and a light spring wagon for the
children and frailer women to ride in, outfitted with everything essential to a new life in a new land."

Margaret Carruth Cahoon, Mary J. Howard and others
record the incident alike.

A STORY WITHIN A STORY

It seems most fitting to digress somewhat from our narrative and include at this point, an incident that should be
of deepest interest to us. It is the reference to a blessing
pronounced upon the head of our grandfather Andrew Cahoon
by the Patriarch, John Smith. May we be mindful that many
of these glorious promises were literally fulfilled during the
life of Andrew upon this earth. These promises are sacred
and we appreciate the fact that this blessing has been preserved for us. It is with humility and reverence to an All-
Wise Father that these words are re-written.

Great Salt Lake City, May 27, 1849

Brother Andrew, I place my hands on your head by the virtue of the Priesthood and seal a Patriarchal blessing upon you
in the name of Jesus of Nazareth Thou art of the Blood of
Ephraim and lawful heir to the Priesthood with all the blessings
which were sealed upon the children of Joseph by Jacob, his
father, to the uttermost bounds of the everlasting hills In-as-
much-as thou hast been faithful in the cause of truth and
obedient to the counsel of the servants of the Lord, your name
is recorded in the Book of Names of the sanctified Thou has
seen some trials and may see many more The Lord hath called
thee to preach the Gospel to the nations of the earth, to the
islands of the sea and He will give you power to accomplish a
mighty work in gathering the remnants of Jacob in leading
them to Zion, and shall establish them in a peaceful land

Thou shalt have the power to rebuke the winds and waves of
the sea, even to turn rivers out of their course, to feed a multitude in the wilderness by the power of the Priesthood and to
do every miracle which was ever done upon the earth, for the
angels shall take charge of thee and will ever be ready to deliver
thee out of the hands of thine enemies

Thou shalt raise up sons and daughters that shall be mighty
in moving the Redeemer's Kingdom on the Earth They shall
multiply so they cannot be numbered Thy name shall be had
in honorable remembrance in the House of the Lord Thy
wisdom shall be great and thine understanding shall reach to
the heavens so as to be able to comprehend the most high, for
no good thing shall be withheld from thee, and inasmuch as
thou art faithful and endure to the end, not a word of this
blessing shall fail Even so — Amen

J. S Smith, Recorder

Fulfillment of Andrew's Patriarchal Blessing

The fulfillment of these blessings is best known, only to Andrew Cahoon, the recipient, however the incidents in the life of this great man, testify to the truthfulness of the blessing. May we reflect upon these various prophecies:

"To preach the Gospel . . . power to accomplish a mighty work . . . lead them to Zion . . establish them in a peaceful land "

His history thus far has authenticated this in every detail. He did preach the Gospel to the nations of the earth and to the islands of the sea. He did bring many people to America (Zion) then to Salt Lake Valley and he did greatly assist these people in the establishment of their new homes in a peaceful land.

"Power To Rebuke The Winds and Waves"

Let us recall the incidents in his voyages across the ocean. Andrew Cahoon and Orson Spencer sailed from New York across the Atlantic to fulfill their mission to the British Isles. The ship had encountered such terrific storms that it had been reported "Lost and all on board perished." However, we are informed, "After a protracted voyage of about forty days, encountering storms and gales, by the kindness of a Father's care, they were all preserved from any serious disaster."

Then again, the return voyage of Andrew bringing one-hundred-twenty Saints to America:

"For thirteen days the 'Carnatic' was tossed violently about in the Channel and the Irish Sea, the vessel was beating off Milford and it was proposed to put to Haven. Several times she ran so close upon the rocks and shoals she rolled and wallowed in the sea with apparent madness."

Surely it is reasonable to conclude that through the faith and prayers of Elder Andrew Cahoon and his Christian friends, they did receive Divine assistance, to "Rebuke the winds and waves."

"Feed a Multitude in the Wilderness "

"At Winter Quarters," Margaret writes, "we met Andrew's father, mother, brothers and their families. They were in very destitute circumstances. Andrew took the merchandise and provisions we had purchased at St. Louis and divided them among all of his father's family.

"In 1849, a meeting was called to find out how much food there was. Mary J. Howard tells us that Janet Young Cahoon had three hundred pounds of flour. It was the only full barrel between Omaha and San Francisco. Janet announced that any sick or elderly person who could not eat the coarse corn-meal, could have one quart of her flour at any time and it lasted until the emigrants arrived in the Fall who had flour with them. Janet also had a barrel of potatoes. They used all they needed to plant and then the rest of the potatoes were put in a large kettle and all the neighbors were invited to a feast. Some had not tasted a potato for more than a year."

Was it not through Andrew and his friends and relatives that it was possible to feed a multitude in the wilderness?

"Even to Turn Rivers Out of Their Course"

Our Church history tells us that in 1865, Andrew Cahoon was chosen Director of the company whose purpose was to supply additional water to the city for irrigation. He was qualified in his chosen vocation as a Civil Engineer, and aided in perfecting plans whereby one-half of the water of the Jordan River could be taken out of the river for use in the city and farms. He assisted in constructing a ten-mile canal and the rivers were actually turned out of their course.

"Thy Wisdom Shall Be Great"

"Andrew did speak with a great wisdom," says Janet W. Taylor. "He was a man of fine character, unusual physical strength, precocious as a child. He had exceptional mental prowess, had taught an adult grammar school at age of thirteen and had fluent command of seven languages."

As to the fulfillment of the words of the Patriarchal Blessing given to Andrew Cahoon, the reader may draw his own conclusion.

RECEPTION IN THE PROMISED LAND

"To Your Tents, O Israel!" That was the greeting to the Saints from Scotland. Yes, Andrew and the Carruth family were among those stalwart Saints numbered in that great exodus — no less a task than when the children of Israel went from under the oppression of Egypt out into the wilderness to journey to the promised land. Knowing they had another Moses to lead them from their persecutors, these Saints of the Latter-days left their homes from far and near.

> Leaving home was not so easy, Loving hearts were left behind. Graves were scattered on the highway; Left where none but God could find. Tho' they're gone, we won't forget them, Nor the trials they past thru They have made the Desert blossom, Like a rose for me and you It was just a wind-blown desert when they reached the Great Salt Lake But it was their Land of Promise, It was theirs to freely take. So they laughed and danced together, Just to drive away their fears — Let us honor and revere them, That Brave Band of Pioneers.

A LONG AND TEDIOUS JOURNEY

(Returning Again to the Margaret Carruth Story)

"We stayed at Winter Quarters a week or ten days and fixed our wagons for the journey. Then about May 1st 1848, we left Winter Quarters with eighteen yoke of oxen, six cows, two horses, seven wagons, and a spring-wagon which my sister, Janet and her three children rode in. We traveled in President Brigham Young's Company in the fore part of the journey. But when the feed began to get scarce the large company was divided into smaller ones and then we were in (Father) Morley's company and others.

"We had a long and tedious journey and not being acquainted with the road made it much worse for us. The roads were very bad or in fact, there were scarcely any roads except those we made ourselves.

"Sometimes we stopped and camped on the road a half day or sometimes a whole day and the brethren would go out and kill game, buffalo and other wild animals for the company to use as food. While they were hunting, the sisters stayed at camp and washed clothes, baked bread and prepared to start on the journey the following day.

"When we reached Sweetwater, we encountered a very heavy snow storm and were compelled to camp. It was here that a great many of our cattle died. While we were at the Sweetwater, President Young wished the Saints to send back some of their wagons and oxen to assist the poor Saints at Winter Quarters on the journey the following season. We sent back two wagons, four yoke of oxen and two young men teamsters who had driven our wagons for us.

"We sent these wagons and oxen to William F. and Daniel S. Cahoon and their families to bring them on to the valley. These were Andrew's brothers, but Andrew's father, mother, and two unmarried children traveled in the same companies as we.

"During our journey across the plains men were obliged to stand guard every night to protect our cattle and camp from the Indians, who were very destructive and treacherous at that time."

A whole city of moving people, wagons, herds of cattle, sheep, pigs and chickens — such was a company of Mormon Pioneers; and may we pause to pay tribute to the Carruth brothers and sisters for the unselfish assistance they gave to their new relatives and friends. They shared their provisions, wagons, oxen and all they possessed.

Marriage on the Prairie

And now, we arrive at the date, July 17, 1848, the events of which supersede all others, especially in the lives of Mary, Margaret and Janet Carruth. It is July 17th, just July 17, 1848!

Were we to choose a title for this episode, probably the most appropriate one would be:

"Andrew And His Three Brides"

The place — Chimney Rock, Nebraska, in a Camp of Mormon Pioneers

The Cast

A Young Mormon Man .... Andrew Cahoon
(Mary's husband)
A Young Scotch Bride ....Mary Carruth Cahoon
(Andrew's wife)
A Young Scotch Lassie .... Margaret Carruth
(Mary's younger sister)
A Young Scotch Widow .... Janet Carruth Young
(Mary's elder sister)

Chimney Rock was so named because it was atop a majestic point and resembled a tall chimney towering to the sky.

Pres. Brigham Young had arrived in Salt Lake Valley with the first pioneers in 1847 and was traveling back to the camp at Chimney Rock, Nebraska to assist the Carruth and Cahoon families, the second company of pioneers of 1848. Before Pres Young reached the camp, he had sent word ahead to tell Andrew and Reynolds Cahoon he wished them to meet him in advance, that he had a message for Andrew.

Special Greetings To Andrew Cahoon
(From President Brigham Young)

"The Best Advice I can Give to Any Young Man, Worthy As You, Andrew, is to Accept and Live the Principle of Plural Marriage and I Advise You to Marry Those other Two Carruth Sisters "

The day had been warm on the prairie and Andrew returns to his home, a low tent on the bank of the Platte River, a camp of the Mormon Pioneers. He had received his message and understood its meaning. He had studied his Bible, he had searched the scriptures and thus he deliberates:

God had at times and under certain conditions commanded that His people live the law of Plural Marriage. Abraham was so commanded and Sarah gave Hagar to Abraham to wife because this was the law and from Hagar sprang many people. Was Abraham therefore under condemnation? The Lord had answered this question to Joseph Smith, "Nay, for I The Lord Commanded It"

"Abraham had been promised that his children should continue in this world and in the next as innumerable as the stars . . . Isaac and Jacob did none other than what the Lord commanded them, also Solomon and Moses, and of David it is said, that David's wives were given him of the Lord by the hand of Nathan, the servant of God, and others of the Prophets have had the Keys to this Power."

The Latter-day Saint Gospel had taught Andrew that there were many spirits in the spirit-world who were waiting to receive their bodies that they might pass through this earthly life experience, and was not this a practical solution? They believed that children were the heritage of the Lord. They believed in large families and raising righteous children unto the Lord.

"Yes," said Andrew, "the outside world will criticize this principle but the Christian world can never make successful

warfare upon or against polygamy unless they first lay down
and discard the Bible as the Word of God. There is no law
against the practice of polygamy. The Lord has again revealed
and commanded this principle and it is my business to accept it."

THE PROBLEM OF PLURAL MARRIAGE

Andrew has made his own decision, he must relate to his
wife, Mary, the advice from their leader Brigham Young.
She and Andrew must alone determine the answer to this
complex problem.

Dear Aunt Mary! She probably spent hours in meditation.
She truly loved her husband, she also loved her sisters. She
felt that if she had a willing heart to do all that she had
been commanded to do, that God would give her the strength
to encounter any ordeal.

Margaret, her younger sister was now a young lady of
sixteen years and if she so desired she could marry Andrew
in celestial marriage as she herself had done. To share the
blessing of the Celestial Kingdom with Margaret and Andrew,
this, Mary would gladly do. Then there was her widowed
sister Janet and her three little girls. Mary also thought of
Janet's fine husband, James Young who had recently died
and they had buried in Scotland.

Now enters into the life of Janet — that glorious principle,
"Ordinance Work for the Dead." Mary understood that principle. She knew that through and by "Proxy," James Young
could be sealed to Janet by the "New and Everlasting Covenant" of marriage — a plan of God again revealed for the
baptism, salvation and exaltation of the dead. Mary knew
that in accordance with the Gospel Plan, Andrew could marry
Janet and care for her and her children in this life and should
he and Janet have children, these children would be sealed
to Janet and James for all eternity.

How unselfish must one become? What greater sacrifices
and trials could be endured than those experienced by these
early pioneers who accepted this new domestic way of life
. . . a way new to them but as old as the ages?

These three sisters had known Elder Andrew Cahoon for
a long time and he had proven himself to be a fine gentle-
man, always kind and considerate; and too, there was not

in the Mormon Ceremony, an "Obedience" clause, only as
the husband "Obeys God's Laws". Oh yes, the man is the
head of his family as Christ is the Head of His Church,
but this did not mean over-lordship in the home, no spirit
of dominating one another. Marriage in the Mormon teaching
is a mutual agreement, an equal partnership, each observing
the rights belonging to the other. Under this way of life,
could not three families enjoy the blessings of a happy life
just as one family could?

Such were the thoughts of Mary as she strolls out to
locate her two sisters. They have been busy mending clothes,
washing dishes, baking bread or doing one of a hundred duties
important to the pioneers. Mary relates to them Pres. Brigham Young's message to Andrew.

We may be sure that these three Carruth sisters enter
into a most serious discussion; their answer is in the affirmative. All doubt has swept from the minds of Mary, Margaret
and Janet as together their voices echo a perfect understanding, and as the day emerges into dusk, Margaret records:

"On the evening of July 17th, 1848, on the banks of the
Platte River in Nebraska Territory, Andrew Cahoon married as his second wife, Margaret Carruth in Celestial Covenant and his third wife, Janet Carruth Young for 'Time'
only. These marriages were performed by Brigham Young."

The subduing of this great Western Desert we now enjoy, was not Man's Work Alone; self-sacrificing and cour-
ageous women such as Mary, Margaret and Janet played
their part in accomplishing that great task. They were among
those most willing to serve. Their homes were of the better
class and they made every sacrifice to instill the spirit and
influence of a home rich in love and harmony.

Arrival in Salt Lake Valley

("Zion" is Reached After Eight Long Months of Travel)
"We arrived in Salt Lake Valley in the evening of September 23, 1848," writes Margaret in her autobiography, "eight
months since we left our home in Scotland. You may be
assured that this new country was very wild and desolate-
looking at that time. The Saints who had entered the valley
before us, were all living in forts which were built as protec-

tion from the troublesome Indians who were very numerous.

"We bought a double log house on the south fort and lived there until the following Spring. Janet and her three children occupying one side; Mary, Andrew and myself occupying the other . . . In the Spring of 1849 we all drew city lots. Janet, Andrew and my brothers James and William Carruth all got lots joining each other in the Eleventh Ward. Andrew's father, Reynolds, had his lots in the Thirteenth Ward, the place where the Salt Lake Theatre was built. William F. and Daniel S. Cahoon received their lots in the Twelfth Ward."

Janet Woolley Taylor, granddaughter of Andrew writes:

"Andrew's lot formed the corner of the Eleventh Ward. It was impractical to make a survey at that time and as chance would have it, Andrew, the Civil Engineer, who was to spend much of his time surveying and laying out townsites, discovered presently that he had erected a fine log house in the middle of Commercial Street. Of course the city had not been completely surveyed at the time and this was as much of a surprise to Andrew as to any one, so we will have to excuse Andrew for that."

CRICKETS DEVOUR CROPS

In 1849 Andrew farmed his land in the "Big Field" but the crickets were so numerous they ate up all the crops. Five thousand acres of farm land had been planted in the valley by the pioneers; the grain was growing fine when in May and June, came swarms of crickets devouring every growing thing. Countless millions of these insects came down from the mountains.

The pioneers fought them as best they could. It seemed hopeless. Their crops were fast disappearing. Their prayers ascended to God and when hope had been given up, in from the lake came great flocks of white birds — the Seagulls. They settled down on the fields and gorged themselves with crickets and then flew to the lake and disgorged, returning to the fields to eat again Day after day the Seagulls repeated this until the crickets were destroyed and part of the crop was saved. The Seagull Monument, erected on Salt Lake Temple Square, pays tribute to these birds.

The pioneer families lived on rations; food as well as clothing were scarce. Many people lived for weeks on "greens" and the roots of the Sego Lily and Thistle. A kind of soup was made by cooking rawhides.

Janet and Her Visitor

Janet Cahoon's first real home was near Fort Pioneer Park. She bought a lot in the Eleventh Ward One night Janet was awakened by something crawling over her bed She kept very quiet and in the morning she found a large snake under her pillow. It had crawled over her and her baby in the night and had comfortably coiled itself beneath her pillow. The story concludes, "She was admired for her courage and well-deserved praises were given her for her bravery through this frightening ordeal."

Until the year 1869, Janet had never worn a hat that had not been made by her own hands. She cut the wheat with a cycle, wrapped it in a wet cloth until she had time to handle it, then made straw braids and sewed them into shape. Out of rushes, she made the bottoms of chairs for her house. She had sheep and carded the wool. She kept a vat for wood ashes, bacon rinds and fat for soap. This kind of work was usually done at night. She parched peas and ground them to make coffee. She kept her own garden, milked her cows, cared for chickens, ducks, and geese, pulled weeds for pigs, was up at four-thirty or five o'clock each morning and worked very late at night.

When the pioneer ladies rested, they were always knitting, darning or mending. These Carruth sisters were worthy pioneers and loved by all who knew them; had much to endure but never complained and were always willing to do their share in every way.

Andrew Cahoon Seeks Gold in California

During the years 1850, 51 and 52, we find Andrew Cahoon residing in California. According to Margaret's History, "Andrew, in 1850, when gold was discovered in California, took a notion that he would like to try his luck at digging gold, so he fitted out a wagon and started to California, taking with him Mary, his first wife, and his youngest brother Mahonri Moriancumer. They were gone nearly two years.

"While they were gone I made my home part of the time with Andrew's brother, Daniel S. and I went out sewing, washing and doing general house work for a living. Andrew went by the northern route through Carson Valley and returned by the southern route passing through San Bernardino. While he was in San Bernardino he assisted in laying out the city. When they returned in 1852, they brought with them quite a lot of gold which was divided among all of Andrew's family."

William Carruth, brother of the three Carruth sisters, "on 13 Nov. 1849, left for California in a company of about forty brethren bound for the 'Gold diggins.' They took the southern route traveling with ox teams and returned via the northern route arriving in Salt Lake City, 2 June 1851, after an absence of eighteen months."*

CAJON PASS OR CAHOON PASS

It has been called to our attention that the "Cajon Pass" near San Bernardino was in all probability, named in honor of Andrew Cahoon, his wife and brother Mahonri Moriancumer, and some credence can be given this. We have definite knowledge that these Cahoon pioneers did reside in this city or Rancho for the period of two years and that Andrew did assist in surveying and laying out the city of San Bernardino. He was a surveyor, a colonizer, a sturdy pioneer and a qualified engineer.

Andrew and Mahonri M. were at the Rancho a year previous to its purchase for the Church and also before the company of 500 Saints from Salt Lake Valley arrived there In every instance in the Journal History of the Latter-day Saints from 1850 to 1857 where mention is made to this pass, the name is recorded "Cahoon Pass".

The specific dates and notations are as follows:

April 15, 1850 — Elder Pratt speaks of finding gold then adds — "and we came to Cahoon Pass . . ."

November 20, 1850 — Brigham Young in a letter to Dr. Bernhisel, says of Iron County . . . "There is no other feasible route to California from that place than through the Cahoon Pass."

December 4, 1850 — "Be it ordained by the General Assembly . . . as soon as practicable, continuously to intersect a stage route from Cahoon Pass . . ."

*Carruth Family" by H. B Carruth, page 227.

April 7, 1851 — "A. M. Lyman and C. E. Rich are en-route to the Cahoon Pass . . ."

April 21, 1852 — The Deseret News prints: "Elder Rich arrived Wednesday, April 21, in company with 13 others, among them were two brothers Cahoon, direct from San Bernardino, the nearest ranch to the Cahoon Pass where the brothers are settled . . ."

December 12, 1857 — A statement of Wm. Hall reads, "We came on up to the mouth of the Cahoon Pass . . ."

December 23, 1857 — A letter from President Pratt and Benson mentions, "that in passing the Cahoon Pass, Sierra Nevada Mountains . . ."

In the early records of the L.D.S. Church Journal History (1850-1872) the "Cajon Pass" is referred to as "Cahoon Pass", or the Scotch name meaning a "Narrow Wood" or "Sea Coasting Common or Point" to which a description of the lands conform. "Cajon," the Spanish spelling, is pronounced Cahoon, and means "box." However, the true origin of the name of the pass has not yet been established, although there is a strong inference that it was named after the Cahoon Brothers.*

California and the Mormons

Almost from the beginning, California has held an important and significant meaning in the thoughts and lives of the Latter-day Saints. Rich citrus groves cover the marks of the first Mormon plows at San Bernardino. It is idle to conjecture what San Bernardino might be today had those thrifty Mormon Saints remained in possession of those preciously rich areas It is said that the Mormon pioneers gave the Joshua tree its name because it looked like Joshua with out-stretched arms beckoning the weary immigrant on.

Within six years, with success and prosperity already assured, the call came out from Utah for all colonists to return. Johnston's army already was marching west to destroy the fruits of ten years of desperate labor. The Government of the United States had declared war on the Mormon people. Zion must draw in her borders and prepare for the worst.

---

*A Century of Mormon Activities in California, by Muir.

Obedient to the call, in the winter of 1857-58 the Saints of San Bernardino returned to Utah in several companies. "Men, women and children go without a murmur, countenances lighted with stern joy, at the assurance that they are about to fight and destroy their enemies "

The "Los Angeles Star" was generous in its appraisal of the character of the Mormons. It openly testifies to its readers: "From our acquaintances with these people, we must say that we know them to be a peaceable, industrious, law-abiding community. Under great disadvantage they have cultivated their farms and caused the ranch, (San Bernardino) which was before their occupation, almost unproductive, to teem with the choicest products of the field and the garden. We know them to be good citizens, and cheerfully testify to that fact." Thus came the end of San Bernardino, as a religious-social colony of the Church.

Many descendants of Reynolds Cahoon have resided in California and to us, whose homes are now here, the Story of Mormonism in California is rich and interesting. Today, as in the past, this great state is playing its part in the history of the church and finds a high place in the hearts of the Latter-day Saints. Nowhere, outside the state of Utah does one find a greater Mormon population and not even Utah holds her Mormon people in greater esteem Beautiful Mormon chapels and homes adorn every part of this great Pacific slope. A magnificent Latter-day Saint Temple has been constructed at Westwood in Los Angeles, and another to be erected at Oakland, will truly proclaim this portion of our beautiful America, a most desirable "Land of Zion."

ANDREW RETURNS FROM CALIFORNIA

On March 14, 1854, Andrew was ordained a High Priest and Bishop of the South Cottonwood Ward, South Cottonwood Stake, Utah. He was the fourth Bishop of the Ward and held this position from 1854 until 1872. "It was one of the largest Wards in Utah, was organized in 1852," his wife, Margaret writes, "and extended at that time, from the mountains on the east to the Jordan River on the West, Mill-Creek on the North to Draper on the South, and was first known as Cottonwood, later changed to South Cottonwood.

ANDREW CALLED TO LAS VEGAS

"In the Spring of 1856, while in the capacity of a bishop, Andrew was chosen by President Brigham Young to go with some other brethren to Las Vegas among the Indians and open up a lead mine and also to build furnaces for the purpose of smelting ore, but when they were working it proved to be a failure, so they were called back home late in the same year."

"THE UTAH WAR"

Again came sorrow and trials to the Utah Pioneers. In the years 1857-58 occurred the conflict called the "Utah War." False reports about the Utah people had been made and as they were celebrating, singing National Airs and saluting the Stars and Stripes on their Pioneer Day, July 24, 1857, news came that 2000 U. S. Government Soldiers were coming to destroy them. Loyal Mormon men and boys left immediately to guard their wives, children and homes. Mahonri Cahoon and William Carruth were among those called to protect the Saints and it is quoted in the "Pioneers and Prominent Men of Utah," that our Grandfather Andrew served in the "Echo Canyon Campaign".

Had the President of the United States, James Buchanan, sent an officer to investigate these false reports, he would have learned the truth. However, acting on the spur of the moment, he sent troops on their way. The only recourse the Mormon people had was to organize themselves, fortify Echo Canyon and do everything in their power to prevent the soldiers from reaching their City until President Buchanan could learn the truth and the danger of a conflict be averted.

Capt Van Vliet told Brigham Young the intention of the army was to help his people, but President Young remembered only too well, their experiences in Missouri and Illinois and knew not what to expect now. The Saints left their homes in Salt Lake City and moved south into Utah Valley.

Gen Kane, that staunch friend of the Mormon people, upon hearing of the troubles in Utah, though feeble in health, went to the President in Washington, and offered to go to Utah with the newly appointed Gov. Cumming and make a peaceable settlement. This he did and when the Governor's wife arrived and saw the towns lonely and deserted, she burst into tears and pleaded with her husband to bring the people

back. Thirty-thousand people had taken their goods and
moved from Salt Lake City. They had gone northward and
far away to the south.

Gov. Cumming found the records and books of the court
safe, and satisfied himself that the reports which had led
the President to send an army were not true. "Johnston's
Army marched through Salt Lake City on June 26, 1858
and all day long the noise of horses hoofs and the roll of
wagons could be heard; the city seemed as if dead. Col. Cooke,
once the Commander of the Mormon Battalion, bared his head
as he rode through the streets in honor of the brave Mormon boys who had marched under his command." Johnston's
Army continued to Cedar Valley and two years later returned to the East to take part in the great Civil War, on
the side of the South. Johnston fell in the battle of Shiloh.

CAHOON FAMILIES RETURN FROM THE SOUTH

"My husband, Andrew, and our families moved to Lehi
and lived there in covered wagons all summer, then after
the army had passed through Salt Lake City, we moved back
to our homes in Salt Lake Valley," says Margaret, and then
continues:

"In 1860, Andrew sold his house located west of the old
Germania Smelter in Murray, Utah He then built an adobe
house on State Street and there the family went to live.
Andrew's father, Reyonlds Cahoon, died and Andrew's mother, Thirza Stiles Cahoon went to live with Andrew, where
she remained until her death."

WATER AND IRRIGATION

Many important issues came before the people for their
consideration and we find Andrew Cahoon prominent in helping solve these public problems. On August 27, 1862, Andrew
is chosen as one of the members to represent "The Deseret
Agricultural and Manufacturing Agents". In 1864 he is Director of the company, whose purpose it was to supply additional water to the city for navigation and irrigation.

"Growing interests of the country imperatively demand an
increase of water on the farms and city lots," the pioneers
said, and such men as Miller, Brinton, Hunter, Young, Taylor
and Cahoon were chosen unanimously as the committee to per-

fect plans whereby half the water of the Jordan River could be taken from the river for use in the city and on the farms. They drafted resolutions of the Convention and were among those entitled to a seat at the Convention to discuss the problem of "Water and Irrigation".

Andrew being an engineer, was selected as a Trustee for the construction of a ten-mile canal and to levy a tax on all lands to be watered by it. In 1867, Brigham Young, Andrew Cahoon and others were appointed members of a corporation to construct canals for irrigation, and to open navigable communication from Utah Lake by way of Salt Lake City. This act was approved by the Legislature and was known as "An act incorporating the Deseret Irrigation and Navigation Company". The estimated cost to reclaim 17,000 acres of desert was estimated to be $500,000. If the company deemed it necessary, the Capital Stock could be increased to any sum not exceeding one million, two hundred thousand dollars

As one would suppose, these positions entailed enormous responsibilities. Andrew not only willingly accepted these civic obligations but served faithfully for eighteen years as the Bishop of an extensive Ward. The editorial below suggests how great were the duties of the Bishop in the pioneer days.

IMPORTANT SYSTEM IN AGRICULTURE

A motion was carried that the Bishops were to instruct the farmers what crops to exclude from their lots. Bishop Andrew Cahoon and others were appointed a committee . . . "Every person who knows anything about agriculture must be aware that more system in the cultivation of the land in this section is a crying necessity. Our aims are high in agriculture as in everything else and we should have the best cultivated land of any people upon the earth. What is needed is More System . . . the proper men to introduce more systematic measures are the Bishops. They are the leaders of the people and should feel that fatherly care belongs to their office, and ought to be as familiar with the business and products of his ward as if they were his own. They can, by consulting men of greatest experience in their wards, decide upon the best grains, seeds, etc., to cultivate and also what portions of the lands are best adapted to the raising of these products."

A pioneer's life was not all work, there was some play. Andrew arranges and conducts the annual cattle drive, an honored custom of gathering up stock which are running at large on public domain, and he makes a good job of it. During his spare moments he supervises Church Receptions in the spacious bowery in Bishop Cahoon's Ward, the following evening he addresses the School of the Prophets in the Tabernacle, and a few weeks later he must deliver the sermon at the "Closing Exercises" of the Normal School.

The wives of the pioneer Bishops are also equally occupied. Janet Young Cahoon was chosen President of the Relief Society in South Cottonwood on May 17, 1868 and Margaret Cahoon was chosen head teacher. Margaret held the position in Primary as President from April 22, 1889 until 1896, and later was appointed President of Murray Ward Relief Society serving until Oct. 29, 1902 when she resigned because of ill health.

Margaret leaves these words to her children: "My life's experiences may seem as very severe hardships, but my belief in my Church teachings and my love for my family brought me comfort I wish you all to investigate the teachings of the Mormon Church."

Dear Aunt Mary Carruth Cahoon was one of the finest of ladies, and "is remembered by all who knew her for her lovable disposition, her thoughtfulness and her Christian life " She had been promised all the blessings of the Priesthood with her husband in the Temple: that she would inherit a kingdom that would never pass away; that all the hidden mysteries of the Redeemer's Kingdom would be revealed unto her; that she would have power to heal the sick in her house by prayer and faith, and drive the destroyer from her habitation; that she would have every desire of her heart; and that with her husband, would be privileged to redeem her father's house back to the days of Noah. She was told that she was the blood and lineage of her husband, that her posterity would be numerous and bear her name in remembrance until the end of time and "this blessing shall not fail!"

ANDREW CHOSEN ON NOMINATING CONVENTION

"Finances are in a Healthy Condition and Debts Do Not Exist." This was the report of Utah in 1870, given at the nominating convention. Andrew is one of the committee to select nominees for the next national election and no greater tribute can be paid these Utah pioneers than to refer to the qualifications of the nominees whom they selected. Their report of Saturday, July 16, 1870 reads.

"There is one feature about the political affairs of the Territory (of Utah) which is worthy of note. The men whose names have been presented to the people for their votes have not sought the office . . . Instances of men seeking offices have been exceedingly rare, the result has been that we have officers who have labored for the welfare of the people, conscientiously, and to promote public weal . . . not adventurers who have intrigued for office for the sake of the spoils, but staid and reliable men whose interests have been intensified with the Territory, and in many instances, have assumed its cares and responsibilities at the sacrifice of personal convenience and profit; prompted solely by the feeling that it was the duty of every citizen to serve the State to the best of his ability whenever, in the opinion of his fellow-citizens, his services were required.

"All have been selected with a view to their fitness . . . Men of known character and influence who had reputations to sustain them and who were possessed of means aside from the pay of the office, have as a rule been selected. The result is that in no portion of the Republic, has there been so little speculation, fraud and misappropriation of public funds . . . Finances are in a healthy condition. It has proven advantageous for the office to seek the man instead of the man to seek the office . . ."

ANDREW RELEASED AS BISHOP OF COTTONWOOD WARD

On Jan. 7, 1872, Andrew received an honorable release from his position as Bishop of his Ward, after nearly twenty years of faithful, efficient service for the Lord and his fellowman. Approximately three years after this honorable release, an incident occurs which concerns us greatly. Andrew separates himself from his church.

There is very little information as to the cause of this and no explanation appears in any of Andrew's available writings. Many times the remark is made that a member leaves the Church, when in fact, the Church in its progress, leaves that certain member behind because of his own indifference

We must understand that the Mormon people were at this time practicing polygamy, there being no law of the United States prohibiting such practice; however, the procedure of allowing a man who had been disfellowshipped or who had apostatized, to have but one wife was only a rule of the church.

Margaret tells us that the date of this incident was October 8, 1874, Brigham Young being President of the Church at the time. She says, "This was a very hard blow to me, and as Andrew had then no right to have more than one wife, I, therefore had no right to live with him as his wife . . ." Margaret and Janet received their divorces May 15, 1883, a rule of their church when such unforeseen circumstances intervened.

Margaret later resided in a beautiful little cottage built for her by her son John P. Cahoon. She was blessed with the companionship of a wonderful young lady, Eliza Lester. After Eliza married, Margaret moved to Provo, Utah to reside with her daughter Maria Antionette Mackay. Janet, Andrew's third wife, made her home in Pleasant Green with her daughter Mary B. Spencer, and Mary, Andrew's first wife, remained with him as his wife, in their home in Murray, Utah. After his death, she lived with her daughter, Mary Emma Winder.

Let us remember that these experiences were not considered as small by the Pioneers themselves, nor should they be so considered by us. In relating these happenings, there is no disposition to revive that which has long since been forgotten and which has been in every possible manner made right again — except, by omitting this event, much of the special value of Andrew's life-experiences would be lost.

We know that in those days of the Church, the trials of these Mormon people in the desert, were almost beyond mortal and physical endurance. Many were the misunderstandings during their troubles and toils, and at times, these misunderstandings, which had no connection with Church principles, but with their own personal concerns, such as business affairs, caused some of the members to apostatize or separate themselves from the church.

The Church Giveth, The Church Taketh Away,

And The Church Restoreth; Blessed Be The Church!

We are indeed grateful to one of the faithful and honored Patriarchs of our Church, and a personal friend of the Cahoon family, President U. G. Miller for giving us the following message:

"I have definite knowledge and am a living witness to the fact that Andrew Cahoon's differences were not so much with the principles of the Church of Jesus Christ of Latter-day Saints, but that his troubles were of a personal nature with Brigham Young."

After the death of grandfather Andrew, grandmother Margaret, Daniel Farrington Cahoon, son of Andrew and Margaret, and other members of the family went into the Holy Temple of God and "by Proxy," Daniel F. performed the Temple ordinances which restored his father Andrew's authority in the Melchizedek Priesthood. Margaret had the divorce annulled and through Margaret and Daniel F., all the former blessings that had previously existed were restored to Andrew, to his wives, and to his children.

The Lord Giveth, The Lord Taketh Away,

And The Lord Restoreth; Blessed Be The Lord.

PROMISE AND BLESSING OF THE PRIESTHOOD

"What is Sealed on Earth Shall be Sealed in Heaven and What is Loosed on Earth Shall be Loosed in The Heavens."

Those who understand the wonderful principles of Vicarious Work for the Dead in the Temple of God, have explained to us as follows·

"Andrew will never lose the reward for the great good he did in the early days of the church and he will yet stand in the midst of the leaders of the Saints and rejoice with them . . . I repeat that you may well be proud of your ancestors, and try to emulate their greatness instead of dwelling on the hour of weakness of Andrew when he left the Church. Undoubtedly, he has long since repented of that and is carrying on the work of the Lord in the Unseen World; and is trying with all his power to impress you with the truth of the matter so that his descendants will not make the mistake he did, and to tell you that he has repented of that hour of weakness and is doing a wonderful work in the Spirit World.

"We know that Andrew Cahoon has been restored to his authority in the Melchizedek Priesthood, because his son has had the work done for him in the temple. Whether Andrew will be made a Bishop or to whatever office he may be ordained in the Spirit World, depends upon himself and the decision of the brethren in charge there. The Church is completely organized there the same as it is here and there is a Mighty Work to do there as well as here."

Mary remained Andrew's wife, Janet had been married and sealed to James Young, now after this divorce, what plight will be Margaret's, the youngest of these three sisters?

In her journal Margaret records:

"I was the mother of eight children, five sons and three daughters. After Andrew was cut off the Church, I was compelled to get a divorce from him . . . Andrew was very good to us, giving us a house and a portion of land."

Let us evoke, if we may, a mental picture — a loving family, a devoted father and mother, a happy home. Love was their link, their tie. These parents must now destroy those ties, a father must forsake his children and wife. Could their love be a mere incident?

MARGARET — LOVE ETERNAL

True love is eternal, and with her greying hair, Margaret loved Andrew as much as when, with her youthful heart, she became his bride. Devotedly, she had been Andrew's wife for many years. Must this reality become a dream?

She loved wisely, which gives to each, the power of working miracles. It made obedience to the principles of the gospel she honored, seem lighter. Her faith like light, was simple and unbending; her love like warmth, bent to every necessity. She watched while her brother slept.

Grandmother Margaret was attractive with such a sweet attractiveness that continual peace and contentment beamed from her beautiful face. For forty years she remained a

widow, and when the verdict was given that Andrew's Priesthood and all his former blessings would be restored to him,
she requested an annullment of their divorce On September
2, 1922, President Heber J. Grant granted this annullment
to her, and, obedient to her wishes, he performed the Celestial
marriage of Andrew and Margaret. In the Holy Temple "by
Proxy" Margaret became Andrew's wife for Eternity With
faith, hope and assurance, she loved as few women in this
whole world could love.

ANDREW'S GRANDCHILDREN REFER TO THE INCIDENT

From notes of Mary J. Howard, great granddaughter
of Janet Carruth Young Cahoon, we quote:

"Andrew Cahoon was released as Bishop 1872 and was
cut off from the Church 1874. Before his death he acknowledged his mistakes and stated that he knew that the church
was right."

Janet Woolley Taylor, daughter of Rachel Cahoon, daughter of Andrew, writes.

"I have been informed that the president of the Church
was interviewed by a member of the Cahoon family regarding the trouble between Andrew and the L D.S. Church which
resulted in Andrew's excommunication, and after careful investigation of his case through church records, this president
stated:

'After careful investigation, I see nothing in the life of
Brother Cahoon to justify his removal from the Church and
I recommend that he be restored to his priesthood and to
all its powers which were formerly his'. "

Janet continues, "In my memory, Grandfather Cahoon
holds a sacred place. I often recall my mother's grief at the
time of her father's unfortunate experience."

Upon numerous occasions, after grandfather Andrew left
the church, he paid tribute and honor to his Church and its
principles. In closing his life's story, we can best judge his
views and feelings by quoting his own words as published in
"The Herald," August 16, 1884, as the question of polygamy
was being debated.

MORMON POLYGAMY BY ANDREW CAHOON

The Herald, Saturday, August 16, 1884

There has been much said and written first and last about Utah and the Mormons When reading these productions, I have frequently felt like writing something myself I was born in Ohio, 1824 Forty years of my life I was a faithful adherent of the Mormon religion. . . . my experience has given me opportunity to know all about the people, their religion and their entire history To my certain knowledge they have been in many respects grossly misrepresented and lied about They are naturally a good people, their religious tenets are all strictly Bible Doctrines; no intelligent person will deny this　. .

I regard this warfare made upon the Mormons as the result of religious jealousy, religious antipathy . . 　I have had three wives myself, raised a family by each one, mostly men and women now grown and respected as good members of society and seem to be as much attracted to each other as own brothers and sisters, and I have yet to see that nature's laws have been so grievously violated as some pretend.

I married these wives outside the limits of the territory of the United States in the year 1848, fourteen years before the passage of the law forbidding it For this offense, without any hearing, trial or conviction, myself and wives all taxpayers, have been disfranchised Whether we are yet to be fined, imprisoned or butchered, I cannot say; the only thing I can say, I could not now desert and disown these faithful wives and good children to accommodate public opinion or any act of Parliament I must live and die with their affections and memories engraven on my heart

The Christian world can never make successful warfare upon or against Polygamy and the Mormons until they first lay down and discard the Bible as the word of God . . . They should not hold up the Bible as the word of God and condemn those who most sincerely and strictly adhere to and practice its principles The Mormons have the Bible on their side, most decidedly, because they claim that plural marriage is an antidote against prostituiton, mistress-keeping and illegiitmacy Of course Congress must be doing something and it is an easy matter for them to declare any act a crime, but the real question is whether it is a sin against laws Congress itself is made the tool of the sectarian churches in legislature against the Mormons, and this is regarded by the Mormons as persecution

Proper selection and happy unions in polygamy may be more in harmony with Nature's Laws than countless thousands of the wretched, unhappy marriages that exist in monogamy and far more to be preferred than celibacy and mistress-keeping.

What higher motive can a man have than the perpetuation and improvement of the human race? What greater crime can a man commit than putting away a kind and devoted wife for barreness, a constitutional defect for which she is not in the least to blame? Is it not worse than having two wives and might not society consent to some more human and national remedy in such a case, than a cruel divorce?

In reading the history of the Great Napoleon, I always date his ruin and downfall from the time of the divorce of Josephine She would have endured anything rather than the pangs of that cruel separation Through the ambition of Napoleon and the demands of Society, the heartless separation was consummated Napoleon fell and the French people were humbled.

"But!" says one, "Public opinion is Monarch and must be obeyed." Well! what is public opinion? Is it not always changing, and who is to say that it is always right? The time was when public opinion was opposed to Free Government, but, was it right? . It may be that the time will come when public opinion will be a better guide than it is today.

I think our Nation is robust enough to allow some freedom of thought and action so long as no person's rights are infringed upon leave truth and error to grapple without too much legislative interference, and trust a little in eternal laws of the universe, 'that truth will eventually become uppermost' and the fittest survive.

I have not written this as an advocate of polygamy, but as a defense against the unjust attacks of religious and political bigots Polygamy is called some very hard names by some very smart men whose morals are not above reproach and by some whose morals are of a very low grade It is said to be a step backward; perhaps it is. In the course of human progress it may be necessary sometimes, to take a step backward to gain momentum to go ahead Who can say that this Mormon Polygamy has not been inaugurated under the guise of a revelation from God as a rebuke to the awful abuses and slavery of the women under our present monogamic marriage laws?

ANDREW CAHOON

This editorial by Andrew is recopied, not to defend the principles of polygamy, but rather to impress upon us that although our dear ancestor, had at this time been separated from his Church for many years, he pays tribute to the Latter-day Saints and maintains that "Their Doctrines are strictly Bible Doctrine." The editorial was written a short time after his dear wives, Margaret and Janet were separated from him, and he expresses here his sentiments of deep remorse because of these cruel divorces.

Let us keep in our memories, the high ideals of Andrew Cahoon, and add the following lines, which best express his own beautiful thoughts of love, marriage, home, parents and children:

> *"So long as there are homes to which we turn at close of day,*
> *So long as there are homes where children are and women stay,*
> *If love and loyalty and faith be found across those sills,*
> *A stricken Nation can recover from its ills."*

OBITUARY OF ANDREW CAHOON

Andrew Cahoon died December 13, 1900 at Murray, Salt Lake County, Utah.

"Largely attended funeral over the remains of Andrew Cahoon was held at the family residence at Murray. Hundreds of neighbors and friends gathered at the home; only half of the crowd could gain entrance into the house. The deceased was praised for his strong, rugged honesty of purpose and motive, and for his justice in dealing with his fellowmen. That seemed to be the trend of all the remarks which were made by the speakers. The funeral cortege was a mile long. The pallbearers were the six sons of the deceased, James W., John P., Albert E., Reynolds, Daniel F., and Joseph C. Cahoon."

Andrew Cahoon was the father of nineteen children * To Andrew and Mary Barr Carruth, his first wife, were born· Thirza Lucina (died infant), Joseph Carruth, George Arthur (died age 8 years), Mary Emma, Lerona (died infant), and Louisa.

The children of Andrew and Margaret Barr Carruth, his second wife, were: Andrew Alonzo, John Pulaski, Albert Elkana, Reynolds, Daniel Farrington, Maria Antoinette, Margaret Melissa (died infant), and Lucy Caroline

The children of Andrew and Janet Barr Carruth (Young), his third wife, were: Rachel, James William, Jane Elizabeth, Reuben, and Marion (died infant).

---

*See The Cahoon Story for biographies of children

MAHONRI
MORIANCUMER
CAHOON

RAIS BELL
CASSEN R.
CAHOON

SARAH ROMNEY
CAHOON
*Wife of Mahonri M.
Cahoon*

MARY CHARLOTTE
JOHNSON CAHOON
*Wife of Rais Bell
Cahoon*

MAHONRI MORIANCUMER CAHOON

Ask and It Shall Be Given You; Seek, and Ye Shall Find,
Knock, and It Shall Be Opened Unto You.
—ST MATTHEW

Mahonri Moriancumer Cahoon was the seventh child of Reynolds and Thirza. He was born July 26, 1834, in Kirtland, Geaugo County, Ohio and died Jan. 24, 1888, in Murray, Salt Lake County, Utah. He married Sarah Romney Nov 22, 1853 in Salt Lake City June 18, 1867, they were sealed in the Endowment House at Salt Lake City

The name of Mahonri Moriancumer is of special significance to us as a family and also important in the history of the Book of Mormon. In most instances, revelation came to the Prophet Joseph Smith in answer to his prayers, uttered or unexpressed. Probably during his translating of the Book of Mormon, Joseph had often pondered in his heart, "Who was the brother of Jared, and what was his name!"

In the humble cottage of Reynolds and Thirza Cahoon dwelt peace and order where the Spirit of God could dictate The opportune time had arrived when the Lord desired to reveal these answers. Into the Cahoon family was born their seventh child and they decided to ask the Prophet Joseph Smith to select the name for their little boy, and bless him.

Here is the story·

BLESSED AND NAMED BY THE PROPHET JOSEPH SMITH

"While residing in Kirtland, Elder Reynolds Cahoon had a son born to him. One day when President Joseph Smith was passing his door, he called the Prophet in, and asked him to bless and name the baby. Joseph did so and gave the boy the name of Mahonri Moriancumer. When he had finished the blessing, he laid the child on the bed and turning to Elder Cahoon, said: 'The name I have just given your son is the name of the brother of Jared. The Lord has just shown (or revealed) it to me ' Elder William F. Cahoon who was standing near heard the Prophet make this statement to his father, and this was the first time the name of the brother of Jared was known in the Church in this dispensation."*

The above story answered many questions which had been asked by Book of Mormon students This revelation pertaining to the name of the Brother of Jared is also related in Reynolds Cahoon's history in this book. (See page 21)

Improvement Era, Vol 8, page 704 Also *Juvenile Instructor*, Vol 27, page 282

Joseph Smith had now announced the name of the Brother of Jared and had given it to the Cahoon baby. The bewildered mother must have repeated time and time again, "Mahonri Moriancumer such an unusual name!, a Revelation! Why such importance to this name?"

THE BROTHER OF JARED AND THE JAREDITES

The Book of Mormon gives us a very interesting though brief history of the Jaredites, the first colonists of this American Continent. Throughout its early history one person figures more prominently than any other. He acted as Revelator; was blessed with great faith that he not only conversed with the Lord but saw Him in His Spiritual Body. In fact, he was the first mortal man to whom the Lord Jesus Christ ever revealed Himself. The Lord showed the brother of Jared all things which were to transpire from the day to the end of the earth.

Ora Pate Stewart in her book, God Planted A Tree, wrote:

"Jared and his righteous brother, Mahonri Moriancumer, and about eighty persons of their families and friends, Shemites, were directed to return in eight barges to the 'land choice above all other lands.' They left Babylon about two hundred years after the flood and settled in North America. Although these people, known to us as the Jaredites, were blessed with a civilization and enlightenment that its height exceeded our own, they failed to live up to the lease of the land — 'I will be their God and they shall be my people — and after sixteen hundred years in America they were destroyed to a man, in the greatest civil war recorded in our history. Theirs is a fascinating, important story to be read in the fifteen short chapters of the Book of Ether within the Book of Mormon."

In December 1952, one of the most beautiful and dramatic paintings ever made of a Latter-day Saint subject was given distribution. The painting is by the famed Church Artist, Arnold Friberg, and is entitled, "The Brother of Jared Sees The Finger of The Lord." — Deseret News, December, 1952.

PIONEER OF CALIFORNIA

Mahonri M. Cahoon, lad of twelve, traveled from Nauvoo with his parents to Utah. After residing in Salt Lake Valley about two years, Mahonri M. at the age of sixteen, decided to go to California with his older brother, Andrew Cahoon. They wanted to "Try their luck at digging gold." Mary Barr Carruth Cahoon, wife of Andrew went with him They resided at the Rancho San Bernardino for two years, 1850-1852. While there, they assisted in surveying and laying out the town of San Bernardino. They found considerable gold which they took back to Salt Lake City and divided among members of the Cahoon family. They returned April 21, 1852 with Elder Rich and others who had been at the Rancho. Although the true origin of the name of the "Cajon Pass" has not yet been established, there is a strong inference that it was named after the Cahoon brothers. See History of Andrew Cahoon, pages 123, 124, 125.

It was after his return to Salt Lake Valley, at the age of nineteen that Mahonri married Sarah Romney, who in 1850 had arrived in Utah with her parents Mahonri and Sarah resided in Murray, Utah, later moving to Coalville Many were the exciting encounters they experienced with the Indians, at times narrowly escaping death. Some of these thrilling stories related by Sarah are given here:

"The first time I saw an Indian was in Nauvoo while Joseph Smith was preaching," she said. Many terrifying experiences occurred later, however, in which lives were endangered and courage and ingenuity were strained to the breaking point. (See Stories Retold By Cloe Winchester Sanders below.)

Mahonri held the office of a Seventy and was active in civic affairs. He was committeeman for the July 4th, 1865 celebration. In his advanced years he resided with his daughter, Nancy Roselle Winchester.

In a grave in Murray City Cemetery lie the remains of Mahonri Moriancumer Cahoon. A white marble stone marks the spot. The inscription on it is scarcely discernible At the request of the compiler of this book, the sexton carefully examined the letters and figures which were almost obliterated. They read: Born — July, 1834 Died — Jan. 1888.

SARAH ROMNEY CAHOON

(From Stories Retold by Cloe Winchester Sanders, Granddaughter)

Sarah Romney was born Feb. 22, 1836 in Penwortham, Lanshire County, England and died January 8, 1909 in Rexburg, Madison County, Idaho She was married to Mahonri Moriancumer Cahoon Nov. 22, 1853, at the age of seventeen.

"Miles Romney, father of Sarah was born July 13, 1806 in Dalton, Lancashire England. He married Elizabeth Gaskell, born Jan. 8, 1808. She was the daughter of Joseph Gaskell and Elizabeth Slater. Miles Romney was the son of George Romney and Sarah King.*

"Miles became a member of the L.D.S. Church in 1837. He was an Elder in the Preston Conference. On 27 Feb. 1841, Miles and his family sailed from Liverpool on the ship 'Sheffield', arriving seven weeks later at New Orleans Sarah, their daughter, who became the wife of Mahonri Moriancumer Cahoon, was only five years old when she crossed the ocean with her parents.

"When the family arrived at New Orleans, they went by boat up the Mississippi River. When they arrived at Nauvoo, Miles Romney was appointed one of the foremen in the construction of the Nauvoo Temple. In 1846 they left with the Mormon Pioneers and arrived in Salt Lake Valley 18 Oct., 1850. In 1856 he was called on a Mission for the L D S. Church to England. Later in life he went to Dixie or Southern Utah and here he had charge of the woodwork on the St George Temple. He died in St. George, Utah, 8 May, 1877.

"In 1854", Sarah writes, "my husband and I were living near the West Mountains I was alone one lovely afternoon. I was sewing and rocking the cradle with my foot when a huge rattlesnake crossed the floor and went under my bed. This almost paralyzed me. I ran to my neighbors; they were all away, the doors all locked except the one where the hired man slept.

"Well, I hadn't been there long when I heard whoops and howls These I knew to be from Indians. I did not know what to do; I had no gun and there being no lock on the door, I fastened it best I could and with the baby, hid myself on the floor in one corner of the room. They were coming from the East and entered my own home first taking all our bread

*See Archibald F Bennett "A Guide for Genealogical Research." Chapters 18, 19, 20

and whatever they wished, then started to see where I was hiding I was frightened almost to death.

"Just at that moment I heard my husband's voice telling me not to be afraid. He and the hired man had seen the Indians coming; put spurs to their horses and arrived there in time to save us. I hugged my baby to my breast and thanked God!'"

Many were the exciting encounters with the Indians, narrowly escaping death. At one time when she and a neighbor lady were alone, the Indians, angry because they could not make the mothers understand what they wanted, drew their guns and would have killed their little babies playing on the floor, had not the husbands come in time.

"Oh! the horrors of those moments! We could only pray and have faith in Divine protection."

At one time the bullet from an Indian's gun tore through the coat Grandfather Mahonri was wearing and another bullet lodged in his hat closely striking his head. His hair was singed as if by fire. These were the experiences of those pioneers.

Sarah again relates:

"While living in Coalville, Utah, word came that the Indians had stolen a little girl from Cache Valley. My husband Mahonri, with others, followed the Indians. He was nearly three months trying to find trace of the child. These men suffered many hardships in the search but were never able to locate the child."

After the death of her husband Sarah moved to Rexburg, Idaho to live with her three sons She was selected First Counselor in the Primary organiation in Fremont Stake. This was a very large Stake but not too large for these faithful Sisters to travel miles in a wagon, often fording the Snake River to visit the Primary. She died in Rexburg, Jan. 8, 1909.

The children of Mahonri Moriancumer and Sarah Romney Cahoon were: Mahonri M. Jr (died age two years), Elizabeth Thirza, Miles Reynolds, John Farrington, Nancy Roselle, Sarah Lorett and George Ernest.*

*See "The Cahoon Story" for biographies of children

RAIS BELL CASSEN REYNOLDS CAHOON

The Christian Is The Highest Style of Man —YOUNG

Rais Bell C. R. Cahoon was the ninth child of Reynolds Cahoon. The mother of Rais Bell was Lucina Roberts, the second wife of Reynolds. Lucina was a widow. She had previously married Peter Johnson.

Rais Bell was born Oct. 13, 1845 or 6, in Nauvoo, Hancock County, Illinois and died Feb. 28, 1911 in Thatcher, Idaho. He was married Nov. 16, 1867 to Mary Charlotte Johnson who was born Dec. 14, 1850 and who died April 27, 1915 in Thatcher, Idaho.

Mary Charlotte was the daughter of Jarvis Johnson and Hester Ann Jackson. Jarvis Johnson, born July 6, 1829, Lincoln County, Vermont, died Jan. 28, 1898 in Beaver Dam, Utah. He was the son of Lucina Roberts and Peter Johnson. Hester Ann Jackson, born Sept. 25, 1834, Knox County, Ohio, died May 11, 1859, Otto County, Nebraska. She was the daughter of William Jackson.

GRANDCHILDREN GIVE HIGHLIGHTS

Annie Panter Hymas, granddaughter of Rais Bell C. R. Cahoon comments:

This relationship is quite complicated. My great grandfather is Jarvis Johnson, son of Peter Johnson and Lucina Roberts. My grandfather, Rais Bell C. R. Cahoon, married Mary Charlotte Johnson, the daughter of his half-brother, Jarvis Johnson. By the marriage of Reynolds Cahoon to Lucina Roberts, widow of Peter Johnson, Reynolds became the step-grandfather of Mary Charlotte Johnson, wife of Rais Bell C. R Cahoon, son of Reynolds." (See Notes of Lucina Roberts In Reynolds Cahoon's Life Story, page 77.)

Rais Bell was an infant just a few months old when his parents left Nauvoo for their pioneer trek to the Rocky Mountains with the Mormon people. He lived in Salt Lake City until a grown man and then went to Brigham City, Utah where he resided for some time, later moving to Thatcher or Gentile Valley, Idaho. The old homestead is on the banks of the Bear River. Here he remained until his death.

He had been blessed with the special privilege of assisting in gathering the "Scattered Members Of Israel." He was also promised further blessings that "if he would sit in council with his brethren and exhort them to faithfulness and comfort the hearts of the destitute, he would be entitled to the gift of the Priesthood and Blessings of the New and Everlasting Covenant." The Patriarch John Smith said to him: "The eyes of the Lord are upon thee and He has a work for thee to do and thy faith shall not fail. Thou shall comfort the hearts of the destitute and thy name shall be held in honorable remembrance."

Mary Ellen Tolman, daughter of Rais Bell writes:

"My father was a good father and a good Latter-day Saint all his life. I remember my father telling me about Brigham Young sending him with others to go back from Salt Lake for the emigrants . . .

"For years he played a drum in the Band organized in Brigham City. He worked in a saw-mill getting timber for the mill. He was one of the first to enter the 'United Order' when the people lived the Order in Brigham City, Utah He was always ready and willing to do all he could for the Gospel."

Eleven children were born to Rais Bell and his wife, Mary Charlotte. They were: Sarah Lucina, Mary Ellen, Margaret Rosella, Esther Melisa, Chloe Estella, Rais John Reynolds, William Jarvis, Mabel Alveretta, Alonzo Alvero, Joseph Leroy, and Charles Alphus.*

*See "The Cahoon Story" for biographies of children

TRUMAN CARLOS CAHOON
Youngest Child of Reynolds Cahoon

None but God can satisfy the longing of the immortal soul; as the heart was made for Him, He only can fill it — TRENCH

Truman Carlos Cahoon was the tenth child of Reynolds Cahoon. His mother was Lucina Roberts Johnson, the second wife of Reynolds. Truman was born Jan. 18, 1850 in Salt Lake City, Utah, and died Feb. 4, 1911 at Pleasant Green, Utah. He never married.

A COMPLETE WAY OF LIFE

Now we close the story of Reynolds Cahoon and his stalwart sons. What a dramatic story it is! Accounts by the very men and women who lived these momentous events have been recorded here — not interpretations but exciting first-hand stories that give us a glimpse into their minds and hearts — stories penned by men and women bent with age, boys and girls young in heart and high in spirit, who not too long ago fought for their very existence.

In this book we have traveled with Reynolds and his family from their homes in New York to Kirtland, Ohio; into Jackson County, Missouri and then to Nauvoo, Illinois — many times at "the point of a gun." In 1846, we encamped with them during the icy, winter months at Winter Quarters, and later relived those historic events at Chimney Rock, Nebraska, traveling on until in the year of 1848, we arrived with them in the Salt Lake Valley.

They had accepted, not just another creed but a complete way of life, built on a solid, spiritual foundation of Love, Hope and Truth — "Knowing this first," as did Peter, "that no prophecy of the scripture is of any private interpretation. For the prophecy came not in old times by the will of man; but holy men of God spake as they were moved by the Holy Ghost." (II Peter 1, 20-21)

Such inspired men as these guided the memorable migration of the Utah Pioneers. With faith and confidence in their Latter-day Prophets; with love for God and their fellowman, under the spiritual leadership of men with creative abilities, these pioneers built bridges, roads and houses, cleared forests, forged rivers and subdued the prairies and hot desert sands.

Through the diaries, personal letters, autobiographies and records of our Cahoon pioneers, we have gained a new concept of our American heritage, and with such a heritage, goes a sacred duty to perpetuate the glorious traditions which have made America strong and free. We have wept with them and we have rejoiced with them We have learned why and how their influence has shaped the destiny of this great land of ours. Stories from eye-witnesses have helped us understand the miracles which have placed the State of Utah and the Mormon Pioneers among the foremost people of the world.

A TRIBUTE TO THE MORMONS

What could be more fitting as a conclusion to our story of Reynolds Cahoon and the Utah Pioneers than to quote from an article by Hartzell Spence, The Story of Religion in America, printed in Look Magazine January 28th, 1958 In this commentary he commends the vision, industry, and aspirations of a great people, who surviving hatred and persecution, walked in dignity and left for all time their indelible mark of greatness

Of the Mormons he writes:

"Since, in the Mormon belief, achieving divinity involves supreme knowledge, the Church pays unusual attention to education. Utah is not exceeded by any state in its rate of college graduates, and Mormons have a higher rate of listings in *Who's Who in America* and on the registers of Scientific honor societies than that of any other faith.

"The list of prominent Mormons is impressive. In Government, it includes Secretary of Agriculture Eza Taft Benson and U. S. Treasurer Ivy Baker Priest In science, there are the television pioneer Philo Farnsworth; a chemist, Dr. Henry Eyring, whom the *Saturday Review* has called one of America's 10 outstanding scientists, and Dr. Harvey Fletcher, author of 52 textbooks on electricity and acoustics In business, the list includes the financier, Mariner S Eccles; a past president of the U S Junior Chamber of Commerce, E. Lamar Buckner; the president of Standard Oil of California, Theodore S. Petersen, and the president of American Motors, George Romney

"Among many prominent artists, is Arnold Friberg, a designer of costumes for the Cecil B. DeMille picture "The Ten Commandments." Mormon accent on sports and entertainment has produced a middleweight boxing champion . , Miss America of 1952 . ., America's prettiest schoolgirl of 1955 . ., Miss U. S A of 1957 . . ., and the 'All American Family' of 1957.

"The Church of Jesus Christ of Latter-day Saints is a thoroughly American institution," Hartzell Spence continues. "It emerged during the period of great religious upheaval after the Revolutionary War, when men challenged their Christian tradition. . . . The larger denominations openly competed with one another, until a mighty din of religious controversy reverberated, particularly along the frontier.

"Greatly disturbed by this hubbub was a 14-year-old boy. . . . His name was Joseph Smith Jr. He was a handsome, tall, flaxen-haired youngster with intense, hazel eyes mellowed by unusually long lashes. He was a strong wrestler, a handy axman, sure in the saddle, an outdoorsman. He had other qualities too — a surprisingly gentle voice and a friendly smile, which disguised a strong streak of stubborness. . . .

"One day in 1820, having meditated on James I:5, he went into the woods to decide what to accept from this babel of tongues. He had a vision of God the Father and His Son, Jesus Christ, who appeared to him in a shining light and told him not to join any established Church . .   Christ would restore His original precepts and Joseph Smith would be the instrument of the restoration.

"The Prophet Joseph Smith's original concept was as simple as the Sermon on the Mount. It restored not only Galilean Christianity, but the familiar cast of Biblical characters· saints, prophets and apostles . . . Its appeal to converts was that it answered every controversy then raging in the Christian world On direct revelation from God, the Prophet Joseph Smith could assure his followers that what he said was true

"The Church is rich. It has grown far beyond its isolated valley. At times, its members have been labeled a 'strange people', but they are not strange They are different, yes, but the right to be different is the essence of the American dream

. .   They have insisted on their right to pursue happiness in their own way.

"This they have done, and it has, indeed, made them happy."

ADDENDA

CAHOON ARCHITECTS AND BUILDERS

CAHOON-RELATED FAMILIES

RELATIVES AID IN ERECTING MONUMENT

GROUND BROKEN FOR MEMORIAL THEATRE

HISTORICAL SKETCHES OF MORMON TEMPLES

LAND OF OUR FOREFATHERS

IN RETROSPECT

CAHOON ARCHITECTS AND BUILDERS

When we build, let us think that we build forever. Let it not be for present delight, nor for present use alone. Let it be such work as our descendants will thank us for, and let us think, as we lay stone on stone, that a time is to come when these stones will be held sacred because our hands have touched them, and men will say, as they look upon the labor and wrought substance of them· 'See this our Fathers did for us' — Ruskin.

Should we ask the question, "What was the vocation, the work, the profession of Reynolds and his sons?", the most probable answer would be that they were architects and builders and that the outstanding achievement of Reynolds was the erecting of the magnificent temple at Kirtland, Ohio and the one at Nauvoo, Illinois. His sons assisted in the construction of those two edifices and also other temples. Today, in many parts of the country, their descendants are prominent engineers, architects, designers and builders of beautiful homes, chapels and other notable edifices.

"The Cahoon Story" contains the names, biographies, activities and accomplishments of many of these descendants. We pay tribute to all of them and in this book we list a few who have followed the profession of their ancestor, Reynolds Cahoon and also include some related members who are interested in construction and engineering.

The late John Pulaski Cahoon, pioneer brick manufacturer and builder of Utah, organized the company now known as the Interstate Brick Company, at the present time being operated by his sons. Reynolds Cahoon, brother of John P., Lewis A Copeland and other members of the family were active in this prominent Utah enterprise.

John Frederick Heath of the Mahonri M. family is an engineer in Utah and Leonard Cahoon of Salt Lake City, great grandson of Reynolds, received outstanding recognition as a structural engineer. In Deseret, Utah, Daniel S. Cahoon and his sons built the smelter there In Utah and Arizona, are Franklin Byron Johnson, Mechanical Engineer, his brother Richard Johnson, Architect and their cousin, Lee Stringham Mackay, Contractor and Builder. David Orson Mackay III is an interior decorator and assisted in many L D.S. temples.

Harold P. Cahoon received his Ph.D. in Ceramic Engineering. Theron M. Lambert is Vice President of Engineering and Research at Electro Ceramics Incorporated. He was senior Electronics Engineer, U. S. Navy Electronics Laboratory and Head of the Transducer Branch. Theron served on National

Committees and is a member of the Utah State Committee on Industry and Education.*

The descendants of George E Cahoon in Utah are among those interested in building and engineering. William W. Golay is a mason contractor and general builder. Kenneth B and Georgene Cahoon Evans are active in real estate. Lynn E. Cahoon is sales engineer for the Gustin-Bacon Mfg. Co , manufacturing Glass Fiber Insulation Products. We mention also Major David A. Wettstein, the pilot on the eventful trip of Vice President Richard M. Nixon to South America

Spencer Reid of Utah and California, held the position of General Superintendent of the American Smelting and Refining Co. Rex Leroy Cahoon of Ogden, Utah, descendant of the Rais Bell Cahoon family, is employed at the Marquardt Aircraft Co., and Commissioner, Lorenzo Clark Romney is in charge of Salt Lake City's eight million dollar airport terminal building and jet landing field.

In Bramwell, Idaho, David O. Mackay supervised and financed the construction of the Church Chapel. In Pocatello, Idaho, William Roscoe Cahoon, President of Pocatello Stake, is a general contractor and builder. His father, William Dennison Cahoon of Boise, Idaho, is also a builder. In Boise, Idaho, Edward Lish Hoagland and his sons, descendants of Andrew Cahoon, assisted in the construction of the Railroad Cut-off from Black Creek to Boise.

In California, Eldon Barr Shurtleff, great great grandson of Reynolds, is a contractor and builder of beautiful homes. Harry M. Fiske of California and Jack Cahoon Fiske of Illinois, husband and son of Lucile Cahoon Fiske, descendant of Andrew, are asssociated with the Ingersoll Rand Company, internationally prominent as manufacturers and distributors of engineering and construction equipment Zollie Leigh James, electrical engineer, is employed at Point Arguello Naval Missile Facility Base, Lompoc, California

In Canada, James Cordon Cahoon and his brother George Edward were pioneer builders and lumber dealers in Alberta. Lloyd D Cahoon, son of James C. is now manager of this business. Jay A. Cahoon, son of George E. is a constructor of Chapels for the Latter-day Saints Church throughout Canada and the United States.

---

*Theron is the son of J R and Winnie Lambert To Winnie and Theron the compilers acknowledge appreciation for every kindness and assistance

CAHOON-RELATED FAMILIES

In his private journal, Reynolds Cahoon tells about his association with many families whose descendants, at a later date, married descendants of the Cahoon family. Reynolds was a missionary companion of Hyrum and Samuel Smith and in his journal, he refers to these related families as follows:

"I held meetings with Brother Stiles and Brother Covey. I remained a short time at Brother Covey's home. On March 29, 1832, I consulted with Brother Thomas Cohoon . . ."

Lucy Mack Smith, mother of the Prophet, has written much regarding these missions and the association of her sons Joseph, Hyrum and Samuel, with Reynolds Cahoon. Until the death of Joseph and Hyrum, their lives were inseparable. A great granddaughter of Reynolds married a great, great grandson of Hyrum Smith.

Reynolds also refers in his journal to the families of Young, Sharp, Spencer, Gordon, Romney, Johnson, Angell and many Cahoon-related families. May we pause to pay tribute to these wonderful families whose lives were an integral part of the history of the Cahoon Pioneers.

THE CORBETT FAMILY*

Walter Colvin Corbett, born December 16, 1906, great, great grandson of Hyrum Smith, married Annie J. Mackay born October 20, 1906, great granddaughter of Reynolds Cahoon. Annie J was the daughter of David O. Mackay and Maria Antoinette Cahoon, daughter of Andrew, son of Reynolds.

Hyrum Smith, son of Joseph Smith, Sr. and Lucy Mack, married Mary Fielding. Mary was Hyrum's second wife, they had two children, Martha Ann Smith and Joseph F. Smith.

After the martyrdom of Hyrum, Mary took her two children to Utah. Her son, Joseph F. became one of the presidents of the Church of Jesus Christ of Latter-day Saints and her daughter, Martha Ann, married William Jasper Harris. Their daughter, Mary Emily Harris, married Walter Sutton Corbett, whose son, Walter Harris Corbett married Irene Colvin. Their son, Walter Colvin Corbett married December 16, 1933, to Annie J. Mackay, descendant of Reynolds Cahoon.

---

*Information furnished by Walter Colvin Corbett. See "Tales of a Triumphant People", by Daughters of the Utah Pioneers.

THE SPENCER FAMILY

Hyrum Theron Spencer, sometimes spelled Hirum, was born Nov. 13, 1838 in West Bridge, Mass. He married March 31, 1857 to Mary Barr Young, born May 19, 1841 in Glasgow, Scotland. She was the daughter of James Young, Jr. and Janet Barr Carruth. James Young died and Janet married her second husband, Andrew Cahoon. Hyrum T. Spencer and Mary Barr Young were married by her stepfather, Andrew Cahoon, when she was sixteen years old. She was a sister of Grace Christy Young and Janet Carruth Young who married Enoch Covey. Hyrum T. Spencer was a brother of Martha and Jane Amanda who married Daniel Stiles Cahoon, son of Reynolds.*

THE COVEY FAMILY
By Grace Covey Jorgensen

"Benjamin Covey joined the Mormon Church in New York. He was the son of Walter Covey and Sarah Hatch. Benjamin was born in 1792 in Fredrickstown, Dutchess County, New York. He married Almira Mack, widow of William Scoby, October, 1836 in Kirtland, Ohio. Almira was born April 28, 1805 in Tunbridge, Orange County, Vermont and died March 10, 1886 in Salt Lake City, Utah. She was the daughter of Captain Stephen Andrew Mack and Temperance Bond. Stephen was the brother of Lucy Mack, the mother of the prophet Joseph Smith, therefore Almira was a cousin of Joseph Smith.

Lucy Mack, in her book "The Prophet Joseph Smith," writes: "Stephen Mack was known as Major Mack, having a commission in the army during the war with England . . . he was a soldier at the age of fourteen . . . He was prominent in the settlement of Detroit and acquired considerable wealth. He died November 11, 1826. Mrs. Stephen Mack, at the age of 77 years crossed the plains to Utah with her daughter Almira Mack and family. Almira was the wife of Benjamin Covey. They traveled in Brigham Young's Company of 1848. Benjamin was captain of 10 wagons in Lorenzo Snow's Company.

---

*See Daniel Stiles Cahoon History, pages 96 to 98

"Benjamin Covey and Almira Mack had four children. The oldest son, Enoch Covey, born August 26, 1827 in Caldwell County, Missouri, married Grace Christie (Christy) Young and her sister Jannette Carruth Young . . ."

The wives of Enoch Covey are the daughters of Janet Carruth and James Young, Jr They are cousins of the children of Mary and Margaret Carruth Cahoon, who married Andrew Cahoon, son of Reynolds Cahoon.

THE SHARP FAMILY
By Mary Belle C. Briggs

"Brigham called for volunteers to go south to settle "Dixie", as St. George was then called. John Farrington Cahoon and Margaret Sharp, my grandparents, left on this mission with two small children. They had many hardships but through their humility and faithfulness, God blessed them and they performed a glorious mission.

"Margaret Sharp was born in Scotland in 1845. She and her two brothers came to America with their parents, and later crossed the plains with the Mormon Pioneers. They traveled with the John Sharp Company arriving in Utah September 1, 1850. John F. Cahoon was the son of William F., son of Reynolds Many of the descendants of John F. have resided in Bountiful, Utah, others traveled to various parts of the country. Margaret, Mrs. Lee M. Rumph, and family reside in Wichita, Kansas. She is a descendant of the John F. and Margaret Sharp Cahoon family.

THE GORDON FAMILY
By Mildred K. Gordon Shuey

"James P. Gordon and Mary Ballantyne, both of Scotland, emigrated to America and settled in Nauvoo, Illinois in the early forties, which place was then the hearquarters of the Mormon Church. Here they were married by Hyrum Smith, brother of the Prophet, Joseph Smith, Jr.

"The Gordons and Smiths became close friends and when the Prophet was arrested and taken to prison, James P. gave him substantial evidence of his friendship. It was while the Gordon family was at breakfast, that James P. observed the Prophet being taken past his house to the jail and after a short consultation with his wife, went out and gave the

Prophet ten dollars which he had received the day before from the sale of a cow. This money, though a small sum, represented much to James P., who was a poor man

"Joseph was deeply affected by this proof of friendship and placing his hand on James P he thanked him warmly and assured him that he would never want for means, which prophecy was amply fulfilled

"My great grandfather, James P. Gordon, accumulated a comfortable competence, being the owner of several farms. He settled first on a farm on the Little Cottonwood, later moved to State Street, where he purchased one hundred sixty acres of land which he cultivated to a high degree, building several houses on it He built a beautiful brick residence and nine children were born to them.

"James P. Gordon was born March 15, 1819 in Houston, Renfrew Scotland, died October 1, 1892 He was a son of F. Joseph and Jane Gordon. James P. married Mary Ballentyne, born August 17, 1817, in Selkirkshire, Scotland, died November 28, 1878 She was the daughter of John and Jeanette Ballentyne."

Their son, John Gordon, born December 20, 1852, married Elizabeth Thirza Cahoon, daughter of Mahonri Moriancumer Cahoon and Sarah Romney. Their daughter, Elizabeth Gordon, born April 22, 1856, married John Pulaski Cahoon, son of Andrew Cahoon and Margaret Carruth

The Cahoon-Brinton Family
By Bishop David Branson Brinton

Chester P. Cahoon, great grandson of Reynolds, married Sept. 22, 1908 to Melvina Brinton, daughter of David Branson Brinton and Susan Erepta Huffaker Chester and Melvina had three sons Arthur, their oldest son died at the age of twelve. Melvina was a member of the Granite Stake Sunday School Board and taught the youth of Zion for many years She died April 12, 1941 She was descendant of John Brinton and Priscilla Branson.

David Brinton, born 1814 in Pennsylvania, son of John, joined the Mormon Church in 1840. David's wife, Sarah Piersol, died in 1843. His second wife, Elizabeth G. Hoopes and her child died in 1846 in Winter Quarters, Nebraska. He married in 1848 to Harriet Wollerton Dilworth. David, his wife, Harriet, and his three sons, Evans Piersol Brinton, Caleb Dilworth Brinton, and David Branson Brinton, were pioneers to Utah in 1850. David, his son, grandson and great grandson held positions as bishops of the church. Bishop David B. and his wife, Ethel Simons Brinton, officiated in the Salt Lake Temple.

THE CAHOON-BENNION FAMILY
By Aurelia Bennion Cahoon

On June 11, 1950, Chester P. Cahoon married Aurelia Bennion, daughter of Harden Bennion and Vilate Kimball Nebeker, daughter of George Nebeker and Elizabeth Dilworth. Through relationship in the Dilworth family, Aurelia Bennion Cahoon and Melvina Brinton Cahoon are second cousins. Aurelia served on the Sunday School Stake Board and was a member of the Y.L.M.I.A. General Board.

John Bennion, born 1823 in Wales, son of John and Elizabeth Roberts, married Esther Birch. John Bennion and George Nebeker were Utah pioneers in 1847. John was called in 1868 by the Mormon Church to go to West Point, Nevada, a village on the Muddy, to handle herds of cattle intrusted to him by the pioneers. He was also a missionary. Harden Bennion, son of John and Esther Birch, was a member of the Utah State Legislature, Board of Equalization, and Commissioner on Taxation and Revenue. In 1916, he became Secretary of the State of Utah In 1925, was Commissioner of Agriculture.

OUR CAHOON COUSINS IN CANADA
THE ROCHE FAMILY

Enid Cahoon Roche, great granddaughter of Reynolds, and her husband Maurice A. Roche have resided in Flin Flon, Manitoba, Canada since 1926. Maurice is a graduate Engineer and holds the position of Assistant to the General Manager of the Hudson Bay Mining and Smelting Company. His son, Maurice John Roche is a Chemical Engineer at A. V. Roe Jet Plane Manufacturing Company in Toronto, Canada.

LEAVITT FAMILY IN CANADA

"Leavitt" is a family-name place and in this settlement reside many of the Cahoon family. They are farmers, teachers, musicans, University graduates, and occupy important positions in the church and government.

Leslie C C. Cahoon, son of James C. C married Mary Leavitt. Their home is in Leavitt, Alberta, Canada and on this nice farm, they have been blessed with ten fine children, two sets of twins. Mary's father, Thomas R. Leavitt, founded this hamlet. Bishop George Edward Cahoon and family resided here for many years. See other families pages 171, 172.

THE STORY OF THE NAME "LEAVITT"
By Lervae Cahoon

"Thomas Rowell Leavitt, Sr., founded the hamlet of Leavitt. At the time of the trouble of the Mormon people in the U. S. A., he fled into Canada. He built the first house in Cardston, Alberta, Canada. On one of his trips to the mountains, he came over the rim of this valley and prophetically stated he would like his sons to establish themselves in this beautiful valley, then called 'Buffalo Flat'.

"Thomas R had families by three wives and most all of his sons have lived here at sometime. Many of his descendants remained at Leavitt and did establish their homes in this valley.

"They are a fine family, the name is a great one and is teeming with genealogical interest right back to the early settlements of America. They have been strong in the Latter-day Faith from the beginning " Lervae then adds: "My wife is Joyce Broadbent. She is the great granddaughter of the above named founder of Leavitt."

CAHOON-RELATED FAMILIES IN CALIFORNIA

The Cahoon-related families and also the direct pioneer descendants of Reynolds Cahoon who reside in California are too numerous to list in this book. Let us relate the following incident and if the reply given in this story is correct, one would hesitate to enumerate all the descendants

At a dancing party given in California by the Sons of the Utah Pioneers, three young ladies, Marianne, Barbara and Loretta Shurtleff, descendants of eight Utah Pioneers including Reynolds Cahoon, entertained on the program. At the conclusion of their dancing number, one child in the audience asked another this question: "Who are their Pioneer Ancestors?", and Behold! This was the reply: "Oh, all the pioneers of Utah and all the pioneers of California are their ancestors."

We shall mention the following families in California: A Ray Cahoon and families; Grover Peter Hansen, his wife, Eva Cahoon and their families; also the Fiske, James, French and Freeze and other families, descendants of Andrew Cahoon.

In Los Angeles, reside Brent Farrington Cahoon, his lovely wife, Nelle Lloyd Cahoon, their daughter, Jennie Romayne Dowd and family. To Nelle, the compilers express their sincere appreciation for assisting in the proof-reading of this book.

Brent and Nelle lived in New York City for many years where their daughter Romayne, was educated After a colorful career as stewardess for Pan American Airways, Romayne was married in London, England, to John J. Dowd of New York City. Shortly after their marriage John was transferred to Frankfort, Germany as Sales Manager for Pan American Airways One year later he and Romayne returned to New York City where their daughter, Ellen Romayne, was born January 10, 1948. John is now a stock broker in Los Angeles, California

In Santa Ana and Garden Grove are James L Drake, a government civil service employee and family; also Donald J. Leytham and family who are descendants of LaVon Drake James, descendant of Andrew Cahoon. To Alma LaVon Leytham, the compilers say "Special Thanks," for assisting in typing many pages of this Pioneer History.

In Albany, California resides the family of Damon T. and Vaudis Erda Cahoon Kilker, and in Pasadena, the Cahoon-related families, Fervegeon and Wolmer, were among the earliest pioneers in that city.

CAHOON RELATIVES AID IN ERECTING MEMORIAL

For years it had been the desire of Kate B Carter, National President of the Daughters of Utah Pioneers to honor in San Diego, the noble men and women of the Mormon Battalion and we pay tribute to our Cahoon Cousins who, with other members of the San Diego Camps, worked so diligently in raising the necessary funds for its completion

Thomas B. Mawson, who served fifteen years as Boy Scout Master in San Diego, dug the hole for the footing of the Monument and had charge of mixing and pouring the cement. Verda Cahoon Mawson, 1st Vice-Captain to the County President, also a member of the Choir, had charge of making fifty bonnets and caps for the choir. Lavenia Cahoon Dunlap was County Chorister and Lazelle Cahoon Boucher was 1st Captain of the La Mesa Camp, all holding these offices at the time of the dedication of the monument. These three girls, all sisters, are granddaughters of Andrew Cahoon and daughters of James William Jr. and Lavenia Brown Cahoon of Utah.

SAN DIEGO HONORS WOMEN OF MORMON
BATTALION

The Mormon Battalion arrived in San Diego, California, January 29, 1847. They were accompanied by four of the wives. One hundred and thirteen years later, on January 29, 1960, at the site of Ft. Stockton in Presidio Park, San Diego, a five-foot granite shaft, bearing two bronze plaques was dedicated to honor the women and children who marched from Council Bluffs to Pueblo, Colorado, and the four women who traveled the entire distance here.

One plaque lists the names of all the women On the second plaque is inscribed:

"Mormon women were anxious to reach the glorious west and any means offered seemed an answer to prayer to help them on their way. When it was learned four laundresses would be allowed each of the five companies, the wives of the soldiers made application and twenty were chosen. Men who could meet the expenses were permitted to take their families, hence nearly eighty women and children accompanied the battalion. They endured the hardships of the journey, knowing hunger and thirst. Four wives, Susan M. Davis, Lydia Hunter, Phebe D. P Brown, and Melissa B. Coray, traveled the entire distance arriving in San Diego 29 January, 1847. Mrs. Hunter gave birth to a son April 20, 1847, the first white child born in San Diego She died two weeks later."[*]

CEREMONY OF DEDICATION

A color guard in Mormon Battalion uniforms, opened the ceremony, which included several anvil salutes and music by the Latter-day Saints Singing Mothers' Choir of San Diego East Stake. Presentation of the Colors by the Sons of Mormon Battalion of Salt Lake City, Utah, was followed by the Story of the Marker, a dramatic skit, with Valerie Wagstaff as narrator. The Marker was unveiled by Charles Jones and Gordon A. Pugmire, Battalion descendants. A Dedicatory prayer was offered and remarks were made by Kate B. Carter, President of the Daughters of Utah Pioneers, and by the special speaker, Fred Curtis of the Sons of Mormon Battalion. Following the presentation of the Monument to Charles C. Dail, Mayor of San Diego, by Alice Jones, D. U. P. President of San Diego, and its acceptance by the Mayor, this memorial

[*]An Individual History of these four wives has been published and is in the Library of the Daughters of Utah Pioneers in Salt Lake City, Utah

ceremony was concluded with a song by the Singing Mothers' Chorus.

GROUND BROKEN FOR MEMORIAL THEATRE

Ground-breaking Ceremonies for the Pioneer Memorial Theatre were held on the University of Utah Campus July 1, 1960 exactly ninety-nine years after the ground was broken for the original Salt Lake Theatre, July 1, 1861.

Wielding copper shovels donated by the Kennecott Copper Corporation, were Leland B Flint, one of its directors; Dr. A. Ray Olpin, president of the University of Utah; David O McKay, president of the Church of Jesus Christ of Latter-day Saints and Governor George D. Clyde.

President David O. McKay turned the first shovelful of earth; Henry D. Moyle of the First Presidency of the Church offered the invocation. The University of Utah Summer Festival Chorus rendered the favorite Mormon hymn, "Come, Come Ye Saints," after which several inspiring addresses were given.

President David O. McKay commented:

"This is more than a ground-breaking ceremony, it is an opportunity to express our appreciation for the service of others."

He paid tribute to all those who had made possible the erection of the Memorial Theatre, and referring to the fact that in spite of their struggles for survival, the Utah Pioneers did not forget the cultural side of life. "The old Salt Lake Theatre," he said, "was a 'Spiritual Oasis' that took on the character of a monument to their struggles.

Dr. Olpin pointed out that the Memorial Theatre was not to be a replica of the old Salt Lake "Play-House," but would resemble it on the outside only, with the inside consisting of the most modern type theatre, including facilities for study.

Governor Clyde described the project as a replica of the cultural objectives of the old theatre rather than that of brick and mortar and referred to the appropriation made by the State as an "investment in the future of its people."

In addition to the appropriation by the State of Utah, funds for this Memorial Theatre were donated by the Church of Jesus Christ of Latter-day Saints, the Kennecott Copper Corporation and by many firms and individuals.

HISTORICAL SKETCHES OF MORMON TEMPLES

CAHOON FAMILIES PLAY IMPORTANT PARTS

This part of the addenda contains a brief history of each of the fourteen Latter-day Saint Temples built previous to the year 1960, also comments concerning several Cahoon-related families whose lives were closely connected with the histories of these temples. The descriptions, the dimensions, and other pertinent facts regarding the temples have been taken from The Improvement Era "Special Temple Issue" November, 1955; "Temples of the Most High" and from other publications.

It is desirable and important that these histories be included. First, because our Utah Pioneer Reynolds Cahoon, his sons and their descendants were active in the erection of many of these edifices; Second, because many related families played important roles in connection with them, several of whom held prominent positions; Third, because the history of the London and Swiss Temples contain a most interesting narrative regarding the country of our forefathers.

THE KIRTLAND TEMPLE

Dedicated March 27, 1836 by the Prophet Joseph Smith, Jr.

Yes, this was the first temple erected in this dispensation of time. Reynolds Cahoon was one of those "three appointed and ordained unto this power."* The size was eighty by fifty-nine feet; the walls fifty feet high, and the tower one hundred and ten feet. The two main halls were fifty-five feet in width and sixty-five feet in length in the inner court and built after the manner "Shown Unto Three."

Greater and more costly temples were erected, but we are told that none so taxed the energies of the people as the Kirtland Temple. The men worked unceasingly, with no thought of pay and the women were seldom equalled in the world's history for utter unselfishness. At the end of the building operations, the committee was some $13,000 in debt. The people were poor and the sacrifices were great.

*Doctrine and Covenants, Section 96, Verse 14. Also see Pages 23, 24, 25, herein

THE NAUVOO TEMPLE

Dedicated May 1, 1846 by Elder Orson Hyde

"For a baptismal font there is not upon the earth, that they, my saints, may be baptized for those who are dead. . . . But I command you, all ye my saints, to build a house unto me, and I will grant you a sufficient time."*

The Nauvoo Temple was the second temple built Reynolds Cahoon was appointed as one of the three members of the committee to supervise the building of this magnificent edifice. His sons took an active part in its construction. This book, "Reynolds Cahoon and His Stalwart Sons," contains a detailed account of the building of these first two temples in Kirtland and Nauvoo. (See Pages 33, 35, 37, 49, 51.)

THE ST. GEORGE TEMPLE

Dedicated April 6, 1877 by Daniel H. Wells.

This temple at St. George in southern Utah, was the third temple to be dedicated. President Wilford Woodruff stated at the fall Conference, 1877, that "the spirits of the dead gathered around him and asked why we did not redeem them. . . . These were the spirits of the Signers of the Declaration of Independence."

President Woodruff was then president of the temple. He went into the baptismal font and asked Brother McAllister to baptize him for them and for other eminent men The names of these men are on the temple records.

SPIRITUAL MANIFESTATIONS

In recording the biographies of Reynolds Cahoon and his Sons, and in the historical events incident to their temples, much has been mentioned as to the manifestations of spiritual beings — the visitation to the Temple of Jesus, Angels, Peter, James, and John, Elias, Elijah, and other heavenly beings.

We may ponder and ask the question: What about these spiritual visitations, these revelations and these manifestations? Did Reynolds Cahoon and our Mormon Pioneer ancestors believe in such?

---

*Doctrine and Covenants, Section 124, Verses 29-31.

Yes, we claim they did! In a much different manner, however, than the "Knocking and writing mediums or clairvoyance." The Latter-day Saints claim that the Gospel was again restored through direct revelation and visitation from God and other heavenly beings. They accept the principle, the philosophy of communication between worlds and believe that "the living may hear from the dead."

These Mormon people are members of the Church of Jesus Christ of Latter-day Saints, and as the name signifies, they accept Jesus Christ as their head and their medium and the only name under Heaven through which they may approach God, the Eternal Father. Bible history is replete with incidents of God and Heavenly beings, walking and talking with the Prophets and Saints of former days

One of the purposes for which they build their temples, is that this House of the Lord or Holy Temple on earth, when prepared and dedicated to the Lord, may be a sanctuary of Holy Communication between God or his angels and men.

This, then, may briefly explain the differences between spiritual manifestations of the so-called "mediums" and the manner in which prophets and Holy men of any dispensation, receive revelations and communications from God.

In the St George Temple, many Cahoon relatives have performed ordinances for their loved ones, and many descendants of Reynolds Cahoon were among the earliest settlers there when the pioneers were called to build that part of the State of Utah.

THE LOGAN TEMPLE
Dedicated May 17, 1884 by President John Taylor

The Logan Temple is located in the northern part of the State of Utah. It was the fourth temple dedicated in this dispensation. Elder Truman O. Angell was the architect. Elder George Q. Cannon remarked at the laying of the cornerstones, that every temple that was completed weakened the power of Satan on earth. There are many personal testimonies that the adversary made every attempt to discourage the workmen of this temple

Similar to the School of the Prophets at the Kirtland Temple, a school was organized at the Logan Temple where various subjects from theology to science were taught.

Newell Spencer Cahoon of the Daniel S. Cahoon family* resides at Logan. He has served as a Bishop of the Church and his wife, Hortense Terry Cahoon, has been an ordinance worker in the temple for many years.

Among the temple and genealogical workers of the Logan and Salt Lake Temples are the descendants of William F. Cahoon,* son of Reynolds The related members of the Cahoon family are the Durfee, Sharp, Angell, Smith, Ensign, Irons, Young, Curtis, Buck, Nelson, Briggs, Underlick, Moss, Tingey, Harris, Price, and Richardson families. Many of these families reside at Bountiful, Utah. They have fulfilled L.D.S. missions and do work at the temples.

CAHOON-TAYLOR FAMILY

President John Taylor's son, Apostle John W. Taylor, married Janet Woolley, daughter of Rachel Cahoon and Samuel W. Woolley. The children of Janet and Apostle Taylor are grandchildren of President John Taylor who dedicated this beautiful temple.

**President John Taylor is a direct descendant of Edward I of England and Eleanor of Castile. Edward I had a daughter, Princess Joan of Arc, who married a second husband, Ralph de Monthermer. It is through Joan of Arc and her second husband that the Taylor line is traced.

President Brigham Young and the Prophet Joseph Smith are descendants through Princess Joan of Arc and her first husband, Gilbert de Clare.

THE MANTI TEMPLE
Dedicated May 21, 1888 by Elder Lorenzo Snow

This is the fifth beautiful temple. It is built upon a solid hill or mountain of Rock. Daniel H Wells was the first President of the Temple Brigham Young, in selecting the site, stated: "Here is the spot where the prophet Moroni stood and dedicated this piece of ground for a temple site and that is the reason why the location is made here, and we can't move it from this spot .."

---

*See biographies and genealogies in "The Cahoon Story."
**Joseph Sudweek's "The Principles and Practice of Genealogy", page 45. (Arc also spelled Acre.)

The cost of this temple was about $1,000,000. W H Folsom was the architect and superintendent. William Farrington Cahoon, son of Reynolds, was one of the speakers at the time of the dedication.

Many spiritual manifestations have been experienced in this beautiful temple On the first day, voices of a heavenly choir were heard by many and visitations by the earlier prophets, signified its acceptance.

To this little valley, came a grandson of Reynolds Cahoon, James Cordon Cassen Cahoon, son of William F Cahoon James C. C. was born October 9, 1847 at Winter Quarters, Nebraska and was a pioneer with Brigham Young's Company in 1848. He was City Sexton for six years at Manti, where he resided from 1861 until 1901, when he moved to Canada.

Margaret Ellen Cahoon, daughter of James C. C. married Leonard Adelbert Shomaker in the Manti Temple Oct. 29, 1890. In 1897, they traveled by team to Canada but later returned to Manti. In 1914, she was left a widow. In 1931, she was called as an ordinance worker in the Manti Temple, which position she held for 15 years.

Members of the Daniel Stiles Cahoon* family reside in Manti, Hinckley, Oasis, Delta, Fillmore and Deseret, Millard County, Utah. The numerous posterity of the Maxfield and Bishop families also reside there Of these are the related families of Larson, Shales, Johnson, Stocks, Bennett, Black and many others.

The children of George Weight Cahoon and Angie Harmon reside in Deseret, Millard County, Utah, their son Dr Garth Arthur and family are at Riverside, California at the present time Children of Henry Wise Hawley were born at Oasis and Deseret, Utah Their daughter, Vera Hawley, married Rulon Clark McMurrin, son of President Joseph W. McMurrin, of the California Mission. Vera and Rulon reside in Los Angeles, California.

The children of Raymond S. Bishop and his wife Annie Maria Hilton were born in Deseret, Delta and Hinckley, Utah These parents and children have performed many L.D.S. Missions. Their son, Verdell Ray, served on a mission to Czechoslovakia and later was appointed Bishop of Hinckley Ward. John R. Bennett and his wife Margaret Cahoon have done

---

*See biographies and genealogies of these families in "The Cahoon Story"

much genealogical and temple work. Their children were born in Deseret.

The Cahoon-related families of Argyle, Child, Peay, Bingham, Patten, Christensen, Manwill, Mendenhall and others reside in the vicinity of Spanish Fork. Reid S Cahoon and wife Belva Darling, now of Spanish Fork, Utah, resided for many years in Manti, Utah, and performed ordinance work at the Manti Temple. Royal Brinkerhoff and wife Beatrice of Bicknell, Utah, are missionaries and temple workers. Probably some members of the Daniel Stiles Cahoon family also reside near St. George, Utah.

THE SALT LAKE TEMPLE
Dedicated April 6, 1893 by President Wilford Woodruff

The Salt Lake Temple was the sixth great temple to be dedicated. Regarding it, Brigham Young stated "This temple must stand through the Millennium. We shall build it of the best materials that can be obtained in the mountains of North America."

"We moved westward," said Brigham Young, "and being led by Jehovah, we arrived at this place. Of our journey hither, we need say nothing, only God led us. Of the sufferings of those who were compelled to, and did, leave Nauvoo in the winter of 1846, we need say nothing. Those who experienced it know it and those who did not, to tell them of it would be like exhibiting a beautiful painting to a blind man."

The Salt Lake Temple was built as it was shown to Brigham Young in vision. Twice in the forty years required to build it the entire excavation was filled in and rebuilt. Those Utah Pioneers never tired, they never ceased. Well might it stand through a thousand years. The walls are built of solid granite blocks and are sixteen feet thick at the foundation, tapering to six feet at the top. There are four spiral staircases, 172 granite steps, each step is 6 ft long and weighs over 1,700 pounds. The entire area is 21,850 feet.

A statue of the angel Moroni, blowing a trumpet, proclaiming the restoration of the Gospel, rests upon the center tower of the temple. It is of hammered copper, heavily gilded with pure gold leaf, and is twelve feet five and one-half inches in height. The cost of the temple was $4,000,000. Truman O. Angell was the architect. This temple and the organ in the Tabernacle have become world famous.

Naamah Tripp Cahoon and Daniel Farrington Cahoon
Salt Lake Temple Workers
Family Historians and Genealogists

Naamah Tripp, wife of Daniel F. Cahoon and daughter of Enoch Bartlett Tripp and Jessie Smith Eddins, compiled an extensive genealogical and historical record of the Tripp and Eddins families. Naamah and Daniel F. were temple workers in the Salt Lake Temple.

Daniel F. spent many years searching out genealogy and histories of the Cahoon and Carruth families of America and of Scotland. First, as a hobby, then being convinced of the importance of preserving family records, Daniel F. endeavored to compile a most complete historical account of his kinfolk.

The information from his family records has been his generous, unselfish contribution to this Utah Pioneer Story — and to him this book is dedicated.

See pages 2, 52, 56, 133.

Family of James Cordon Cassen Cahoon

Descendants of William F. Cahoon

Pioneers of Utah and Canada — Temple Workers and Temple Builders

James C. C. Cahoon* married Ellen Spencer Wilson, first wife, and Martha Braithwaite, second wife. By them he had sixteen children. In the above picture taken about year 1917, some members of this pioneer family are shown. The younger children are now married.

Back Row: Maggie M. Nelson, Della C. Lenz, Martha Nielsen, James C. Cahoon and Baby Ellen, Barbara Dietrick Cahoon, Mary M. Hall, Margaret E. Shomaker, Annie L. Alder Cahoon. Second Row: LeMaughn Cahoon, Francis F. Nielsen, Joseph Hall, George E. Cahoon, Leonard Cahoon, Edward Hall. Third Row: Martha H. Braithwaite Cahoon, James Cordon Cassen Cahoon, Mrs. Dietrick. Front Row: Roy D. Cahoon, Thelma D. Cahoon (Court), Cordon C. Cahoon, Annie D. Cahoon (Romney), Lloyd D. Cahoon.

Sons of Leslie C. and Mary Leavitt Cahoon

Pioneers of Leavitt, Canada.

(Story of Leavitt, Alberta, Canada, page 157.)

Back Row,
James Dewey
Edwin T.
Edward C.
Golden L.

Front Row:
Lawrence
Leslie C.
Jerald Lavar

In this temple are recorded visitations of heavenly personages. The Lord, Jesus Christ, our Saviour, appeared and conversed with President Lorenzo Snow. President Snow leaves us his testimony that the Lord came to the temple in answer to his fervent prayer asking for the Lord's guidance and instructions; that he talked with the Lord face to face, that the Lord stood before him in beautiful White Robes. His hands, feet and countenance were of a glorious whiteness and brightness He stood about three feet above the floor as though on a plate of solid gold.

CAHOON-ANGELL FAMILY*
By Mrs Ermina Angell Naff

"Two daughters of William Farrington Cahoon married two sons of Solomon Angell and Eunice C. Young. Prudence Sarah Ermina Cahoon, daughter of William F., married John Osborn Angell and her sister Thirza Vilate Cahoon, daughter of William F., married Albert Angell. John O. and Albert are nephews of Truman O. Angell, architect of the Salt Lake Temple."

Ermina Angell Naff continues· "I have traced my lineage to Thomas Angell, the New England Pilgrim. Thomas came on the first boat with Roger Williams. I am the daughter of Solomon Angell of John Osborn, of Solomon, of James Williams, son of Thomas Angell." Mary Ann Angell, daughter of James Williams Angell, married Brigham Young.

CAHOON-EREKSON FAMILY
By Mary L. S Putnam

Andrew Alonzo Cahoon, son of Andrew and Margaret Carruth Cahoon, married Mary Ann Erekson*, daughter of Jonas Erekson, pioneer of 1849 and Mary Powell, pioneer of 1848 Alonzo and Jonas were engaged in mining and in sheep and cattle raising in Utah. Jonas was one of the first merchants in Murray, Utah Mary Powell, wife of Jonas, was a prominent professional nurse and doctor. Norman W Erekson, son of Jonas, spent many years as a temple worker at the Salt Lake Temple. Zelph Young Erekson and William Shirley Erekson, grandsons of Jonas Erekson and his second wife, Isabella Markham Benbow, have served as mission presidents in the Australian and Swiss missions, respectively.

*See "The Cahoon Story" for biographies and genealogy

Raymond Spencer Cahoon and his wife, Louie Morrison Cahoon were ordinance workers for nine years at the temple. Raymond S. was the son of Orson Spencer Cahoon, son of Daniel Stiles, son of Reynolds. Raymond S. was Assistant Chief of Police in Salt Lake City and is now Chief of Police in Blanding, San Juan County, Utah.

A large majority of the descendants of Andrew Cahoon* reside near Salt Lake City and neighboring settlements. The Carruth, Stiles, Young and the Cahoon-related families are too numerous to mention in this volume. Their genealogies and biographies are recorded in the "The Cahoon Story." Andrew Cahoon had nineteen children. He married three Carruth sisters and through each came a large posterity. Andrew's children intermarried with families of McOmie, Copeland, Winder, Gordon, Erekson, Davis, Tripp, Bernhardt, Mackay, Carlisle, Woolley, Proctor, Haynes, Morgan, Covey and Spencer. Many of these family members have done ordinance work in the Salt Lake Temple.

THE HAWAIIAN TEMPLE
Dedicated November 27, 1919 by President Heber J. Grant.

This temple is the seventh temple and is located on the Island of Oahu at Laie, one of the northern groups of the Hawaiian Islands. It is on a moderately high hill with a beautiful view of the Pacific Ocean. In 1864, the Latter-day Saints Church purchased a 6500-acre tract located about thirty-two miles north of Honolulu, known as the "Plantation of Laie." Here a temple costing about $265,000 was built.

The land was dry and it was a most foreboding place. The few people there lived near a small streamlet in the hills. In 1884, President Joseph F. Smith blessed the land and prophesied that there would be water upon the land and that it would be a gathering place for the Saints. Wells were drilled for water and now the land has irrigating streams and wells of flowing water *

In 1916 construction work on the temple was begun Ralph Edwin Woolley was the builder; the architects were Pope and Burton. Crushed volcanic rock, reinforced with steel, was used

---

*Information furnished by Preston Parkinson and also by Ray E Dillman, former president of the Temple. See also "The Cahoon Story"

as a concrete, hence, the building is a monolith of artificial stone — a cream-white structure which may be said to be literally hewn out of a single stone. It is built in the form of a Greek Cross. Its artistic landscaping, cement walks and three oblong pool terraces, descending the gentle slope to the sands of the Beach, with one large circular pool just above the highway of the sanded beach, presents a beautiful picture.

Elder Samuel Edwin Woolley who was completing almost a quarter century of presiding over the Latter-day Saints of the Hawaiian Mission, was a speaker at the dedication of the temple. His remarks at this time, 1919, were printed in the Improvement Era of November 1955. They were as follows:

"This land, the land of Laie, was one of the cities of refuge in olden times and now it is a city of refuge indeed, both to the spirit and body of man. . . When President George Q. Cannon visited here, fifty years after the gospel had been established, he told us, both at Laie and Honolulu, that the time would soon come when we would have a house in which to perform the ordinances necessary for the salvation of the living and the dead."

William W. Waddoups was appointed first President of the Temple, serving from 1919 to 1930. Ralph Edwin Woolley was fourth president, 1935 to 1936 and also ninth president, 1944 to 1953. Ray E Dillman was president in 1956.

Samuel Edwin Woolley Family

Samuel Edwin Woolley, born October 22, 1859, in Salt Lake City, Utah, was the son of Samuel Wickersham Woolley and Maria Angell. Samuel E. is a half-brother to the children of Rachel Cahoon Woolley, daughter of Andrew Cahoon, son of Reynolds Cahoon.*

Samuel Edwin Woolley married Alice Rowberry of Grantsville on May 6, 1895 and on August 9, 1895 he was appointed to preside over the Hawaiian Mission. Here he resided with his family for twenty-four years. He directed the labors of hundreds of missionaries, had charge of the erection of the temple and operated the affairs of the pineapple plantation of the church at Laie T. H. He was honorably released July 1, 1922 and returned to Utah, where he died April 3, 1925.

---

*History taken from the Daniel F. Cahoon Family Records, also from the Family Records of Samuel E and Ralph E. Woolley, kept by Mrs Ralph E Woolley.

Ralph Edwin Woolley, son of Samuel E., was born March 4, 1886, in Grantsville, Utah. When he was nine years old, he accompanied his parents to the Sandwich Islands He returned to Utah to complete his education, graduating from the University of Utah with the degree of a civil engineer. He became one of the best known contractors and builders in the Islands. He was the building constructor of the Hawaiian L.D.S. Temple, the Oahu Stake Center at Honolulu, the Royal Hawaiian Hotel and many other buildings.

December 8, 1920 he married Jeanette Romania Hyde, born August 2, 1892 at Salt Lake City, Utah, daughter of Joseph Smith Hyde and Jeanette L. Alcord Romania had been living with her parents in Hawaii while her mother held an appointment as collector of customs of the port of Honolulu.

Romania is a granddaughter of Orson Hyde, one of the early apostles of the Latter-day Saints Church.

The first Latter-day Saint stake off the mainland of North America was organized June 30, 1935 with Ralph Edwin Woolley as president. He held this position for sixteen years, concurrently holding the position as president of the Temple at Laie. Seldom has the same individual held two such positions. On September 15, 1957, he died in his home on the Islands.

Ralph E. and Romania had one daughter, Virginia Jeanette Woolley, born September 30, 1921 in Honolulu. She was married on June 6, 1942 to Jay Ambrose Quealy Jr , born April 3, 1919, son of Jay Ambrose Quealy and Lottie Jacketta McCune. After serving as bishop of Waikiki, Jay A. Quealy Jr , was appointed President of the Honolulu Stake.

Thousands of visitors go to Honolulu annually and their tour of the Island includes the "Mormon Temple". Here they are given literature and information concerning the temple and the gospel. The Latter-day Saints feel that their leaders were inspired when they decided to build a temple on one of the Hawaiian Islands.

THE CANADIAN TEMPLE
Dedicated August 26, 1923 by President Heber J. Grant

The Canadian Temple is the eighth temple built by the Church. It is located in Cardston, Alberta, Canada. The architectural design of this beautiful temple is unique and impressive. It is described as having "a Grecian massiveness, a Peruvian touch and is similar only to the ancient temples of the Aztecs and other aborigines of Central and South America " About thirty feet from the sidewalk is an artistic frieze of cast concrete, the subject is that of Jesus and "The Samaritan Woman at the Well " It has ornamental flower beds, small fish ponds and a roof garden over the first floor.

The cost of this temple was $1,000,000 Our Cahoon cousins, descendants of Reynolds, were most active in its construction and in the building of the city of Cardston, Alberta and the outlying settlements

Apostle John W Taylor, who married Janet Woolley, daughter of Rachel Cahoon, daughter of Andrew Cahoon, was one of the first settlers of Cardston It was John W. who prophesied the exact spot of the Temple Regarding the country of Alberta, Canada he said:

"This land will be the breadbasket of the world; and this temple shall be reared to the worship of Almighty God "

James Cordon Casson Cahoon, son of William F Cahoon, moved with his family, in the year 1901 from Manti, Utah, to Cardston. His first wife Ellen Spencer Wilson died in 1880 leaving a family of young children He married Martha Hannah Braithwaite, his second wife and by his two wives he was the father of sixteen children.

From this honored man, have descended many respected citizens of Utah and Canada· the families of Margaret Shomaker, Mary Maranda Hall, Martha Amelia Nielson, Orah Casson Martin, Della C. Lenz, and the many other fine Cahoon sons and their wives who have been colonizers, builders, civic and religious workers.

James C and his brother George Edward founded the Cahoon Hotel and other places of business George E was a bishop for about eighteen years and his son Lervae now holds his father's position as bishop of Leavitt Ward Lloyd D. Cahoon, son of James C. was appointed to the presidency of the Cardston Temple.

Many descendants of William F.,* son of Reynolds, are workers at this temple. Mary Isabella Martin and husband, John James Coombs reside in Calgary, Alberta, Canada John

---

*See Histories and Genealogies in "The Cahoon Story "

J. was born in Nottingham, England and during his leave as overseas Pilot Officer, he did L.D.S. missionary work there. Mary Isabella and John have served on several missions in Canada. They also were called to the Blackfoot Indians at Gleichen, Alberta. Minnie Amelia Martin and husband, Earl Blaine Gallup reside in Cardston and have done much genealogical and temple work. Earl B. has traced the Gallup family line to the year 1465 when John Gallup "came out of the North" in the fifth year of the reign of Edward IV.

THE ARIZONA TEMPLE

Dedicated October 23, 1927 by President Heber J. Grant

This is the ninth temple. Like the Hawaiian and Canadian Temples it has neither spires nor towers. Its architecture is Colonial in appearance, but it is really an American adaptation of Classic architecture. At night the illumination of the exterior reflects into a mirrored pool creating a replica of this beautiful temple. Work on the temple at Mesa, Arizona was begun November 23, 1923 and in a period of four years it was completed and dedicated.

It is known as the Lamanite Temple, and all the Lamanite records are kept there. It was built especially for the Lamanites (Indians) to receive their endowments whenever they are ready. However, people of all nationalities are doing temple work there the same as in other temples.

Spiritual manifestations and visitations of heavenly nature have occurred, and remarkable confirmations of authentic pedigree history have been made known to the workers at this temple. At the Arizona Temple, as in many other temples, the descendants of Reynolds Cahoon have officiated for their loved ones.

John Boyd Cahoon Jr., and his wife Faye Amelia Tilby, resided in Phoenix, Arizona and performed ordinance work at the Arizona and Los Angeles Temples. Stewart C. Shurtleff, great grandson of Andrew Cahoon served on a Temple Mission to the Arizona Temple and after his return, the genealogical committee of Glendale Stake, California, reported that most of the temple work of the Stake for that period of time, had been done by this one young man. Stewart assisted in tracing the Shurtleff Family ancestral pedigree chart (purportedly) as far back as our first parents, Adam and Eve.

Dell Spencer Cahoon, descendant of Andrew, and Stanley Irven Cahoon, descendant of Daniel S. reside in Scottsdale, Arizona Stanley is the Phoenix branch manager of the Regional Sign Supply Inc of Salt Lake City, Utah.

THE IDAHO FALLS TEMPLE
Dedicated Sept. 23, 1945 by President George Albert Smith

This is the tenth temple. The architecture of this most beautiful edifice is strictly modern in style. On the West, flow the waters of the Snake River and the Temple can be seen from a distance of many miles. Its foundation is a solid bed of lava rock Some of the marble used in its construction came from Utah but most of it was imported from France, Italy and Sweden. Wide cement walks inlaid with blocks of native stone of various colors, lead up to three ponds or lagoons built of concrete. The cost of this edifice, with furnishings and landscaping was $700,000.

This beautiful temple is in the vicinity of numerous homes of the Cahoon descendants, who attend it and enjoy its blessings.

Many of the children of Rais Bell C. R Cahoon and his wife, Mary Charlotte Johnson, have resided in Idaho. Their homes were in Preston, Oneida County; Mink Creek, Franklin County; Gentile Valley, Cache County; Thatcher, Bannock County; Lava Hot Springs; Inkom; and in Idaho Falls, Idaho.

The Panter family, the Hymas family, the Richards, Tolman, Stewart, Byington, Fowler, Allen, Bennett, Walton, Bevens, Jacobson, Eskelson, Hansen, Ranson and other Cahoon-related families* reside in these various communities. Many are genealogical and temple workers.

The family of Mahonri Moriancumer Cahoon also resided in Idaho and many of his descendants are there. The related families,* Winzeler, Timson, Wilson, Anderson, Kempton, Simper, Shuey, Driscoll, Youngblood, Donnelly, Paget, Meyer, Dillinger, Bertoch, Lenroot, Camphouse, Gorman, Zollinger, Perry, Fehring, Anderson, Heath, Wilson, Belliston, Hartshorne, Scott, Sine, Hansen, Eby, Edwards, Major, Johnson, Mitchell, Bridge, Thomas, Lawrence, Woolston, Kinsley, Searcy, Browning and others have made their homes in Rexburg, Idaho Falls and the neighboring towns. There are also

---

*See biographies and geneaology in "The Cahoon Story"

the Cahoon-related families of Dundas, Nankervis, Taenger, Hill, Ausherman, Preece, Hutchison, Olsen, Booth, Bronson, Netzley, Galbraith, Garcia, Brown, Aumiller, McMillan, Hansen, Winchester and Stoddard.

Judge Miles R. Cahoon and family resided in Rexburg, Idaho. Dr. Reynolds Fehring Cahoon is an anathesiologist in Salt Lake City. Chloe Winchester of the Mahonri M. family married Orson Sanders who served as Bishop in the Malta Ward, Idaho. Margaret Isabell Mackay, descendant of Andrew Cahoon, her husband Edward Lish Hoagland and their eight sons reside in Melba, Idaho. They are active Temple workers.

May we hesitate and again record the relationship of our Cahoon-Pioneer family members to the Presidencies of the Church of Jesus Christ of Latter-day Saints. One was President George Albert Smith, who dedicated the Idaho Falls temple. The other was John Rex Winder, First Counsellor to President Joseph F. Smith.

CAHOON-WINDER-HORNE-SMITH*

Mary Shepherd Horne, born November 26, 1890, Salt Lake City, Utah, married on December 23, 1916 to Leo Cahoon Winder, born September 20, 1887, Salt Lake City, Utah.

Mary was the daughter of Alice Smith Merrill (Horne) who was the daughter of Bathsheba Smith (Merrill), who was the daughter of President George Albert Smith.

Leo C. was the son of Richard Henry Winder who was the son of John Rex Winder Leo died October 8, 1940. His mother was Mary Emma Cahoon Winder, daughter of Andrew Cahoon and Mary Carruth

Through these prominent leaders of the Church, the children of Mary and Leo C. Winder may trace their ancestry to the very earliest period of time.

THE SWISS TEMPLE
Dedicated Sept. 11, 1955 by President David O. McKay

The Swiss Temple is the eleventh temple erected in this dispensation. It is located about three miles north of Bern in Munchenbuchsee, Zollikofen, Switzerland. The site is higher

---

*For biographies and genealogies of these families see "The Cahoon Story"

than the surrounding area and faces south toward Bern and the Alps. Edward O. Anderson was the architect of the Temple.

HISTORY OF THE SWISS TEMPLE

Excerpts from the Records of Pres. Samuel E. Bringhurst

A conference was held in Copenhagen, Denmark on July 5, 6, 7, 1950. The presidents of ten European Missions were in attendance Elder John A. Widstoe who represented the General Authorities of the Church, asked what could be done to stem the heavy emigration of saints to America. It was the unanimous opinion that a temple in Europe would stop most of it.

April, 1952 the General Authorities agreed that a temple should be built in Switzerland. President Samuel E. Bringhust of the Swiss-Austrian Mission recommended Bern or that area. After continuous praying, searching and inspecting of properties, a visit was made to the castle of a wealthy lady, Fran Elizabeth De Meuron who owned certain property and resided ten miles south of Bern.

The missionaries had been informed that it would be impossible to get an audience with her. President Bringhurst said: "After praying about it, Elder Newman, Elder Hill and I drove out to the castle . . . she was very courteous and invited us in through the outer gates and as she asked us to have Linden Bluten tea with her, she remarked, "I remember you Mormons have your Word of Wisdom which precludes most of the things other people enjoy but I commend you for it." Linden Bluten tea is made from dried blossoms of the Linden tree.

She explained that the court was in control of her property and a recent request had been denied. Several negotiations were made on other properties, each attempt resulting in disappointment. President Bringhurst continues:

"Mr. Schulthess and I inspected property in and around Bern considered large enough and suitable for our use. We selected two pieces but were undecided which one to recommend. We prayed earnestly about it and drove to Basel and took Sister Bringhurst to see them. After looking them over carefully we left When about five miles out, I turned around and drove back over the two properties again. As Sister Bringhurst and I got out of the car and walked across the one, we both had a peaceful satisfied feeling come over us and we were sure that was the place where the Lord wished His Temple built."

President McKay authorized President Bringhurst to purchase this piece of property containing approximately seven acres of land at a total cost of $186,000, including the hard-surfacing of the streets. So when President and Sister Bringhurst were released from the Swiss-Austrian Mission on January 1, 1953, they took to Salt Lake City, the title papers to the Temple Site and delivered them to the First Presidency of the Church.

In April 1953 Elder Bringhurst was sent back to Switzerland to obtain the building permit and close a street running east and west through the property, he was also requested to investigate availability of building materials. A burnt tile material manufactured in Germany was chosen for facing

SITE DEDICATION AND GROUND-BREAKING CEREMONIES

The sun came up clear and bright August 5, 1953. President and Sister McKay, Dr. Lewelyn R. McKay, their son, and President William F. Pershon were driven to the temple site by Elder Samuel Bringhurst. Describing this, Elder Bringhurst writes: "We drove around and upon the site. With the little town of Zollikofen in the immediate foreground, the City of Bern beyond, the wonderful Alps in the distance, with the sun shining on their snow-capped peaks and the beautiful forest in the rear, it presented a picture that will be remembered and especially by President McKay and others who were seeing it for the first time.

"Then President McKay put both hands on my shoulders and looked at me with those wonderful piercing eyes and said, 'I thank you for this accomplishment. It is wonderful, even more than we had hoped.' Those words lifted a tremendous load of responsibility I had carried for more than a year and I shall always be grateful to President McKay for them."

President David O. McKay offered the Dedicatory Prayer at the Ground-Breaking Ceremonies William Zimmer, William F. Pershon, A. Hamer Reiser, Samuel E. Bringhurst, Dr. Llewelyn McKay, and Edward O. Anderson made remarks. Two hymns were sung and a solo, "The Holy City" was rendered by Sister J. Gotzenberger.

At the spot designated as the southeast corner of the Temple, ground was broken President McKay removed the first shovelful of dirt and asked Samuel E Bringhurst to remove the second. Mayor Dr. Walter Rauber, Recorder Schneider, Mr. Herman Schulthess, Mr. Hans Jordi and approximately six hundred missionaries and members were in attendance.

November 13, 1954 the cornerstone was laid Each article to be placed in the cornerstone was inspected by President Stephen L. Richards. President William F. Perschon handed these articles to Samuel E. Bringhurst who placed them in the copper box after reading each one in English. President Pershon read them in German. Between five and six hundred people were present. President Richards spoke and Elder Peter Loscher translated. Brother Bringhurst offered the closing prayer.

June 10, 1955 Brother Henry D Moyle of the Council of Twelve and Samuel E Bringhurst began to check and revise the German translation of the Temple Ordinances, which required considerable time and was all done in the Salt Lake Temple. Elder Richard L. Evans and Brother Gordon B. Hinckley were given the responsibility of filming the Temple Ceremony in the various foreign languages.

June 30, 1955 Elder Bringhurst was told it was the unanimous decision of the First Presidency that he should be the first president of the Swiss Temple and President David O. McKay set him apart for this position.

"Of all positions to which I have been called," Elder Bringhurst writes, "being first President of the first European Temple was the most sobering one of my life "

Referring to the Temple he states, "This is the first of a new type of Temple. We remain in one room and the changes are made by projecting them on the screen and we leave it only when we go through the Veil into the Celestial room. The responsibility of this position is tremendous and frightening, but with the help of the Lord and the humble willing people we will succeed "

Approximately two thousand non-members including City, County and Government officials were shown through the Temple during the two days of September 8th and 9th. More than twenty thousand visited the building during construction, and several were baptized as a result.

DEDICATION OF THE SWISS TEMPLE

"The day of the dedication had arrived It was Sunday, September 11, 1955 and the surrounding lawn and flowers were glorious As President David O. McKay and Sister McKay entered the building, the missionaries, standing in reverent silence, formed a pathway for them. The services were held in the Celestial room, the Salt Lake Tabernacle Choir was seated in a circle around this room and in the main assembly room.

President McKay presided and conducted the meeting. He announced the first hymn to be sung in the sacred edifice — "The Morning Breaks, the Shadows Flee." Invocation was offered by President William F. Pershon, after which the choir sang, "Holiness Becomes the House of the Lord." Addresses were given by President Samuel E Bringhurst and Elder Ezra Taft Benson, after which President McKay delivered the dedicatory address and the Dedicatory Prayer. Miss Ewan Harbrecht, soloist with the choir, sang, "Bless This House."

The General Authorities of the Church in attendance were: President McKay who presided and conducted, Elder Spencer Kimball, Ezra Taft Benson, Elder Henry D. Moyle and Elder Richard L. Evans Nine sessions were held and at each session President McKay gave the Dedicatory Prayer.

In closing the history of the Swiss Temple, we wish to add that President Samuel E. Bringhurst is the nephew of Daniel Farrington and Naamah Tripp Cahoon. He is the son of John B and Emma Frances Tripp Bringhurst. Namah and Emma were sisters. President Bringhurst was born Jan. 27, 1890. He was married in the Salt Lake Temple, Dec. 9, 1909, to Lenora Kemp, born Feb. 14, 1892, the daughter of William Kemp and Adaline Carter.

Samuel E. and Lenora have held many responsible positions of the L.D.S. Church. They reside in Murray, Utah and have four children.

THE LOS ANGELES TEMPLE
Dedicated March 11, 1956 by David O McKay

On a prominent hill, near Westwood, Los Angeles, California, the twelfth Latter-day Saints' Temple was built The spire of this magnificent temple can be seen from such distant points as San Pedro, Catalina Island and from ships twenty-five miles out at sea. The spire is 257 feet above the first floor, the temple is 364 feet wide and 241 feet deep and contains 190,-614 square feet of floor space, or approximately four and one half acres The temple contains ninety rooms; the largest is the assembly room seating 2,600 people Edward O. Anderson was the architect.

The task of raising a million dollars required to build it seemed a tremendous project, but the people of Southern California never hesitated. The response was immediate and overwhelming In April 1952, the Stake President reported not $1,000,000, but that $1,648,613.17 had been received in money and pledges.

The exterior of the temple is covered with Mo-Sai stone facing of crushed quartz and white Portland cement "The quartz of cast stone and the quartz in the granite are in harmony and each gives the same life to the wall surface in daylight; they sparkle in the sunshine, and glow in the flood-lights at night " The statue of the Angel Moroni is the creation of Millard F. Malin. It is of cast aluminum covered with gold leaf.

The murals inside the temple are unbelievably beautiful — planted areas filled with potted flowers and plants blend harmoniously with the murals. Carpets and draperies are of highest grade and blend into a symphony of indescribable beauty. One is impressed with the magnitude and beauty of the building and grounds, with the pool, the rose gardens and the fountains.

In 1937, the Church purchased the Harold Lloyd estate which comprised 24.23 acres. The temple site now includes thirteen acres. The remainder of the ground is occupied by a Bureau of Information, a heating plant, the California Mission home and the Westwood Ward chapel.

"In the process of time the shores of the Pacific may yet be overlooked from the temple of the Lord " This message which contains a note of prophecy, was part of an epistle sent from Brigham Young and Willard Richards from the Salt Lake Valley in August 1847, to the Saints in California

Now the Saints on the "shores of the Pacific" have every reason to rejoice. Many of the descendants of the Utah Cahoon pioneers come from far distances to perform temple work. During the weeks the temple was open for visitors numerous volunteers assisted in the temple. The compiler of this book was at the temple many days escorting visitors and after the dedication of the temple, assisted in various departments.

Laurain Shomaker and Lydia Elizabeth Walburger, his wife, were among the first appointed ordinance workers of the temple. Laurain is the son of Margaret Cahoon Shoemaker who served fifteen years in the Manti Temple.

John Cahoon Franz and his wife Eva Burton have done much genealogical research and temple work John C, born September 16, 1908, was the son of Albert Luke Franz and Florence Adelaide Cahoon. He is a descendant of William Cahoon through Joseph and Hannah Kent Cahoon. Florence A., born November 2, 1908, is the daughter of Arthur Fielding Burton and Kittie Calpurnia Dixon. John C. and family reside in Berkeley, California.

THE NEW ZEALAND TEMPLE

Dedicated April 20, 1958 by President David O. McKay

This temple is the thirteenth temple and is referred to as a "Temple in the South Pacific." It is situated in the land of the Moari, near Hamilton, an inland city on the northern isle. The architect was Edward O. Anderson.

President David O. McKay assigned President Wendell B Mendenhall of the San Joaquin Stake to the special mission of investigatnig possible temple sites in these beautiful lands of the South Seas He investigated available lands near Auckland, New Zealand, where mission headquarters are located. He visited the college near Auckland and upon the majestic, beautiful hill nearby, he envisioned the Temple. This was the only strip of property separating the college grounds from the extensive Church farm lands.

The purchasing and erecting of this temple is truly a story of prophecy, vision and inspiration from God. When President David O McKay viewed the property, he said, "This is the place to build the temple." When the owners refused to sell, President McKay said: "They will sell it; They will sell it." The owners did agree to sell and the price asked was accepted by the Church.

Again, when a telephone message was received at their "hui tau", the annual all-mission conference, that the First Presidency desired a temple to be built, and that it was to be built, as was the college, entirely through volunteer missionary labor, all four thousand native members raised their hands and with tears of joy in their eyes, solemnly sustained the proposal.

Like some of the pioneers in Salt Lake Valley who learned their crafts while working on the Assembly Hall, a similar story is being written in New Zealand and many native workmen will be trained for specialized occupations.

The Polynesian Saints have long been a faithful, devoted people and now the members from the Australian, Samoan, Tongan and Tahitian Latter-day Saints Missions attend their beautiful temple, serving a membership of over 40,000 Saints.

Three brothers, Robert, William and John Carruth emigrated from Loanhead, Renfrewshire, Scotland to New Zealand in 1839. Robert died in South Australia, William died in Kamo, New Zealand and John died near Auckland, New Zealand William was one of the oldest colonists of the Whangarei district. He was an elder in the Presbyterian Church and one of its most liberal supporters. These brothers were relatives of the Carruth-Cahoon sisters and the Carruth Utah pioneers.

THE LONDON TEMPLE*
Dedicated September 7, 1958 by President David O. McKay

This temple is the fourteenth temple built by the Latter-day Saints. It is located at Newchapel, Surrey, England which is about twenty-five miles south of London. Newchapel was an old Elizabethan farm, and the remains of the old farmhouse can be seen in the present house which stands on the estate. This present house on the property although Elizabethan in style is only about thirty years old. Beautiful formal gardens occupy about one-third of the property, which is a site of natural beauty the year around.

The earliest record of Newchapel appears to be found in William the Conqueror's Doomsday Book The story of Newchapel, the site of the London Temple is a fascinating one A branch of the church has been established at Newchapel, and the genealogical offices of the British Mission have been moved to a remodeled building on the grounds.

---

*Improvement Era, November 1955

President Selvoy J. Boyer was appointed first president of the Temple. Elder Edward O. Anderson was the Temple architect, and Sir Thomas Bennett was the supervising architect of the British Temple

GROUND-BREAKING SERVICES OF LONDON TEMPLE

At ground-breaking services for the London Temple, Saturday, August 27, 1955, President McKay turned the first shovelful of earth and pronounced his benediction and blessing. Little did the people know that a prophet of God was in their midst. Official guests were there. The choir rendered the music. President McKay remarked: "The Tabernacle Choir, on its initial European tour, has already established a number of firsts. For the first time in the history of the Church, a group of members of the Church of Jesus Christ of Latter-day Saints was welcomed at Greenock by the Provost and Lady, uniformed band, bagpipes, kilts. For the first time, the Lord Provost and Lady of Glasgow greeted an organization of the Church in the Municipal Hall. For the first time in the history of the Church, the London County Council greeted members and officials of the choir..

"But this is not the first time that we have held ground-breaking ceremonies for a house of the Lord. . . . It is the first time in Great Britain. . . . We have now completed or have under construction fourteen temples in the Church and others are under consideration "

THE LAND OF OUR FOREFATHERS

In 1955, during the months of August and September, the Mormon Tabernacle Choir was on a Concert Tour, and it had been arranged that the European Tour would coincide with the Ground-Breaking ceremonies of the London Temple on August 27, and also the Dedication of The Swiss Temple on September eleventh.

President David O McKay and his party arrived in Scotland Thursday, August 18th where President Reiser and several Elders of the British Mission met them A sprig of Scotch heather was pinned on each one and a hearty welcome extended to all. How thrilled they were to be on Scotch soil! The President's party was formally received in the private chambers of the Lord and Lady Provost.

On the docks at Greenock, Scotland, the President's Party met the Tabernacle Choir which arrived on the S S Saxonia With the last boatload, came a Scotch bagpipe band in full regalia The Provost (mayor) of the city of Greenock and President McKay officially greeted the choir members and its representatives. On the docks along the Clyde River, the choir included in its songs the heart-touching "Come, Come, Ye Saints," and "On the Bonny, Bonny Banks of Loch Lomond." The Scots as well as Church members were deeply moved.

That afternoon the Choir, President McKay and party were graciously entertained by Mr. and Mrs. Andrew Hood, the Lord and Lady Provost of Glasgow. In the beautiful marble hall, the Lord Provost gave an address of welcome He stated in his remarks that this "is the first time that a body of Latter-day Saints has been formally received in Glasgow " He decried the prejudice, ignorance, and injustice of the past toward our people, and stated that the days of persecution no longer exist in Scotland

President McKay responded by telling of his great love for Scotland and of his deep appreciation for the cordial welcome that had been extended the Choir and his party. No one in the room realized better than President McKay how bitter the persecution of the past had been He recalled that fifty-eight years before he would "hardly have dared set foot on the steps of the City Chambers of Glasgow." When he visited Stirling Castle, he pointed out the plaque and repeated the words, "Whate'er Thou Art, Act Well Thy Part." He recalled that as a discouraged and homesick missionary this motto was a direct message to him.

Yes, in Rossdhu, Luss, Loch Lomond, the hereditary chiefs o fthe Colquhoun Clan have resided since the year 1160 They were a home-loving people, however during Oliver Cromwell's regime, these political refugees moved to Ulster, Ireland where they remained for one hundred years. Many Scots migrated to Sweden, Germany, England and America, where the spelling "Colquhoun" is found in various forms Our Carruth, Barr, Young and Stewart family ancestors resided in Renfrewshire. Margaret Carruth tells us that we are descendants of Mary, Queen of Scots.

How thrilled was President McKay to visit Robert Burns Memorial Cottage, Sir Walter Scott's Monument and the house from which John Knox preached his sermons. Scotland, the land of our forbears!

IN RETROSPECT

As we relate the events of this glorious tour of the Tabernacle Choir in 1955, the cordial welcome extended to them and to President McKay and his party by the Lord and Lady Provost and people of Europe, may our thoughts return to the incidents of 1846. One hundred and nine years prior to this date, a young Mormon missionary, Andrew Cahoon, sailed from New York to Scotland to serve on his European mission.

Saying farewell to loved ones and with little money for his expenses, he embarked on his voyage. For forty days the ship on which he sailed encountered terrific storms and after it had been reported "Lost and All on Board Drowned," he arrived in Great Britain among strangers, where the teachings of Mormonism had been grossly misrepresented.

Again, let us recall the voyage to America made by our Cahoon and Carruth pioneer ancestors, one hundred-twelve years ago. In Scotland, in 1847, the Carruths became members of the Church of Jesus Christ of Latter-day Saints and accepted its teachings as the true gospel again restored to earth With a great desire to go to Zion (America) and dwell with the Saints, they left their loved ones and their beautiful homes.

They knew nothing of our modern facilities of traveling — our present-day speed, convenience and luxuries After a tiresome journey to Greenock, Scotland, where some of the younger members were baptized in the icy waters of the Atlantic Ocean, they set sail on the ship "Carnatic" for America.

For thirteen days the ship tossed unceasingly. It rocked and rolled with such madness that all passengers on board became violently ill. After sixty-one days of this treacherous voyage, they arrived in New Orleans, joined the Latter-day Saints at Winter Quarters and from there they traveled West with the Mormon Pioneers.

Finally, at the end of a journey of eight months from their beautiful homeland, they reached their destination, September 23rd, 1848, to be greeted only by a strange, wild and desolate valley — a valley later to become the fertile soil of a great people, nurtured by their tears, sanctified by their faith, consecrated by a high and noble purpose in the service of their God.

INDEX

185

CAHOON (Cont'd)

Amelia Ann Larson Cahoon, 165

Harold P , s of John B. & Vera C Cahoon, & h Priscilla Johnson, 150

Henry Reynolds, s of William F & h of Anna Durfee, 92

Hortense Terry, w. of Newell Spencer Cahoon, 164

Hyrum Spencer, s of Daniel S , & h of Amelia Ann Larson, 98

James Cordon Cassen, s of William F & h of Ellen S Wilson, & h of Martha H Braithwaite, 92, 156, 165, 167, 171

James C , s of James C C & h of Barbara Deitrick, 151, 167, 171

James W , s of Andrew, & h of Martha Ellen Proctor, 79, 138

James W , Jr s of James W , & h of Lavenia Brown, 158

Jane Elizabeth, d of Andrew, & w of Harry Haynes, 138

Janet Carruth, see Janet Carruth Young

Jay A., s of George E & Annie Louise Alder Cahoon, & h of Ada Layne Brown, 151, 167

Jennie Romayne, d of Brent F. & Nelle L Cahoon & w of John J Dowd, 158

John Boyd, s of John P. & Elizabeth Gordon Cahoon, 150

John Boyd, Jr , s of John B & Vera Carlson Cahoon, & h of Faye A Tilby, 172

John Farrington, s of William F , & h of Margaret Sharp, 91, 92, 154

John Farrington, s of Mahonri M , & h of Magdalena Hansen, 143,

John Pulaski, or John P , s of Andrew, & h of Elizabeth Gordon, 95, 132, 138, 150, 155

Joseph, s of William & h of Elizabeth . . . . , & h of Hannah Kent, 2

Joseph Carruth, s of Andrew, & h of Mary Ann McComie, 138

Joseph Leroy, s of Rais B , & h of Lona Bennett & of Lucile Walton, 145

Joseph Mahonri, s of William F & h of Mary Emma Ensign, 92

Julia, d of Daniel S & Martha S. Cahoon, 98

Julia Amina, d of Reynolds Cahoon, died child, 78

CAHOON (Cont'd)

Lavenia, w of Kelse Dunlap, 158

Lazelle, w. of James W. Boucher, 158

Le Maughn, s of James C & Barbara Cahoon, 167

Leonard, s of Andrew Alonzo Cahoon & h of Matilda Watts, 150

Leonard, des. of Wm F., 167

Lerona Eliza, d of William F , & w of Myron B. Durfee, 92

Lerona, (died infant), d of Andrew Cahoon, 138

Lerona Eliza, d of Reynolds Cahoon, see Lerona Eliza Cahoon Stanley

Lervae, s of George E & Louise Alder Cahoon, 157, 167, 171

Leslie C , s of James C C , & h. of Mary Leavett, 156, also Sons of, 167

Lloyd D , s of James C. & Barbara Dietrick Cahoon, & h of Laura Duce, 151, 167

Louisa, d of Andrew & Mary C. Cahoon, & w of Lewis A Copeland, 138

Lucile Naamah, d of Daniel F & Naamah Cahoon, see Lucile C Fiske

Lucina Roberts (Johnson), w of Reynolds Cahoon, 74, 77, 78, 144

Lucina Johnson, d of Reynolds Cahoon, died child, 78

Lucy Caroline, d of Andrew Cahoon, see Lucy Caroline Cahoon Carlisle

Lynn E , s of George E. & Viola Gyllenskog Cahoon, & h of Davona Bennett, 150

Mabel Alveretta, d of Rais Cahoon, & w of Anton Stewart, 145

Maggie M (Nelson), d. of Joseph & Mary M. Cahoon Hall, 167

Mahonri Moriancumer, s of Reynolds & Thirza Stiles Cahoon, 21, 62, 78, 123, 124, 127, 139, 140, 141, 142, 155, 173, 174

Mahonri M , Jr , s of Mahonri M & Sarah Romney Cahoon, died age 2, 143

Margaret Ellen, w of Leonard Adelbert Shomaker, 165, 167, 171, 180

Margaret, d of Daniel S , & w. of John R Bennett, 98, 165

188

CAHOON (Cont'd)
    & w. of Robert Quarton Max-
      field, 98
    Sarah Lucina, d. of Rais B &
      Mary C Johnson Cahoon, 145
    Sarah Lorett or Janet, d of Ma-
      honri M Cahoon, died child,
      143
    Stanley Irven, s of Theron Ca-
      hoon, & h of Irene Manville,
      173
    Stephen Tiffany, s of William F
      & Nancy M Cahoon & h of
      Anna Irons, 92
    Stella, see Stella Cahoon Shurt-
      leff
    Thelma D., (Court), 167
    Theron, s. of Daniel S & Jane A.
      Cahoon, & h of Eliza Chris-
      tena Johnson or Hansen, 98
    Thirza Lucina, d. of Andrew Ca-
      hoon, died infant, 138
    Thirza Stiles, w of Reynolds Ca-
      hoon, 3, 4, 21, 22, 49, 62, 70,
      71, 73, 74, 75, 76, 77, 78, 79, 94,
      95, 96, 99, 128, 139
    Thirza Vilate, w of Albert An-
      gell, 92 167
    Thurza Elizabeth, d of Pulaski
      S Cahoon, died child, 95
    Truman Carlos, s of Reynolds
      & Lucina Roberts Cahoon, 62,
      78, 145
    Vaudis Erda, d of John P. & Eli-
      zabeth Gordon Cahoon, & w of
      Damon T. Kilker, 158
    Verda, w. of Thomas B Maw-
      son, 158
    Venus, w. of W W. Golay, 151
    William (spelled Cahoone) of
      Block Island, Rhode Island, 1,
      2
    William Dennison, s of Henry
      Reynolds & Annie Durfee Ca-
      hoon, & h of Jessie Richard-
      son, 151
    William Farrington or William
      F, 2, 19, 21, 22, 28 31. 32,
      35, 36, 38, 53, 62, 63, 70, 78, 79,
      80, 81, 82, 84, 85, 86, 91, 92, 93,
      94, 96, 99, 118, 122, 164, 165,
      167, 171
    William Jarvis. s of Rais B, &
      h of Agnes Hansen, 145
    William, Jr, father of Reynolds
      Cahoon & h of Mehitable
      Hodge or Hodges, 1, 2, 73
    William Marion, s. of Wm F &
      Nancy M Cahoon, & h of
      Martitia R Smith, 92
    William Roscoe, s of William
      Dennison & Jessie Richardson

CAHOON (Cont'd)
    Cahoon & h. of Venitta Call,
      151
CALHOUN, John C, 39, 42
CAMERON
    Alan B, s. of Charles C & Mary
      Louisa Cahoon Cameron, 95
    Charles Conrad, h of Mary
      Louisa Cahoon, 95
CANNON, George Q (Pres &
    Elder), 82, 84, 163, 169
CARLISLE, Lucy Caroline Ca-
    hoon, w of Harvey C Carlisle,
    138
CARLSON, Vera, w of John Boyd
    Cahoon, 150
CARRUTH
    James, 109, 110, 113, 122
    Janet, see Janet Carruth Young
      Cahoon
    John, 181
    Margaret, see Margaret Carruth
      Cahoon
    Mary, see Mary Carruth Cahoon
    Robert, 181
    William, Jr, 109, 110, 113, 122,
      124
    William, 181
CARTER
    Adaline, w of Wm Kemp, 178
    Jared, 13, 14, 18, 19, 23, 92
    Kate B, Nat Pres D U.P, 158,
      159
    Prudence, w. of Aaron Gibbs, 92
CASSON, Mary or Mary Dugdale
    Cassen, w of Wm F. Cahoon, &
    widow of James Cassen, 92
CLAY, Henry (candidate), 42
CLAYTON
    Brother, 47
    William, 35, 53
CLYDE, Geo D (Governor), 160
COHOON, Thomas, 152
COLE, Zera (father), 82
COLQUHOUN, Clan, 106, 183
COLTON, Zebedee, 81
COLVIN, Irene, w of Walter Har-
    ris Corbett, 152
COOKE
    Col, 128
    Phillip St George (Lt Col), 54
COOLEDGE, J. W, 38
COOMBS, John James, 171
COPELAND, Lewis A, 150
CORAY, Melissa B, 159
CORBETT
    Annie J Mackay, d of David O
      & Maria Antoinette Cahoon
      Mackay & w of Walter Calvin
      Corbett, 152
    Walter Colvin, s of Walter Har-
      ris & Irene Colvin Corbett, 152

190

TAYLOR (Cont'd)
Thirza Lerona Stanley, w of Hil-
liard B Taylor, 93, 94
William Burnham, see Hilliard
Burnham Tayor
TILBY, Faye Amelia, w. of John
Boyd Cahoon, Jr, 172
TRIPP
Emma Frances, w of John B
Bringhurst, 178
Enoch Bartlett, s of William Jr
& Naamah Hall Bartlett
Tripp, 2, 52, 166
Jessie Eddins (or Eddings), 2,
56, 166
Naamah, see Naamah Tripp Ca-
hoon
TOLMAN, Joseph H, h of Mary
Ellen Cahoon, 145
TYLER, President, 43

VAN BUREN, (Candidate), 42

WADDOUPS, William W, 169
WALBURGER, Lydia Elizabeth,
w of Laurain Shomaker, 180
WALLACE, George B, 69
WASSON, L. D, 45
WATSON, Mary, w of Jacob
Hooper, 95
WATTS, Elder, 105
WELLS
Daniel H, 59, 65, 71, 162, 164
General, 63, 64
WENTWORTH, John, 7
WETTSTEIN, David A (Major
U S M C), h of Nathalia E.
Cahoon, 151
WHEELOCK, C H, 111
WHITMORE, David, 11
WHITNEY
Bishop, 4, 16
Newel, 26
Newel K., 27
WIDSTOE, John A. (Elder), 175
WIGHT, Lyman, 4, 28, 30
WILLETT, Hugh C (Dr.), 55
WILLIAMS, Frederick G, 23
WILSON, General, 31
WINCHESTER
Chloe, (wife of Orson Sanders),
174
Nancy Roselle, see Nancy Ro-
selle Cahoon, w of Henry W.
Winchester
WINDER
John Rex, 174
Leo Cahoon, s of Richard H. &
Mary E. Winder & h of Mary
Horne, 174
Mary Emma Cahoon, w of Rich-
ard Henry Winder, 132, 138,
174

WINDER (Cont'd)
Richard Henry, s of John Rex
Winder & h of Mary Emma
Cahoon, 174
WOODRUFF
Mr, 64
Wiford, (Pres), 162, 166
WOOLLEY
Janet, w of Apostle John W.
Taylor, 164, 171
Jeanette Romania Hyde, d of
Joseph S. Hyde, & w. of Ralph
E Woolley, 170
Rachel Cahoon, d of Andrew
Cahoon, & wife of Samuel W
Woolley, 113, 135, 138, 164,
167, 169, 171
Ralph Edwin, s. of Samuel &
Alice Rowberry Wooley, 168,
170
Ralph E Mrs. (Romania), 169
Samuel Edwin, s of Samuel W.
& Maria Angell Woolley, 169,
170
Samuel Wickersham, h of 1st w.
Maria Angell & 2nd w Rachel
Cahoon, 164, 167, 169
Virginia Jeanette, d of Ralph E.
& J Romania Hyde Woolley,
& w of Jay A Quealy, Jr, 170

YOUNG
Brigham (Pres), 18, 19, 26, 35,
37, 49, 51, 52, 53, 54, 56, 58, 59,
60, 61, 63, 64, 65, 69, 70, 71, 72,
73, 74, 83, 89, 91, 95, 102, 109,
117, 119, 120, 121, 124, 127, 129,
133, 154, 164, 166, 167, 179
Brother, 128
Grace Christy or Christie, d. of
James Young Jr, & Janet Car-
ruth, & w. of Enoch Covey, 154
Janet or Jannette, d of James
Young, Jr, & Janet Carruth, &
w of Enoch Covey, 154
Janet Carruth, d of William &
Mary Barr Carruth, & w of
James Young, Jr., & w of An-
drew Cahoon, see Janet C.
Young Cahoon, 59, 60, 61, 121,
123, 124, 134, 138
James, Jr., h of Janet Carruth,
109, 134, 154
James, Sr, 109, 110, 111
John, 59
Joseph, 49, 91
Mary Barr, d of James Young,
Jr, & Janet Carruth, & w of
Hiram Theron Spencer, 98,
132, 153

ZIMMER, William, 176

195

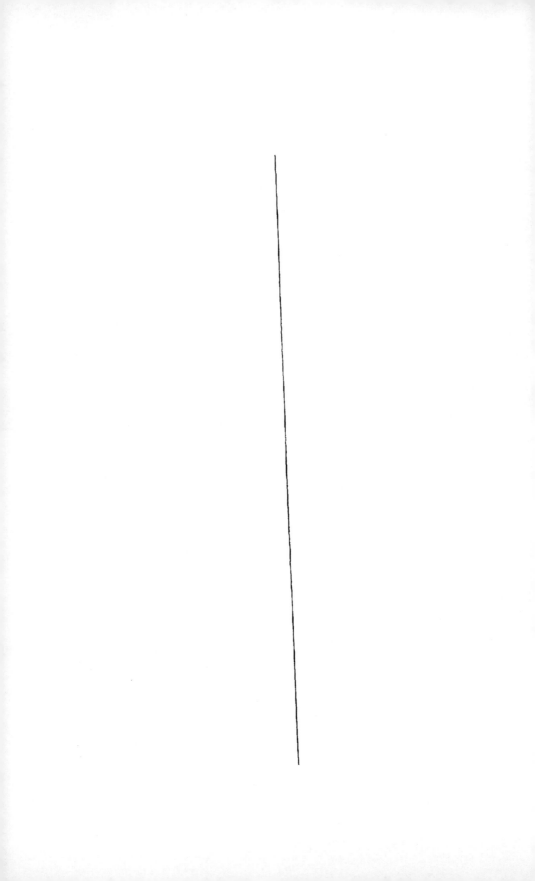

GRA

Feb. 1846 — First Pioneers left Nauvoo, Illinois. Crossed t
    River.

Feb. 5, 1846 — Sugar Creek, Iowa. Organized camps a
    Captains of Tens, Fifties and Hundreds.

Feb. 15, 1846 — William F. and Daniel S. Cahoon left Na
    Nauvoo Band. They camped at Sugar Creek, Iowa.

March 9, 1846 — Reynolds Cahoon and Cutler Compar
    "Roll-Out" their Camps. They traveled with the m

APHIC MAP SHOWING THE EXODUS OF THE MORMON PIONEE

l the Mississippi	May 8, 1846 — Reynolds Cahoon Camp arrived at Garden Gro[e, for Andrew Cahoon carried mail between Garden Grove and Nauv
and appointed	July 6, 1846 — Cahoon and Cutler Camp were three miles [om M Pisgah. They continued to Council Bluffs.
lauvoo with the	July, 1846 — Cahoon Camp crossed Missouri River, arrived [Wint Quarters, Nebraska.
any ordered to main Camp of	November, 1846 — Andrew Cahoon left Winter Quarter[for [urop

NEERS IN 1847, WITH DAILY STOPPING PLACES OF BRIGHAM YOUNG'S

, Iowa.	1847 — Council Bluffs. Daniel S. Cahoon married Martha Spencer. They go to Cutler's Park. Their Celestial Marriage, March 12, 1848, Cahoon's House, Winter Quarters.	July
lauvoo.		
m Mt.	April, 1848 — Andrew Cahoon and Carruth Family arrived at New Orleans from Scotland.	Sept
Winter	Spring of 1848 — Carruth Fam... ...t Rey... lds Cahoon Camp at Wint...	Mar
ropean	Spring of 1848 — Cah... ...t Winter Quarters.	Sep

MPANY

8 — Chimney Rock, Nebraska. Andrew married Margaret Car-
and Janet Carruth Young.

1848 — Cahoon Camp with Carruth Family arrived in Salt
e Valley, Utah.

1, 1849 — William F. and Daniel S. Cahoon Families left
ler's Park and Winter Quarters, Nebraska.

, 1849 — William F. and Daniel S. Cahoon Families arrived
alt Lake Valley, Utah.

Lightning Source UK Ltd.
Milton Keynes UK
UKHW020820300822
408063UK00004B/254